More advance praise for *From Difficult to Disturbed*

"Dr. Laurence Miller is well known as a practicing clinical and forensic psychologist, management consultant, and author. *From Difficult to Disturbed* draws on Dr. Miller's distinctive ability to translate psychological concepts and terms into understandable and useful business terms. It discusses many of the personalities seen in the workforce today and provides managers and employees with the practical tools needed to successfully deal with the people and their problems that can disrupt—and even destroy—a workplace. The true measure of a nonfiction author is the ability to translate difficult theories and complex concepts so that readers may effectively apply them in their own real world; as always, Dr. Miller has succeeded at this exceptionally well."—Dr. James D. Sewell, Assistant Commissioner, retired, Florida Department of Law Enforcement

"Not all problem employees are as simple to deal with as most books on coaching and counseling suggest. There are employees whose personalities are difficult or even seriously disturbed, and textbook solutions aren't likely to help a busy manager. That's why I'm so delighted with Dr. Laurence Miller's book *From Difficult to Disturbed.* He offers practical solutions to dealing with common people problems but he also offers help with more complex problems like overly dependent, histrionic, narcissistic, antisocial workers and even more—employees with mental disorders such as depression, schizophrenia, anxiety, panic disorders, and alcohol and substance abuse. It's a book that belongs on the bookshelves not only of managers but also HR professionals."—Florence Stone, author of *Coaching, Counseling & Mentoring,* 2nd edition

"Thoughtfully and purposefully written, Dr. Laurence Miller's *From Difficult to Disturbed* offers us a down-to-earth guide to dealing effectively with problematic coworkers and bosses in any work setting. Dr. Miller's descriptive analyses of personality styles are easily illuminated via an uncanny ability to translate complicated psychological jargon into everyday language. Our journey through the Histrionic, Avoidant, Dependent, Borderline, Obsessive-Compulsive, Paranoid, Narcissistic, Schizoid, and Passive-Aggressive personality types reveals Dr. Miller's keen insight and breadth of knowledge amassed during his career as a clinical psychologist, management consultant, and law enforcement specialist. *From Difficult to Disturbed* spotlights case studies of employer and employee personality types—and how they affect the work environment—and are presented insightfully along with straightforward "how-to" suggestions for negotiating the human work environment in order to achieve maximum productivity and personal satisfaction. Also offered are sections on employees having general mental and neuropsychological disorders and mind-body syndromes, as well as violence in the workplace, stress and tension in top-level managers, and important suggestions for managing dysfunctional employees. Dr. Miller's *From Difficult to Disturbed* is a *must-read* book for the general public, personnel and human relations departments, school systems, business, and psychology undergraduate and graduate schools within universities. Managers will want to keep a copy handy to use as a reference guide in their daily dealings with the people with whom they work."—Richard L. Levenson, Jr., Psy.D., NYS Licensed Psychologist, editor, *International Journal of Emergency Mental Health*

FROM Difficult
TO *Disturbed*

FROM Difficult
TO *Disturbed*

Understanding and Managing Dysfunctional Employees

Laurence Miller, Ph.D.

AMACOM

American Management Association

New York • Atlanta • Brussels • Chicago • Mexico City • San Francisco
Shanghai • Tokyo • Toronto • Washington, D.C.

Special discounts on bulk quantities of AMACOM books are available to corporations, professional associations, and other organizations. For details, contact Special Sales Department, AMACOM, a division of American Management Association, 1601 Broadway, New York, NY 10019.
Tel.: 212-903-8316. Fax: 212-903-8083.
E-mail: specialsls@amanet.org
Website: www.amacombooks.org/go/specialsales
To view all AMACOM titles go to: www.amacombooks.org

This publication is designed to provide accurate and authoritative information in regard to the subject matter covered. It is sold with the understanding that the publisher is not engaged in rendering legal, accounting, or other professional service. If legal advice or other expert assistance is required, the services of a competent professional person should be sought.

The material in this book is for educational and informational purposes only and is not intended to provide specific clinical or legal advice. All instructions and recommendations for emergency response and crisis intervention should be supplemented by proper training and practice. Readers are advised to consult with appropriately credentialed practitioners for further information and training on these topics.

Library of Congress Cataloging-in-Publication Data

Miller, Laurence, 1951–
    From difficult to disturbed : understanding and managing dysfunctional employees / Laurence Miller.
        p   cm.
    Includes bibliographical references and index.
    ISBN-13: 978–0–8144–0922–0 (hardcover)
    ISBN-10: 0–8144–0922–9 (hardcover)
    1. Problem employees.   2. Personnel management.   3. Supervision of employees.
    I. Title.

    HF5549.5.E42M54   2008
    658.3'045—dc22   2007026895

Printing number

10 9 8 7 6 5 4 3 2 1

Contents

Preface

When I was in high school, a friend and I decided it was time we toughened up, so we pooled our change and bought a book called *Teach Yourself Karate*. This slim drugstore paperback was filled with grainy black-and-white photos of high-kicking men on low-lying mats, supplemented by a thin instructional text. I was skeptical: Can you really learn a complex martial arts technique by reading a book? But my friend was determined and we spent many hours emulating and practicing the kicks, chops, thrusts, and blocks we saw on those pages. After a while, it seemed like we'd gotten down the fundamentals, but eventually I lost interest and let him have the book.

My friend didn't give up, though. He practiced and practiced every move in that book and then went on to take real-life karate training at a local dojo, ultimately earned a black belt, and became a karate instructor himself. Years later, when I discussed the episode with him, he told me that he really learned only the rudimentary basics of karate from the book, but I still remember his words about that little instruction manual:

> "It gave me the foundation, something I could build on. It gave me enough usable knowledge so that I wouldn't feel helpless in a fight because, even though I didn't know everything, I could still

defend myself. It gave me something I could use right away and it gave me the *oomph*."

So it is that I'm often asked if something as critical and complex as business management psychology can be learned from a book or a course. It's the same question that applies to every other area I teach and train: crisis intervention, police psychology, forensic behavioral science, psychotherapy, neuropsychology. It's the same, in fact, with virtually every complex field of human endeavor: medicine, firefighting, military training, airline piloting, sports, music—you can add your own items to this list.

The topics may be complex but the answer is simple: The books and the courses by themselves don't make you an expert. However, they can give you the foundation, the background knowledge, the accumulated wisdom to go on and conquer the field—why do you think doctors go to medical school and managers get MBAs? Continuing to practice and train in simulations and real-life settings will give you the expertise to be a true professional; your motivation to excel will supply the *oomph*.

But you have to start somewhere. And where you start has to give you enough practical information so that you can hit the ground running and feel like you can apply your skills immediately to real-life situations. If this weren't true, there'd be no need for books, courses, or training materials in any field. My friend got his black belt, but he started with a black-and-white paperback.

But we need the *right* training materials. One of my headaches in surveying the current literature on business psychology has been the sheer volume and variety of loopiness that passes for behavioral management theory and practice in this field. Personality types that don't make sense. Syndromes that don't exist. Tests that don't measure anything. Recommendations that apply to virtually no one. Theories based on cherry-picked evidence and misinformed speculation. Underdeveloped ideas and piecemeal applications. And most distressing, books and tapes and courses that talk and talk and talk but don't address the real concerns that today's real managers have in the real business world.

How do I get a lazy employee to work harder? How do I deal with a subordinate who can't follow instructions—or won't? What do I do with a worker who doesn't respond to coaching, counseling, or discipline? How do I encourage personnel to come forward with problems before they escalate to crises? What do I do on the spot if an employee seems to be out of control and about to blow? How can I fine-tune my communication style for maximum impact on employee performance and morale? How can I develop effective leadership qualities and encourage loyalty and team building in my department and organization? How can I use practical management and organizational psychology on a day-to-day basis to enhance the health and productivity of my company and my career?

Of course, you don't have to be a psychologist to be a good manager; otherwise only psychologists would be managers—and, to some, that's a scary thought. But just as understanding how your car or your computer works can make you a better driver or Web user, understanding what makes people tick will allow you to apply your managerial skills more sharply and effectively. No, people are not machines, and that's why this book is a guide, not a numbered instruction manual.

Whether you're a top business executive, midlevel manager, or roll-up-your-sleeves supervisor, *From Difficult to Disturbed: Understanding and Managing Dysfunctional Employees* will provide you with a unique, usable guide to the personality styles and interpersonal dynamics that can motivate your people to perform at their best or their worst. Based on validated principles of clinical, social, and organizational psychology—not psychobabble—this book gives you a practical behavioral science tool that you can apply *right now* to solving people problems and enhancing productivity in your workplace.

I don't want this to be another murky tome you'll thumb through once and then consign to bookshelf purgatory. Whether in the office or on the shop floor, in the service bay or in the boardroom, the book you hold in your hand is a practical resource that you can refer to again and again as you confront the challenges of a complex workplace filled with complex, real live people.

Yet, as confident as I am that this volume will be a valuable asset to your management practice, I'm not going to promise what I can't deliver, what no book can deliver. Just passively reading these pages won't turn you into the Master Manager of the Universe. You have to do the work, practice the kicks and blocks, try out the strategies, be willing to accept honest feedback about your efforts, fine-tune your moves, and try again.

But just because something takes effort doesn't mean it has to be boring or painful. Keep at it and an amazing thing will happen: You'll find yourself managing better and your people will be working harder and smarter for you. Through your psychologically informed interactions with your workforce, your management style will become progressively smoother and less stressful, and your dealings with your people won't seem like a collection of tricks and tactics but will come to represent a real attempt to help them be the best they can be. Gradually, inexorably, from these threads of knowledge, you'll weave your own black belt in people karate. And with continued practice and a willingness to learn, you'll progress from tentative novice to adept practitioner, and finally to the sublime but humble confidence of a true master.

Not just on-site managers and supervisors will find this approach useful. As an EAP coordinator, a human resources administrator, or a company risk-management executive, you can use this book as a guide to protecting your company from unnecessary risks and liabilities, as well as providing the best services for your employees to encourage a healthy corporate culture.

Think of this book, then, as a user-friendly management psychology training manual, a practical guide to understanding all the basic people types and using all the essential people skills you'll need to make your company great and your own job more satisfying and rewarding—a head start and a heads-up toward getting and keeping your managerial *oomph*.

Acknowledgments

Abook like this has many points of convergence and its influences have been many and varied. The professionals I've worked with in the fields of psychology, law enforcement, criminal justice, and business management have provided me with insights and experiences that have hopefully made me a better practitioner and educator. My clinical patients and consulting clients continue to reinforce the importance of seeing people beyond the diagnostic labels and behavioral descriptions that often propel them into my office. The students in my courses and training seminars have allowed me to serve them best when they've challenged me to back up my ideas and present my practical recommendations in clear, convincing, and usable form.

I want to thank book agent James Schiavone for securing a most apt outlet for this work at AMACOM and executive editor Ellen Kadin for first recognizing the value of this book for AMACOM's readership and for passing it along to editor in chief Adrienne Hickey, executive editor Jacquie Flynn, and associate editor Erika Spelman. Adrienne, Jacquie, and Erika have proven to be the kind of editors all good authors want: able to capture a manuscript's essential message and help refine its expression into the practical, usable book you hold in your hand.

Last, but never least, my family earns my gratitude for enduring the prolonged absence of yet another self-imposed exile while completing this book. For better or worse, living with an author who often does his writing after coming home from his day job, they've learned to get used to brief glimpses of me when I pop my head out for air. But I hope they understand that I never stop appreciating their support for the work that I do.

. . . .

CHAPTER 1

Human Nature and the Practical Psychology of Work

As a manager, you work hard. And if you're holding this book in your hand, it means that you want to manage smarter, better, and with a more positive impact on your people and your company. You're also aware that people are complex and you probably have been frustrated by the plethora of one-size-fits-all management guides that treat your employees as if they were cookie-cutter clones.

Welcome to the real world. This introductory chapter outlines the fundamental principles of practical psychology at work that define the manager's task and that will help you understand the challenges you face and how to handle them. This chapter also introduces the basic facts of personality and psychopathology that managers need to know in order to understand and effectively deal with the diverse members of their workforce.

Fundamental Principles of Practical Psychology at Work

Guiding this book is a set of truisms about organizational psychology and human behavior that every successful business manager understands intuitively or comes to learn through experience. Understand, assimilate, and use these principles and you will mold the kind of workforce other managers wish they had.

Every Workplace Is a Village

To survive the harsh natural environments that human beings evolved in and that shaped our mentality, socialization, and culture, we came of age as a species in the context of small bands or family groups. For most of our recorded human history, and for a far longer prehistorical epoch, we were born into and then played, hunted, gathered, mated, raised children, defended ourselves, and died amid no more than a few dozen related village mates. Later, as agriculture allowed larger and larger populations to occupy the same real estate and as specialization of work tasks led to what we now call civilization, basic human nature hardly budged and our hundred-thousand-year-old hominid brain still retains the tribal mentality that a mere few millennia of hieroglyphics and Web links cannot override.

Thus, even today, every workplace is a family, a tribe, a community. It is the place where many of us spend more than half our waking lives, where we form alliances and cultivate friendships, where we joust with rivals and spar with enemies. Work is where we try to realize our loftiest dreams or just get through the day; the place that gives many of us our core identity or just a livelihood. And like families, tribes, and communities everywhere, each workplace has its own norms, cultures, and colorful characters.

People Are Different

You already know this from your own family and friends. People have different temperaments, different styles of reacting to stress and interacting with others. Some people are hard-nosed, others easygoing. Some are generous to a fault, others fault finding and selfish. Some are a joy to work with and others suck the joy out of your workday. If you're a manager for any length of time, at one point or another you'll have most of these types working for you. And if you know how to deal with them—not trick them, not manipulate them, not "play" them, but understand their personality styles and form a mutual rapport at their own level—then they will *want* to give you their best, because making an effort to truly understand someone is one of the highest forms of respect.

Some of the material for this book grew out of my research and experience consulting with law enforcement and other public safety organizations. It is well known to anyone who watches TV cop shows that police officers have to deal with some of society's toughest customers. What may be less familiar is that police officers often *are* the toughest customers for their departments to deal with when it comes to matters of morale, discipline, integrity, honor, leadership, productivity, fairness, and the effects of one's personal life on his or her work life. No, I don't expect you to manage your organization like a sheriff's department or a police precinct, but many of the interpersonal management tools I teach to officers and their leaders can help you deal with your own work staff. Other principles and strategies come directly from corporate management psychology and can be uniquely and creatively applied to your individual company.

Still another source of input for this book came from my experience in clinical counseling and psychotherapy working with employees, managers, and CEOs in settings as diverse as a workers compensation rehab clinic, corporate briefing room, and clinical private practice. In talking with many of these people, I was frequently reminded of Freud's words when asked his view on the purpose of human life. He replied, "To love and to work." Much of the contribution of clinical therapists deals with the first part, but there has been an unfortunate tendency for mental health professionals to neglect or downplay work concerns as a source of stress and conflict in people's lives, often assuming that they are merely ancillary to, or symbolic of, family dynamics.

However, according to the theme of this book, work dynamics replicate family dynamics because they *are* family dynamics. What we see in action in the workplace are the daily operations and malfunctions of the tribal connection processes that have always permitted humans to function as interdependent teams and groups.

The Best Form of Crisis Intervention Is Crisis Prevention

Law enforcement, emergency services, and the workplace all come together in another aspect of my practice: on-site crisis intervention and emergency mental health services to organizations that have been jolted by a sudden tragedy such as a workplace violence incident, an armed robbery, a hostage situation, a natural disaster, or a corporate public relations crisis. It has become clear to me that the ability to make rapid decisions under stress is crucial for managers who want to help their people get through an emergency.

In addition, doing follow-up psychotherapy with traumatized employees has reinforced in my mind how vital it is for companies to let their people know that they will do everything possible to support them and take care of them after a major crisis. As a forensic psychologist and expert witness in work stress, disability, and compensation cases, I've developed a keen appreciation of how proper handling of conflict and stress on the job by knowledgeable managers and executives can sharply reduce disability claims, improve worker health and morale, and—here's the bottom line, literally—increase the productivity and profitability of your company.

These two parallel domains of management practice—fixing a bad situation and making a good situation better—are inextricably entwined. Like renovating a home, you tear down and repair while you build up and improve. Most crises are fluid, organic entities that evolve over a time course that can range from minutes to years, and at each stage, you want to have an established set of measures to prevent a few bad incidents from multiplying exponentially and exploding like a plague onto your organization. Hence, preparation, planning, and training are crucial. It follows that the best way to resolve a crisis is to prevent it from occurring in the first place and hardly a day goes by in the world of work that opportunities for staving off potential calamities do not occur but are, sadly, overlooked.

I often hear managers say, "What do I know about crisis management? Let the professionals handle it." However, as a manager, you are in a unique position to prevent most workplace crises from occurring by observing and intervening in low-level conflicts and confrontations before they become major conflagrations. Those professionals—police, firefighters, and paramedics—are, by definition, *responders* to emergencies that have already begun or escalated. The professionals can react, but they usually can't predict, anticipate, or prevent. Only you know your people as well as you do. Only you have taken the time and effort to understand the diversity of personalities in your workplace and how to manage your workforce in a fair and efficient way. This book will help you continue to do that smarter and better.

20/20 Hindsight = 20/20 Insight = 20/20 Foresight

Because it is often equated with second-guessing, Monday-morning quarterbacking, or useless self-flagellation, 20/20 hindsight has gotten a bum rap. In reality, however, looking back on an unsuccessful action and analyzing how it went down is an essential process for developing any skill—if the *hindsight* analysis leads to a certain degree of *insight* into what went wrong and how it happened. This insight into what happened last time can then be used to create a new set of options and action plans for next time— that is, *foresight*. What we're talking about is basically the concept of learning from experience. All true professionals, managers included, engage in an ongoing process of continuing education and self-improvement—the *culture of knowledge* noted in Chapter 12. This book is intended to contribute to that process.

Personality and Psychopathology: Traits, Types, and Disorders

We all have personality *traits*. Some of us are outgoing and gregarious; others keep to ourselves. Some people are orderly and meticulous and never seem to have an unplanned moment, whereas others enjoy life spontaneously but can't find their shoes. Some are open, trusting souls who love not wisely but too well, whereas others never trust anyone farther than they can throw them.

But when these quirks of personal color begin to grate harmfully on others or to significantly derail a person's own success, psychologists regard these quirks not just as personality traits, but as *personality disorders*. The American Psychiatric Association defines a personality disorder as "an enduring pattern of inner experience and behavior that deviates markedly from the expectations of the individual's culture, is pervasive and inflexible, has an onset in adolescence or early adulthood, is stable over time, and leads to distress or impairment."

Generally, a personality disorder represents a characteristic style of ineffective interactions with other people that persists across situations and is stubbornly resistant to change. Many personality-disordered individuals have little insight into their own behavior or understanding of the adverse impact they have on themselves and others. Often, they justify their self-defeating or offensive behavior as being due to fickle fate or the fault of someone else. Some personalities are characteristically egocentric, seeing things only from their own perspective, and they often have poor impulse control, which impels them to gratify their own needs, often at the expense of others. Other personalities may be self-deprecating to a fault, never seeming to be able to assert themselves or stand up for their rights.

Thus, the *extremes* of their self-perception and conduct toward others are what distinguish personality-disordered individuals from those with milder traits. Another view is that every one of us has a unique set of personality traits, but not everyone has a personality disorder. Yet, as with most such distinctions, the dividing line is rarely a definitive one.

Personality styles and disorders co-occur with, shade into, and influence the expression of more serious mental disorders, such as depression, bipolar disorder, schizophrenia, and even organic brain syndromes like epilepsy or dementia. Personality and psychopathology also interact with substance abuse and problems with the legal system. However, because different individuals with a wide variety of syndromes may possess legitimate skills and talents in many aspects of work, their other more dysfunctional behaviors may be overlooked or tolerated in the workplace—or they may be exploited by other coworkers or supervisors.

In fact, people gravitate toward different kinds of jobs based not only on their training and intellectual skills but also on the basis of their personalities, temperaments, and cognitive styles. This includes whether they feel most comfortable in supervisory versus subordinate roles and accounts for why some otherwise technically brilliant bit-and-byte workers fall to pieces when their promotions require them to interact with flesh-and-blood human beings, or why the verbally nimble public relations front person becomes hopelessly mired in his own scheduling and paperwork. In the ideal case, someone with a particular personality style or disorder will find a comfortable niche in your organization and operate effectively until something changes significantly in the person's job site, assignment, or relationship with coworkers.

Signs and Symptoms of Abnormal Behavior

We clinical folks live in a world of terminology. Unfortunately, many of the clinical labels used by mental health professionals have an unavoidable derogatory ring to them. Throughout this book, I retain the professional mental health terminology for purposes of consistency, while not necessarily endorsing the negative personal connotations these terms are often burdened with when bandied about in common usage. (Who, after all, wants to be called a histrionic or passive-aggressive personality?) Nevertheless, until we can come up with something better, we're stuck with these labels, so please don't take it personally. And, while you certainly don't have to master the arcane lingo of psychology and psychiatry to be an effective manager, some understanding of the behavioral concepts behind the ten-gallon words will provide you with the background and insight to appreciate and profit from the material in the chapters to come.

In medicine, a *sign* is an objective observation or finding on a clinical examination; it's something the physician can see, hear, or feel. Examples include a limp while walking, an abnormal heartbeat through a stethoscope, or disorganized speech during conversation. A *symptom* is an internal, subjective experience that is reported by the patient, such as a pain in the knee, throbbing headaches following exertion, or voices in his head telling him to fight off the evil forces threatening him. When you go to your doctor, he or she asks you about symptoms ("Where does it hurt?") and examines you for signs (lower right abdomen feels swollen and rigid).

A *syndrome* is a standard cluster of signs and symptoms that occur in a regular pattern and are typically associated with a particular etiology (cause) and/or occur in a particular subset of the population. Examples include degenerative arthritis of the knee in a retired NFL player, hypertensive headaches in an overweight woman with a high-salt diet, and paranoid schizophrenia in a homeless young man who abuses amphetamines and alcohol. A syndrome becomes a *disorder* when it interferes with important life functions of the person, such as shortening the life span; decreasing the quality of health and well-being; or interfering with job, family, or social functioning.

Although different syndromes have different symptom clusters, as a manager or coworker, there are some general signs of mental disorder that you should be able to recognize in the people you work with.

General inappropriateness of behavior may be a sign of mental illness, although it may also be due to intoxication or a variety of everyday factors such as fatigue or being overly exuberant. Individuals with mental disorders tend to have their cognitive and behavioral gyroscopes set to extremes, characterized by either inflexibility and rigidity, or impulsivity and unpredictability. Emotions may range from elated to depressed, calm to panicked, and there may be an unnatural changeability of mood that is inconsistent with the circumstances. Attention, concentration, and memory may be impaired, due to either an organic brain syndrome or heightened distractibility from the anxiety of an internal dialogue. Severely disturbed individuals may be disoriented for *time* ("What day is this? Is it morning or afternoon?"), *place* ("Do you know where you are now? Where do you live?"), or *person* ("What's your name? How old are you?").

Speech may be *tangential,* flitting from topic to topic without a clear connection between them, or it may be *circumstantial,* remaining on or returning to the same topic, even after the conversation has moved on. *Perseveration* refers to abnormal persistence or repetition of speech or behavior, repeating the same actions or themes over and over. *Pressured speech* occurs in a rapid, staccato, sometimes jumbled form, words and syllables colliding and blending with others, as if the person is rushing to spill it all out as fast as possible; conversely, speech output may seem *abnormally slow,* as if the person is weighing and measuring every word.

Aphasia refers to a group of organic language disorders due to brain damage that are characterized by disturbances in comprehension and expression. As most commonly seen in elderly people with dementia or stroke-related brain injury, individuals with *receptive aphasia* fail to comprehend normal speech and may appear to be ignoring or defying your instructions. The speech output of people with *expressive aphasia* may seem garbled and confused and in severe cases may be limited to one- or two-word answers that are off the mark. *Aprosodia* refers to an abnormally flat and unexpressive tone and cadence of speech, even where the vocabulary and grammar are essentially intact. Some individuals may remain completely *mute,* due to either organic language disturbance or psychotic fear of saying anything. Remember, too, that perfectly healthy people may clam up to avoid incriminating themselves, because of their own anxiety or just to be obstinate.

What someone is thinking (a symptom) can usually only be inferred from what he or she is saying and doing (signs). *Flight of ideas* refers to a rapid jumping around of thought processes that often occurs in manic states (or as part of the routine of certain stand-up comics). *Paranoia* refers to the belief or feeling that one is being plotted against or harmed (always evaluate if these feelings have a basis in fact). *Grandiose ideas* relate to one's inflated view of his or her own self-importance, and *ideas of reference* cause the person to regard otherwise neutral events as pertaining specifically to him or her.

These four cognitive symptoms often occur together in several types of bipolar manic or schizophrenic syndromes—for example, "They must be out to destroy me [paranoia] because they know I've discovered the secret to world peace [grandiose idea], and the proof is on that TV show about the Vatican where I could tell they were talking about me [idea of reference], and maybe I should go on TV myself or maybe I should get a lawyer and sue the networks or maybe I should network with other people who believe in world peace, because Jesus worked with a net to catch the fishes [circumstantiality and flight of ideas]."

Delusions are false beliefs that are clung to in spite of what would appear to be clear objective evidence to the contrary. *Hallucinations* are abnormal sensory experiences that are most often auditory (involve hearing) in manic and schizophrenic states; visual or tactile (touch) in organic brain syndromes; or, more rarely, may affect the other senses as well. Individuals may have *somatic delusions,* in which they believe their bodies are infected, decaying, or changing in size and shape; these may be accompanied by olfactory (odor) hallucinations. Hallucinations and delusions may occur together, as in paranoid individuals who hear voices telling them that they are targeted for termination consistent with their belief in a government plot to destroy them, or the symptoms may occur separately.

The personal and social behavior of seriously mentally ill people is usually observably abnormal. Social interactions may be suspicious and guarded, or confrontational and combative. Such people may be uncooperative or overly compliant. They may appear confused or disoriented. In some cases, they may show a hair-trigger response to the smallest provocation, becoming terrified or aggressive or both, and require restraint for their own safety and/or that of others. Yet, many of these individuals continue to work at jobs where, as long as their most florid symptoms are controlled by proper treatment, they're able to keep a low profile and earn their living.

How to Use This Book

As the workplace continues to become more diverse, managers will be increasingly called upon to maintain workplace productivity and to resolve workplace problems that emanate from these employee characteristics of personality, psychopathology, background, and culture. This book can provide you with the psychological insight and practical tools necessary to maximize productive relationships among your employees. Personalities and psychopathologies may not be easy to change, but they often can be accommodated. A seemingly obstreperous or hopeless employee may be salvageable if you know how to play to his or her strengths and minimize or overcome his or her interpersonal and job-related weaknesses.

For the purposes of discussion, each trait or syndrome is described separately, as if it is a "pure" type, but bear in mind that these are abstractions and that in the complicated, messy world of human nature, it is common for people to have mixtures and blends of personality traits or disorders. For example, the dependent personality's craving for approval may be expressed through obsessive-compulsive devotion to details for her boss and she will become depressed if she feels his attention isn't forthcoming. Or the paranoid personality's suspicions about being undermined by the substandard work of jealous coworkers may manifest itself in a histrionic display of disciplinary wrath that approaches a delusional psychotic breakdown when his stress level piles up. People are complex, which is why the case histories that illustrate each description are drawn from actual practice.

From Difficult to Disturbed is organized along three interactive dimensions. The first dimension, in Chapters 2 to 6, consists of the personality traits and styles that characterize the diverse group of people you work with. Most of these individuals may not have any kind of serious mental disorder per se, but their unique styles of perceiving, thinking, emoting, and relating may require special skill on your part to manage them effectively. This might entail getting an obsessive-compulsive employee to step back from paralyzing minutiae and to move forward on the broader task. Or it may involve encouraging an avoidant employee to be less fearful of voicing her good ideas at a planning meeting. You might have to convince a narcissistic or paranoid employee that working as part of a team makes sense for his own agenda. These chapters show you how to customize your management, supervision, and communication style for maximum impact on the work output and well-being of these diverse employee personalities.

Sometimes, the problems are more serious because extreme forms of these personalities may predispose certain workers to one or more types of diagnosable mental disorder. This comprises the subject of the second dimension, in Chapters 7 to 9, and, no, I'm not going to try to turn you into a psychodiagnostician. However, the chapters will give you sufficient understanding of these syndromes to recognize how their signs and symptoms may be affecting your employees' performance on the job. Then, we'll discuss practical management strategies for confronting these problems in a sensitive yet forthright way—for example, dealing with a somatizing employee who takes too many sick days, or getting a worker with panic attacks, bipolar disorder, substance abuse, or an organic brain syndrome the right kind of help to salvage his or her otherwise valuable work role and perhaps save that person's career.

The third dimension starts from the place where many managers first confront the issue of problem employees—the problems themselves. Chapters 10 and 11 cover unproductive, misbehaving, and potentially violent employees to help you work backward to the psychological principles you've already learned in order to pinpoint the origin of the problem and develop your own unique, customized prevention and management approach. For example, is your "lazy" employee an entitled narcissist or antisocial slacker who feels that hard work is beneath him, or a situationally depressed worker who is distracted by all his problems but could recover and return to work with the proper assistance? Because you never know when you're going to suddenly find yourself in a potentially lethal situation, I provide some specific guidelines for defusing a potentially violent encounter that could save your life and those of your employees and customers.

Finally, Chapter 12 pulls together ideas and concepts from the rest of the book to explain why competent management always represents the best example of leadership and to show you how to consolidate, reinforce, and expand these leadership skills to manage organizational stress, optimize your company's productivity, and further your personal career goals.

Each chapter in this book begins with a plain-language description of the particular personality style or psychological syndrome under discussion. It shows you how to identify both the strengths and the weaknesses of each type and then provides specific practical guidelines for managing that person (that's right, they're still *people,* not specimens) in the most efficient and respectful way possible. Throughout each chapter are concrete case examples from my own clinical and consulting practice to give the discussion blood, sinew, nerve, and bone. Certain features of identity and circumstance have been changed to protect the privacy of the individuals involved; but, because these are real cases, not every example in this book will represent a pure personality type, illustrate a perfect intervention, or have a happy ending. I think it's far more instructive to show you how things turn out in the real business world than to leave you scratching your head about why your daily experience doesn't match an arbitrary set of prefabricated textbook cases.

Even bosses have bosses, and most real-life managers understand only too well that a huge chunk of their job consists of channeling the demands from above into workable directives below. Accordingly, this book recognizes the crucial need for a guide for managers to productively manage those who manage them—again, not to manipulate, not to trick, but to use effective people skills to enhance communication and reinforce company morale.

And whether you like it or not, you may recognize your *own* personality and interaction patterns within these pages, so a special section of each chapter enables you to refine and improve your own management and communication styles. Often, we learn the most about ourselves from observing others. In addition to learning how to manage your employees, I hope you'll come away from this book with a little insight into your own work psyche, which will, in turn, make you a far more effective steward of the intricate and fascinating work psyches of those whose careers have been placed in your capable hands.

. . . .
Shrinkers and Clingers
Avoidant and Dependent Employees

Most of us prize our ability to socialize and relate to people in a pleasant and constructive way. That is because most of us possess the basic self-confidence and social poise required to negotiate interpersonal encounters smoothly. For some people, communication is a natural skill—they just seem to have been born with a gift for connecting with people and use it buoyantly and enthusiastically. Others have to work at it, but they are still able to master the art of communication sufficiently to navigate their social worlds.

But there are those who regard the prospect of interacting with others as a gut-twisting challenge. The thought of speaking up at a meeting or discussing a project with a boss, a coworker, or even a subordinate fills them with dread. Then there are others who will be only too happy to engage you—and never let go. Although not necessarily unpleasant, these individuals seem to hang on to you for life support, requiring an excessively high level of guidance, supervision, and reassurance.

If one of these individuals works for you, or vice versa, you need to be able to engage the person sufficiently to make the interaction worthwhile, but at the same time not come off as a scary presence that will spook the person into silence or unintentionally encourage him or her to depend on you for every little decision and action.

Avoidant Personality

What They're Thinking

"Keep a low profile. Don't make waves. Don't stick my neck out. People are scary. Just do my job, stay out of trouble, and everything will be all right."

What They're Like

An *avoidant personality* has a pattern of social inhibition, feelings of inadequacy, and hypersensitivity to negative evaluation or criticism. Even relatively neutral or potentially pleasant interactions with people are approached with dread, and any sort of real confrontation is out of the question. These are people who fear people. They are uncomfortable in social situations, don't hang out with the crowd at the coffee urn, and decline invitations to office parties. Yet, they are not antisocial per se and are usually very polite and accommodating in demeanor. In fact, they may secretly long for the very human companionship that they are so fearful of pursuing. They therefore are typically very lonely people.

Others perceive them as being perpetual wallflowers, yet their overall pleasant and deferential style makes them basically likeable. They are rarely rejected outright from social groups, but they are more likely to be simply overlooked or left out. They may develop a small number of close friendships with peers who are relatively nonthreatening and nondemanding, and they possess the basic capacity for empathy and human connection—if only they could get over being so shy.

Because of their fear of social engagement, avoidant workers are usually at a distinct disadvantage in job roles that require any kind of entrepreneurial people skills. Often, their interactions with people create a vicious cycle because their palpable discomfort at conversing makes the other person increasingly antsy and anxious to get out of there. This discomfort is picked up by the avoidant employee, who then becomes even more halting and subdued in his or her communication style, further heightening the tension level for all concerned.

If feeling particularly threatened, the avoidant employee may avoid work altogether, calling in sick or even seeking permanent disability for "job stress" or other ailments. Extreme social phobia also carries the risk of alcohol or substance abuse as a form of self-medication for anxiety, but serious addiction tends to be less of a problem with avoidant workers than with other personality types, such as the antisocial or borderline. Sometimes, avoidant workers may be prone to somatizing their distress in the form of psychosomatic symptoms and illnesses (see Chapter 9). In general, however, their conscientiousness and eagerness to please make them reliable and compliant workers, even if they don't show great independence and initiative or go the proverbial extra mile.

In general, avoidant personality types tend to gravitate toward relatively obscure, low-level occupational roles in which there is little need to interact with others. A well-defined work situation with minimal interpersonal contact can be compatible with this personality type, and under these conditions, they tend to make very stable and reliable workers.

The Avoidant Boss

As might be expected, few individuals with an avoidant personality style actively seek positions of power and authority. Occasionally, however, their otherwise good technical skills may get them appointed to head some project (after all, they could hardly refuse), and thus they'll be thrust, at least temporarily, into the position of leader. In this role, they may function adequately as long as they can stick to the technical aspects of the task and the project is relatively routine and not interpersonally stressful.

If you are working on a project with an avoidant boss, you'll likely feel frustrated by the lack of direction or constructive feedback you get. Try to encourage your boss to outline your task or role as clearly as possible, and make it clear that you view constructive criticism not as a confrontation or challenge but as a way of improving the performance of the whole team. Once you gain the trust and respect of your avoidant boss, you'll probably find him to be a valuable resource, although you'll probably have to keep soliciting his help, rather than expect it to be readily forthcoming.

One danger is that your less scrupulous colleagues may find the avoidant boss an easy mark. The natural tendency of avoidant personalities to sidestep confrontations may allow others to get away with inadequate performances or to engage in frankly unethical and illegal activities (see Chapter 10) that may get the whole company in trouble. If such a potential exists, and your boss won't act, you may have to go above the avoidant supervisor's head and let the higher-ups know—not to get your boss in trouble but just the opposite: to protect him from the unsavory actions of the jerks below.

> ▦ *CASE STUDY.* Alex had a great reputation for being the best catalog designer the BellTex Company had ever worked with. Some people joked that hardly anybody ever saw him come out of his cubicle; they just phoned or e-mailed in what they wanted and out came a finished catalog that was always perfect. So perfect, in fact, that when BellTex wanted to expand operations and hire a bigger production staff, Alex was the logical choice to head up the project, which would involve training and supervising a small team of writers and illustrators.
>
> So it was quite a surprise to Joy, his supervisor, when Alex tried to turn the position down. Was Alex mad at Joy or unhappy at BellTex, she wondered aloud? No, Alex sheepishly replied, he just didn't know if he could handle the "complexity" of working with other people in a larger department. "Look," Joy replied somewhat testily, "we're going to do this expansion and we'd love you to be in charge of the catalog, but if you can't do it, we have to find somebody else. Let me know by five."
>
> Alex didn't want to jeopardize his job, so he reluctantly accepted the assignment. It wasn't long before Joy started getting complaints from the new team that the catalog project was floundering from a lack of direction. "Alex certainly seems to know his stuff in the print and computer aspects," one of the team members told Joy, "but we just can't get him to *tell* us anything. We try to have these design meetings and he just kind of sits there and gives one-word answers to our questions, like he really doesn't want to be there or something. If we fall any further behind, we're going to be late with the spring issue." Joy was troubled. She didn't want to fire or demote Alex, but she was responsible for keeping production on schedule and couldn't let the project collapse.
>
> Fortunately, it was another member of the new design team, Mitch, who stumbled on the solution. Instead of cornering Alex in team meetings, Mitch started e-mailing his questions and suggestions to Alex's workstation. He encouraged another

team member to do so, and within a day or two, the team had set up an informal intranet chat room where they could brainstorm ideas for the catalog and, even better, instantly display their design ideas on-screen for all to critique and comment on. Alex still needed to meet with the team face-to-face once in a while to review the actual hard copy for the print version of the catalog, but this seemed to be tolerable.

The team discovered they actually liked working with Alex, who, from behind his computer screen, was far more comfortable imparting his creative and organizational wisdom. The catalog was completed on schedule; Joy was joyful; the team continued on happily; and Alex, somewhat encouraged by his success in dealing with his team online, actually became a little more confident and easygoing in dealing with them face-to-face. He would never be the life of any party, but he had forged a good working relationship with his design team.

The Avoidant Employee

Give the avoidant employee a specific task to do, keep the supervision brief and positive, let her stay out of the spotlight, and the avoidant worker may be your most reliable and faithful employee. Obviously, few occupations allow workers to be total hermits, but if the work description calls for competent technical, clerical, mechanical, or physical skills without much need for regular human contact, the avoidant employee will usually do a good job.

Most work roles, however, require some kind of periodic supervision or evaluation. Remember, the avoidant personality is not antisocial, just intimidated by people, especially authority figures. So keep the supervision light, more in line with a coaching and counseling approach, rather than as criticism or discipline per se (more on this topic in Chapter 10). Actually, disciplinary problems are the least of your concerns with the avoidant employee; if anything, this person is more likely to underreport problems for fear of "making waves." Left to fester, these problems could potentially corrode company productivity or morale, so you may have to proactively, but nonthreateningly, solicit her feedback. Of course, if the avoidant employee consistently fails to perform up to par and won't respond to gentle encouragement, you may have to be more forceful. If this worker can't tolerate well-intentioned constructive criticism, she will probably eventually just leave the company.

⁝⁝⁝ *CASE STUDY*. This was the third time Judith had found an excuse to postpone her quarterly performance review. When Mr. Lowry finally demanded she meet him in his office, she looked like she was about to face a firing squad. Mr. Lowry saw her distress and tried to be as supportive and calm as he could. As he began going over Judith's acceptable, if not outstanding, performance record for the last quarter, Judith suddenly burst into tears. Upon questioning, she revealed that, for the last six months, she had allowed a brash young salesperson, named Hank, to file incomplete and sometimes altered sales invoices. "He promised he'd come back and finish them later, but he never did," Judith tearfully explained.

Although displeased by this clear breach of rules, Mr. Lowry tried to be understanding. "Why'd you let him get away with that?" he asked. "The first time it happened," said Judith, "Hank was just so loud and talked so fast that by the time I knew it he was out of there and I had the incomplete invoice in front of me. I didn't know what to do, so I filled in a few blanks that seemed right and filed it. When he asked me to do it again, I started to say no, but he came on so forceful about being a 'team player' and how we're supposed to 'cover for each other.' I just got overwhelmed and didn't know what to do, so I just repeated what I did the first time. And then it went on and on and I didn't know what to do."

"Why didn't you come to me and report it?" Mr. Lowry asked. Judith's answer was simple: "I was afraid. I was afraid if I did report it, I'd get in trouble or be fired for helping him, but I was also afraid that if I didn't cover for Hank, he'd make extra trouble for me—he could be so forceful, like he was angry if I didn't do what he wanted. Then, I'd just stand there and not know what to say. Also, I wasn't quite sure how to report it or whom to report it to."

Mr. Lowry thought for a minute. Then, he said, "Judith, we have to treat all employees equally and fairly. Because your actions are a clear violation of company rules, I have to refer this for disciplinary action and it's going to affect this quarter's evaluation rating. But since this is a first offense, you're unlikely to be fired. What I'm going to recommend are a few sessions of job coaching to make sure you clearly understand the company policies and procedures for filing sales invoices and the exact mechanism of filing a breach-of-rules report. If you're ever unsure about something, I want you to feel free to come and ask me—I'm never going to zap anyone for asking an honest question. If you correct the problem, then by next quarter, your review rating will go up. We'll investigate Hank's actions and deal with him as necessary through our disciplinary process. Your assignment for now is just to go back and do your job."

If *You* Are an Avoidant Personality

Reading this book will help you to understand and deal with the personalities you work with. Often, however, the hardest thing to face is the possibility that *you* may be part of the problem. This chapter section requires you to sit back for a moment and engage in a little constructive self-examination. Why? Because, ultimately, the person you have the most control over is yourself. If you can productively modify your own behavior and work style, you'll have a much easier time influencing your coworkers to modify theirs. You may even learn a little about yourself in the process.

Remember the diagnostic labels I'm using here are for convenience, to conform with the terminology used by mental health clinicians. As with applying them to others, don't let the sometimes funky-sounding names throw you; pay more attention to the descriptions and recommendations and learn to apply them to your own improvement in work style.

If You Are an Avoidant Boss

As much as you may enjoy the pay and perks of your new or longstanding supervisory position, you're probably uncomfortable every time you have to interact with a subordinate and you look forward to any kind of conflict or confrontation with sheer dread. Part of the problem is that because interpersonal reactions are characteristically unpleasant for you, you've spent a lifetime sidestepping them, so you really haven't had much practice in dealing with people. This is something psychologists call *avoidance conditioning*. You avoid something you fear, which temporarily reduces your anxiety, so you keep on avoiding it—and more and more situations like it—in order to keep the anxiety at a tolerable level. The problem is that you never give yourself the chance to learn that most interpersonal interactions are not painful or stressful, but are at least neutral and sometimes even enjoyable.

You're not going to be able to rewire your nervous system by reading a book, but here are some practical suggestions for dealing with the people you supervise.

Regularize. As much as possible, keep things to a schedule. If supervisory sessions are part of your responsibilities, try to hold them at certain hours of certain days. Sure, unexpected situations may arise that have to be dealt with on the fly, but most tasks at work can be scheduled as needed. That gives you time to prepare for the next suggestion.

Standardize. You probably think that everybody else does things easily and effortlessly and that you're the only person who has to struggle. In reality, most of those who make it look easy actually have laid the groundwork through careful planning and practice. So can you. In preparation for your regular meetings, have a written-up protocol that you can either refer to on a clipboard or recall from memory. There's no shame in taking notes for any kind of meeting, large or small, and, in fact, doing so shows that you take the encounter seriously and is more likely to garner you respect. As you get accustomed to the routine, you'll need to rely on your notes less and less and others will soon be remarking how "easy" you make the supervisory process seem.

What about unscheduled meetings and other emergencies? Even here, it's unlikely that anything will happen that you can't at least conceive of and prepare a contingency plan for in advance. So keep a file (index cards, ring binder, computer disk, whatever works for you) that covers the typical and unusual scenarios you might have to deal with. Some of these may come straight from your company manual; others you may have to custom design yourself. Go over your notes on a regular basis and practice talking through the various scenarios. The more often you do it, the more comfortable it will feel.

Find a mentor. You know you have a problem getting close to people and trusting them, and that's not going to change overnight. But in the meantime, don't be afraid to seek the aid of those who have gone before you. Most people will be flattered if you ask their advice—to a point. Maybe there is a senior manager or an officer in the company who seems to be basically a good guy or gal and who can be a source of valuable information. Remember, it's a lot less stressful not to have to reinvent the wheel.

If You Are an Avoidant Employee

Chances are, you've found a niche in the work world that allows you to keep a low profile and keep your interactions with others at a minimum. But there may be times when you have to deal with coworkers or supervisors, so here are a few tips to keep the process as painless as possible.

Prepare. You probably have a pretty good idea about what aspects of your job allow you to function independently and what aspects involve some kind of interaction with a colleague or supervisor. Make a list of these situations and write out some possible scenarios for dealing with them. Meetings are probably especially stressful for you, so prepare for each meeting by anticipating the topics to be covered and what your role is likely to be. Remember, as bad as having all those people in the room at one time may seem, this may actually be preferable to some one-on-one encounters because the group meeting allows you to get lost in the crowd, so there might actually be less to prepare for. The downside, of course, is that you and your good ideas may get lost in the shuffle if you don't speak up.

Listen. A lot of anxiety over conversations has to do with the fear of what you'll actually have to say. Because of this, you're probably so preoccupied with thinking of *how* to respond that you barely hear *what* is being said to you; consequently, when it's your turn to speak, you only have partial input to base your answer on. The result is more panic. What you say, then, will have greater import if you first carefully listen to what the other person says. Practice listening to the other speaker, first in nondemanding situations and among people with whom you feel relatively comfortable.

When it's your turn to respond, say what flows naturally. As you become more at ease with the conversational give-and-take, apply these skills to less familiar people and more demanding encounters.

Try to see people as a resource, not a threat. I know—easy for me to say. But you don't have to walk around in fear. At work and outside it, cultivate nonthreatening acquaintances that might eventually lead to friendships. Get used to just being around people without breaking a sweat. Start with people you already know and trust and then gradually expand your social network. Let people into your world and try to become a part of theirs.

Dependent Personality

What They're Thinking

"Just tell me what to do. Show me carefully so I don't make a mistake and disappoint you. Do you still think I'm a good worker? Do you still like me? I don't know what I'd do without this job."

What They're Like

"Neediness" is the word here. The *dependent personality* shows a pattern of submissive and clinging behavior stemming from an excessive need to be taken care of. Whereas avoidant personalities fear people and prefer to be away from them, dependent personalities need people and fear only their rejection or lack of support. Also, while avoidant workers may be reluctant to ask for directions because the interaction makes them nervous, dependent personalities may show the opposite problem: they never *stop* asking.

Dependent personalities look to others to provide guidance and direction and are ready-made followers. As such, they may actually be good, dedicated workers, as long as independent decision making is kept to a minimum. Work interactions are apt to be taken more personally than with other workers, because dependent employees crave positive strokes at work for validation of their essential worthiness and likability as human beings. As such, their feelings are easily hurt, even by seemingly neutral or innocuous constructive criticism, but they are far less likely to nurse a grudge than the narcissistic, paranoid, or borderline worker.

Overdependence on validation from others, hypersensitivity to slights and rejections, and overreaction to real or imagined criticism may combine to make the dependent worker suffer unnecessary stress and strain on the job. Part of this situation is because they tend to overly focus on the emotional effect their task will have on others, sometimes to the neglect of the technical aspects of the assignment itself: "How will this make me look? What will others think of me?" Once in a relatively secure position, any threatened loss of a job may seem like the end of the world and send them into a psychological tailspin. Otherwise, their slavish devotion to supervisors who provide sufficient validation may make them among the most loyal of employees.

The Dependent Boss

As with avoidant personalities, dependent personalities rarely seek out positions of authority and responsibility on their own, yet may be thrust into them by virtue of their technical skills in certain kinds of team projects. As conscripted work team leaders, they are likely to be the kind of bosses who must have as much info as possible before making a decision, and they may become flustered if there is disagreement among team members on how to proceed. Their hesitation does not stem so much from the preoccupation with details that paralyzes the obsessive-compulsive personality, but from the fear of being disliked and disrespected if they make the "wrong" decision and from their emphasis on consensus and harmony above all. A self-fulfilling prophecy may evolve as their fear of losing respect leads to procrastination, which frustrates the subordinate team members, leading to true erosion of authority and a worsening rudderlessness of the project as a whole. Subordinates may complain, "Who's in charge here?"

If you have a dependent boss, try to keep the larger goals of the work team and company in mind. You may have to "carry" the boss in terms of organizing and presenting the work as pretty much already a done deal, and let her rubber-stamp it if necessary. If you have a dependent boss, making her look good may be the only way to make your team look good. In less extreme cases, if you give your dependent boss a little more informational support than usual, as well as the right kind of strokes when appropriate, you may find her to be a fair and loyal ally, and certainly a lot easier to work for than some other kinds of bosses, such as the narcissistic, antisocial, or paranoid types.

▓▓ *CASE STUDY.* "If I hear her say, 'What do *you* think?' one more time, I'm gonna run out of the room screaming. Can't she just make a friggin' decision?" That was the consensus about working for Sophia, the bright and generally cheerful sales manager for a property developer. But as a manager, she never seemed to come to a definitive conclusion about anything. Ironically, there was an engraved plaque on her desk that read, I VALUE YOUR INPUT, but what she couldn't seem to understand was that all the input in the world is useless if you don't use it to come up with a plan of action. Nobody actually disliked working with Sophia; they were just frustrated by her lack of direction.

What seemed to jam up the process was Sophia's continual need for validation and approval. Although supposedly valuing input, she reacted to any kind of well-meaning questioning as a personal attack on her credibility and authority, which could grind the meeting to a halt. Her workers then felt in the position of having to act like "yes-yes" drones to keep the process moving along or risk a stall in the road if they raised a question.

It turned out that Sophia had a particular problem with Brad, the top sales producer, who had cultivated an assertive style that was quite effective in selling homes to prospective buyers. He would listen to his prospects' concerns and counter every point with rapid-fire refutations, delivered in a logical, authoritative tone that seemed to impress most of his would-be clients. Because Brad was basically honest and ethical about the content of his proposals, his manner was taken as forthright and direct. This "let's get down to business" approach worked well in the sales office and on the home sites, but when carried over into the sales meetings, it had the unintended effect of intimidating and paralyzing Sophia, who withheld making any kind of point or giving any direction for fear of Brad's blasting it down.

Fortunately, this interpersonal dynamic was observed by another sales representative, Ken, who was able to convince Brad to soften his style of presentation at the sales meetings. This wouldn't solve the whole problem, though, because it was unreasonable to expect everyone to walk around on eggshells just to avoid spooking Sophia. Finally, after some lunch table discussions, a group of sales reps called a private meeting with Sophia and told her that they really enjoyed working with her, and *did* appreciate that she welcomed their input, but that they would really like some more concrete guidance and that, most important, they didn't expect every decision to be a perfect one.

Through this combination of approaches, Sophia—still showing some hesitancy—was better able to express her opinions at the sales meetings. By including a certain amount of support and reinforcement in their welcomed input, the sales staff was able to turn a vicious cycle into a positive one. Sophia continued to value their input and now they could make better use of more of Sophia's output.

The Dependent Employee

It might seem that this employee's need for approval and eagerness to please would make the dependent personality the ideal assistant or subordinate. And for simple, directed tasks this is usually true. The problem arises when the dependent employee has to take any kind of initiative or make an independent decision. At first gratified by the new employee's seeming eagerness to learn, bosses may eventually become irritated by this person's never-ending quest for re-explanation and reassurance. Coaching and counseling (see Chapter 10) such employees is at first rewarding as they appear, spongelike, to soak up every new idea and suggestion. After a while, however, bosses may feel, "Enough is enough—can't he do *anything* without me holding his hand?" Other employees may resent the extra attention the dependent employee gets, while growing tired themselves of his constant queries for direction and reassurance.

However, if you're able to provide a low-stress, progressive type of corrective supervision that gradually helps the dependent employee master the tasks he needs—and if you can keep the emphasis on reinforcing the good behavior without overcriticizing the bad—this employee may eventually feel secure enough in the work relationship to operate a little more independently and do a good job. Remember that the dependent employee *wants* to do well; approval is his emotional oxygen. If you can train him carefully and dose your encouragement accordingly, you will have a loyal, competent, and stable worker.

::::: *CASE STUDY*. Phil had the potential to be one of the best mechanics at the auto dealer repair shop. His work was always done meticulously and completed on time. The trouble was that every time he had to start a new job, he peppered Carlos, the shop floor manager, with a million questions about what to do and how to do it. "Phil, you don't have to ask me each time you do something," Carlos kept saying. But Phil always seemed to need that go-ahead stamp of approval before starting a new task.

Finally, Carlos had an idea. The vast majority of engine repairs were for routine car problems. Using a set of index cards, Carlos had Phil write out the procedures for each of the more common repair jobs. After reviewing them and making a few minor alterations, Carlos told Phil to consult the cards whenever the repairs were of the usual, routine variety. In these cases, Carlos assured him, Phil would have the manager's complete support and blessing on whatever repair actions he felt were necessary as long as he documented them in his workbook as per the standard procedure. Only if there was something unusual did he have to speak to Carlos directly.

Reluctantly at first, Phil began using the new system and to his and Carlos's delight, he was able to gradually expand the range of repairs that he could work on independently. Phil was even able to show Jorge—a mechanic who had no trouble working alone, but was a little too sloppy and unorganized— how to use the card system to improve his own efficiency.

If *You* Are a Dependent Personality

If You Are a Dependent Boss

Understand that your desire to be liked and fear of disapproval are holding you back from being a successful manager. Worse, your reluctance to supervise effectively may result in a lack of direction and lack of productivity of the whole team or department. Therefore, carefully consider the following recommendations.

Watch your tone and style of communication. It's important to realize that employees far more rarely take offense at the content of a particular message than at the tone and style in which it's delivered. As long as you treat your people with respect—and that doesn't mean being afraid of them—then they will mostly respect you back, even though they may grumble about a particular decision or judgment call you make. Every interaction does not have to be a popularity contest.

Seek reasonable guidance and reassurance from the higher-ups. The operative word here is *reasonable.* Knowing you have the support from your superiors to take the actions you feel are necessary is a good thing, but don't overrely on it. There will be times you have to wing it without specific preapproval from above. If you use your best judgment and are prepared to explain why you did what you did, you will rarely be faulted for taking a good-faith leap.

Encourage feedback from those below you. This doesn't mean asking them how to do your job, but encouraging input that will keep you in the loop so that your decisions and actions reflect the reality of your department. However, understand that encouraging feedback also invites criticism, constructive or otherwise, so be careful not to send a mixed message: Don't tell everyone about your open-door policy, then cringe or bristle when something you don't like comes sailing through the portal. Remember that most people just want to have a pleasant place to work, and if you supervise with respectful authority, you'll get more cooperation than you might have anticipated.

Cultivate diverse relationships and extracurricular activities. The less the work world becomes your whole world, the less you'll have to rely on any one particular person or group for your own validation. Whether it be family members, poker buddies, fellow church members, or a few cherished friends, having people in your corner whom you can be real with away from the job makes it easier to deal with the stresses of management at work.

If You Are a Dependent Employee

You may be so afraid of making the wrong move that you're paralyzing yourself into workplace limbo. It's not even about getting ahead: just staying in your present position requires that you take a certain degree of initiative in your daily work. Here are some ways of doing that without choking.

Find out who knows what. Make sure you ask the right people the right questions. No one likes to be asked a question he or she can't answer. Utilize your company personnel directory and chain-of-command sheet and find out who are the best sources of what kind of information.

Learn as much as you can on your own. This will help you avoid excessive questioning and will hone those questions you do ask into intelligent, targeted information-seeking packets that demonstrate at least as much knowledge as they ask for in return. Actually, you're probably familiar with this process from job interview strategies that advise you to get as much background information on the company you're applying to in order to show that you're a serious contender and that, if hired, you can hit the ground running. Well, the same applies when you're actually *on* the job. Most supervisors will welcome an honest question that represents an effort to extend your knowledge base, but they will grow tired of queries that sound like you want them to tell you how to do your job. Ask, but ask wisely—which leads to the next recommendation.

Learn how to ask for help. If possible, focus on a specific task, not global appeals for help. To minimize the repeat-question phenomenon, make mental or written notes. If you must go back for more information, make each successive query more focused, so it's obvious you're developing a learning curve, not just going on endless fishing expeditions.

Cultivate something you're really good at doing. Away from work, find a sport or hobby at which you can excel. This jolt of confidence will prove a welcome antidote to the toxic ineffectuality you may be feeling after a particularly stressful help-seeking encounter.

CHAPTER 3

Emoters and Reactors

Histrionic and Borderline Employees

You probably know people whose lives seem to be a perpetual drama, men and women who live on an emotional rollercoaster, who seem always to be careening from crisis to crisis. Dealing with such people can range from amusing to maddening and it's possible that you work for some of them or have some of them working for you. On their good days, they may actually be competent, pleasant employees or supervisors; on their bad days, they can be hell on wheels to work with. This chapter will help you get the most out of their positive characteristics and minimize the fallout from the negative.

Histrionic Personality

What They're Thinking

"Don't confuse me with all these details. I think with my heart, go with my gut. If it feels right, it must be right. I love to be the center of attention. Are you sure you like me? When I'm up, the whole world smiles with me; when I'm down, the whole world has come to an end. But life is a cabaret, so look great and have a good time. If my job isn't fun, why do it?"

What They're Like

The *histrionic personality* shows a pattern of excessive emotionality, attention seeking, a need for excitement, flamboyant theatricality in speech and behavior, a nonlogical and impressionistic cognitive style, and the use of exaggeration to maintain largely superficial relationships for the purpose of getting emotional needs met by being cared for by others. When such needs are not met, the histrionic personality may become petulant, angry, depressed, and/or develop psychosomatic ailments and symptoms (see Chapter 9). When she is in an "up" mood, she will be delightful and entertaining to be with—bubbly, flirty, the life of the party. In fact, histrionic personalities naturally gravitate to careers that put them in front of crowds: acting, politics, teaching, sales, and so on. This is the ultimate "people person."

Unlike the overly intense, needy, and edgy persona of the borderline, histrionic personalities typically present themselves as interpersonally engaged and genuinely likeable. Even when snubbed and dissed, they are less likely to nurse a grudge. Hey, anger and gloom are downers, so why dwell on bad feelings! With their quick wit and engaging touchy-feely interpersonal style, histrionic personalities tend to form great first impressions because, for them, this is not an act. They absolutely love getting attention from people and actively seek out such positive interactions.

The problem comes in the follow-through. The histrionic personality is characterized by what has been described as an *impressionistic cognitive style*. In direct contrast to the obsessive-compulsive personality, whose painstaking preoccupation with details causes him to miss the forest for the trees, for the histrionic personality there are *no* trees, only an ever-shifting forest. Decisions tend to be formed on the basis of impressions and intuitions, with rational analysis of facts and details regarded as an intrusive annoyance: "If it feels right, it must be true; don't bother me with piddling facts." In some contexts, this gut-instinct type of decision making may lead to flashes of insight and spontaneous creativity, but without careful follow-up organization and planning, the project may disintegrate into a million directionless pieces.

Worse, without grounding in logic and reason, impressionistically formed opinions and decisions tend to shift abruptly. What feels right and is therefore absolutely true today is completely different than what felt right and was absolutely true yesterday. Ditto for tomorrow. Not surprisingly, then, these individuals can be extremely frustrating to work with.

For these reasons, histrionic personality traits are likely to prevent an employee from moving up very far within a highly structured organization, especially where attention to technical details or management of complex staff relationships is important. The pattern of attention-seeking behavior and the predominance of superficial sizzle over substantive steak soon wears thin. When histrionic employees perceive that their accomplishments have been undervalued—that their workmates and superiors don't *like* them— they may react with anger; depression; or, very characteristic for this personality type, a range of physical symptoms, all expressed with their characteristic flamboyant and theatrical style.

The Histrionic Boss

Potentially, this kind of boss could be a joy to work with—or a misery. As long as she is provided with sufficient support and validation from her employees, and as long as they make her look good to the higher-ups, her department may "feel the love" flowing continually around the workplace. The perky enthusiasm of an "up" histrionic boss may energize the work team around her, especially in those job roles that involve heavy-duty interpersonal contact, such as sales and marketing. One nice thing about histrionic bosses is that they give as good as they get: If they're happy, they want *everyone* to be happy, and they may be gracious and generous to a fault with employees who reciprocate their good feelings. Remember, they want work to be fun, fun, fun!

Real work is rarely all games and giggles, however, and the histrionic boss's cheery leadership style conceals two potential downsides. Downside number one is literally a down side: If the histrionic boss's mood abruptly switches from joy to gloom, she may drag everyone off the cliff with her. Then you might feel like your work environment has suddenly shifted from a theme park to a funeral home. The bright side is that these dour moods rarely last very long and protracted grudges are rarely held— remember, the histrionic personality's guiding priority is to feel good, and she will look for any excuse to forgive and forget as long as she can continue to soak up the adulation of her admirers.

Downside number two comes from the histrionic boss's impressionistic cognitive style. Zippy ideas may come fast and furious, but you may get little practical guidance from your histrionic boss on how to implement the details of these plans to make them workable. This is not due to fear of confrontation, as with the avoidant personality, but more related to the histrionic personality's pitiful lack of organizational skills. However, an assistant who can serve as a detail person can play an indispensable role on the histrionic boss's work team. Just imagine the meticulous campaign manager plotting out the schedule and herding the crowd around the hand-pumping, baby-kissing politician; or the no-nonsense business agent stewarding the career of the flamboyant rock star or celebrity motivational speaker.

Keep your histrionic boss happy by making her look good, express your sincere appreciation and admiration liberally, learn to translate her flashes of brilliance into workable accomplishments, and you will likely have a pleasant, loyal, and generous boss to work for. Remember that unlike many of the other personality types who seem to feed off misery, the histrionic personality genuinely wants to be happy, and if your happiness jives with her happiness, so much the better.

CASE STUDY. At first, the staff at the trendy *New Scene* magazine couldn't believe their good luck. Their former managing editor, competent to be sure, had been a real sourpuss to work for. But now, the rag had hired Caroline, who, at the first meeting, burst into the room like a rolling carnival, colorful clothes, flamboyant gestures, and lilting laugh making the whole room seem to levitate. Unlike her morose predecessor, Caroline seemed the perfect choice for this hip magazine.

Things started out great. Every morning, the daily staff meeting was provisioned with fresh donuts and coffee, there were frequent happy-hour convocations at the local pub, and project planning sessions were informal and ebullient affairs. Work got done and people had fun. But then things started to unravel. Caroline came late to meetings. She failed to show up for her posted office hours to confer with staff. Her characteristic cheeriness seemed to be thinning out; the smiles now seemed forced. Always the fashion plate, lately she appeared to pay less attention to how she looked. Some days she appeared bleary-eyed and her staff couldn't swear to it, but some of them thought she was royally hungover. Then, one day at a meeting, she exploded: "Do I have to do everything around here?"

A manager from another department asked if everything was all right. "That's personal," Caroline snapped back. The good mood of the members of the work group was curdling fast. Worse, their manager's frequent tardiness and absences meant that they had to fend for themselves in design production and deadlines. The situation was approaching mutiny. One Friday, a few senior staffers got together and decided to come up with ideas over the weekend and then meet on Monday to decide what action should be taken.

The next Monday morning, when Caroline again failed to show up for the morning meeting, the work group began discussing how to inform the human resources department—when, to everybody's amazement, Caroline, bedecked and beaming, bounded into the room bearing gourmet coffee and pastries and sat down, ready for business as usual. "Who died?" she quipped when she observed the silent gapes of the stunned staff. After a few moments, however, it was back to the good old days, the recent few weeks' unpleasantness forgotten.

And so up and down it went for the next several months. After enough of these cycles, the magazine's work group developed a contingency plan. When Caroline was in what the staff came to call her "red" mood, she was professional and efficient, bubbly and inspiring, a joy to work with. When, about every other month, she went into her "black" mood for a week or so, the team became skilled at working around her absences and desultory participation. She was good enough during her red periods that the group learned to carry her during the black ones.

Although many team members genuinely liked Caroline and wished she would get some help for her mysterious mood swings, they resigned themselves to taking her as she was, because, overall, she was still far easier to work with than the last slug—or than a new, unknown, managing editor might be. "Better the devil you know," as one staffer put it.

The Histrionic Employee

Good humor is infectious, and your histrionic employee may provide a refreshing dose of levity in an otherwise somber office environment. But sometimes work requires people to cut the comedy and get down to business, and if a weighty matter or outright crisis demands a more serious effort and tone at the workplace, the perennially perky Peter-Pan demeanor of the histrionic employee may soon take on a dyspeptic, saccharine quality. However, if you let the histrionic employee play to his strengths—as a salesperson, marketer, public relations representative, or front office staff person—he may quickly become a credit to your organization because his friendly, helpful style will genuinely make people feel good about themselves and about your company.

In the real world of work, though, just about any job has aspects that involve dealing with dull, ordinary paper-pushing, file-organizing, or housekeeping tasks. Unfortunately, this is not a personality style who takes well to crunching numbers, inputting data, or revising reports; he will quickly get bored and his efficiency will lag. If your histrionic employee is chronically late or messy with his work, appropriate supervision will be necessary. Supervisors need to take a highly supportive approach in describing and reinforcing work-relevant, positive behavior, but they must be able to back off a few emotional steps when excessive praise and attention are sought for their own sake.

Gentle, reality-based guidance ("I really appreciate your effort and enthusiasm, but you need to work a little harder on your own with this project to make sure it's completed according to our protocol and by the deadline") may shield the employee's self-esteem while refocusing his efforts on work-related tasks. Try to provide as much detail as necessary, so that the histrionic employee understands clearly how to carry out the task, but not so much explicit direction that he becomes dependent on your spoon-feeding every step of the project. Overall, if you provide the proper level of instruction and guidance, and lay on the praise when it is genuinely due, you will have an exceptionally loyal and pleasant employee.

> ⠿ CASE STUDY. Maybe Ed, the Halo Pharmaceutical Company sales supervisor, should have been suspicious when Michael insisted on being called "Mikey." But Mikey seemed to be a born sales rep for the new heart medication that the company was launching. That smile—it could charm the hardest-hearted

cardiologist into taking the stethoscope out of his ears to listen to Mikey's pitch. That enthusiasm—Mikey seemed to pulse on like a boundlessly beeping EKG, always ready for the next contact. Those outfits—Mikey was a good-looking young man and dressed like a model to impress the medical office staffs he visited. That patter—to his credit, Mikey did his homework to nail the medical facts and lingo down cold and presented them in a serious, yet engaging manner. It was naturally assumed that he'd have every doctor in his new territory eating out of his hand.

Things got off with a bang. The first few contacts went great and the medical staff at the doctors' offices loved Mikey, especially when he brought in the Halo-sponsored lavish catered lunches that were the mainstay of pharmaceutical sales calls. The doctors were impressed with Mikey's medical acumen and even those docs who didn't place orders right away invited him back for follow-up meetings.

After a while, though, it seemed like the glitter was outpacing the guts. Mikey's suits kept getting sharper and sharper and the catered lunches kept getting fancier and fancier and he seemed to be spending more and more time out in the field. But there seemed to be less and less to show for it in terms of sales numbers. At first, his supervisor suspected that Mikey might be skimming, but an internal audit turned up nothing suspicious.

The real problem soon became apparent. A master of the face-to-face deal, Mikey fell to pieces on the follow-up. He couldn't seem to maintain records and turn in contact sheets as required. This was despite the fact that these oversights and delays affected not just company profits but his own commissions as well.

Mikey was referred to a special company in-service on record-keeping skills and this helped for a while. However, it soon became clear that the paperwork problem was not about a lack of ability—Mikey just couldn't force himself to spend more than a moment of time on anything that didn't involve presenting himself out there and giving a performance. Paperwork was just too damn boring, so he'd procrastinate and then rush through it, making numerous mistakes that then had to be laboriously corrected by the accounting department.

Finally, Ed, the sales supervisor, had to make a decision. Mikey was a born showman, but unless he could do the grunt work and get his paperwork in on time and correctly, he was on his way to becoming a losing proposition. Ed thought of getting Mikey an assistant to clean up his paperwork, but then, every other salesperson would rightly grumble about why Mikey had gotten special treatment. Yet, Mikey was such a damn good sales presenter, it would be a shame to let him go.

Unless . . . a memo had come through the past week about starting a company-based Halo Speakers Bureau that would give presentations to large audiences of both medical professionals and public groups about the new Halo wonder drugs. Although the usual company literature and paraphernalia (brochures, pens, cup holders, and mouse pads) would be distributed, there'd be no actual selling at these meetings. Interested parties would contact the company via mail, telephone, or website and would then be contacted by an individual sales rep who would make the pitch. The only downside for the presenters was that this was a straight salary position, the commissions going to the reps who actually made the sales.

Ed cautiously presented this option to Mikey and was surprised when Mikey seemed positively relieved to have this opportunity to do his out-front stuff without the scut work headache. The speakers program was launched and it wasn't long before Mikey—with his legendary suits, professional yet entertaining patter, and sheer joy of working a room—was reaping company awards for the best presenter. However, both Ed and Mikey never forgot that it was a lucky twist of fate that brought the Speakers Bureau around when it did; otherwise, for all his raw talent, Mikey would likely have been out of a job.

If *You* Are a Histrionic Personality

If You Are a Histrionic Boss

One of the things you probably like best about your supervisory role is the opportunity to hold forth and give people the benefit of your expertise and experience, because helping them do well and feel good makes you feel good. And if that's what you're doing, great. But if your workers have any complaints about you, these probably fall into two categories: (1) You put the gas pedal to the floor, start the ride, marvel at the scenery, but then become distracted and don't know how to follow the map to the journey's end. That is, you generate great enthusiasm and energy but have problems with the follow-through. (2) You have a hard time separating the business from the personal aspects of the job. If someone messes up, you're more likely to take it personally, which puts added pressure on your employees. Or you expect every employee to be your confidante and buddy, even though that makes some of them uncomfortable. Therefore, here are some recommendations for digesting the meat and potatoes of a work project while still leaving room for dessert.

Prepare. Before you embark on a new project, take a deep breath and ask yourself: "What do I actually know about this task? After I present the main idea, what concrete steps will I have to take to guide this project to its completion?" This, in turn, leads to the next recommendation.

Get assistance. Know your limitations and try to compensate for them by enlisting help. As long as you're doing *your* job correctly, there's no shame in asking for assistance in the things at which you're not as proficient. So if there is a detail person on your team, recruit him or her to help carry out the nuts and bolts of the project's execution. Again, don't expect someone else to do *your* job, but be wise enough to delegate appropriately.

Don't take it personally. Look, it might be nice if everybody at work could be all warm and huggy, but unfortunately, in the real world, too much familiarity can lead others to take advantage of you if they perceive that you'll do pretty much anything to be liked. If you're the boss, you may sometimes have to flunk the popularity test in order to pull rank and assert your company's right to have its employees do the jobs they're paid for. When this happens, resist the temptation to see things as all-or-nothing. Firm, responsible supervision on your part doesn't have to fatally impair a good working relationship and may even improve it if employees end up having more respect for you for calling the shots as you see them.

If You Are a Histrionic Employee

There's no law that says your job has to be harder than necessary but remember that it's called "work" for a reason. Even if you love what you're doing, often you're going to have to buckle down, concentrate, and follow a task through to completion. Granted, your creatively spontaneous mind doesn't do well with picayune details, but if you're in a job that regularly requires this kind of meticulousness, you might have to ask yourself if it's really for you. Another danger spot involves relationships at work. You are particularly susceptible to having your good work disrupted by bad relationships, and although it may be hard to keep the boundaries straight, if you don't, it could jeopardize the job you love. Here are some recommendations.

Again, don't take everything personally. This doesn't mean you can't have friends at work. Just don't expect them to suspend the rules of working relationships just because they're your friends. If your boss critiques your work, try to separate this criticism from criticism of you as a person. As a rule, make *objectivity* your default mode at work.

Have all the fun you want—where it's appropriate. It's fine to have fun at the office party, after work, and on weekends. Some coworkers will be your friends; others won't. Again, be aware of the boundaries and do your best to stay within them. A particular danger involves love affairs at work. Sometimes they have a happy ending, but when they don't, guess what? When it ends, you and the other person still have to work there. There's an expression you've heard that I won't repeat here about not commingling two certain activities, but it certainly applies to workplace romances. Please let your heart be guided by your brain.

Borderline Personality

What They're Thinking

"This is the best job I'll ever have; this is the worst place I've ever worked. The people in this office are great; the people who work here are slime. My job is my life; if I lost it, I'd die. No one could possibly understand the true depths of my profound feelings. I didn't lie; I just changed my mind and if you don't believe me, drop dead and go to hell."

What They're Like

A *borderline personality* displays a pattern of instability in interpersonal relationships, fragile self-image, and wild emotional swings. Manic highs of boundless optimism may lead to rash, impulsive actions, which are later regretted with depressive self-loathing, sometimes to the point of suicidal gestures; not surprisingly, bipolar disorder (see Chapter 7) is a frequently accompanying syndrome and the two conditions may in fact be expressions of a common disorder. At extremes, borderline personalities seem to be out of touch with reality: Whatever they feel or believe at the moment is the absolute truth, which may then abruptly shift 180 degrees if a different mood or thought strikes them. This trait can give their behavior and relationships a mercurial Jekyll-and-Hyde quality. In fact, this is where the term "borderline" comes from: At times, these individuals seem to be straddling the border between mere neurotic pathos and outright psychotic craziness.

Their changeability may sometimes be mistaken for phoniness, but unlike the antisocial or paranoid personalities, the borderline is not necessarily consciously lying or manipulating. Like the histrionic personality, with whom it may overlap, the borderline sincerely believes in whatever version of the truth she's telling at the moment, and if she changes her story, she expects you to go along happily with the new version—and gets angry if you don't. At other times, however, she may quite deliberately lie and make up whatever story she thinks will get people to do what she wants; she feels entitled to manipulate people in this way because she feels there is no other way to get them to do what she desperately needs them to. Again, the problem is that even the lies aren't consistent; the story versions keep changing and her audience gets sick and tired of trying to keep up.

This changeability also affects personal and business relationships, a phenomenon known as *alternating idealization and devaluation*. There are no gray areas in borderline personalities' estimation of people; they either love you or hate you, and they may swing from one extreme to the other with equal white-hot intensity. They are supremely passionate people, in both the positive and negative senses of that word. Their mental absolutism also applies to opinions of people, a phenomenon called *splitting*: People are not seen as having textured and complex characters; they're either all good or all bad—again, often the same people at different times. The result is maddening unpredictability, because you never know from one encounter to the next how your borderline workmate will react to you. History means nothing, and context means nothing; whatever the dominant emotion is at the moment colors the borderline's feelings and therefore interactions with the other person, no matter what the objective reality may be.

Part of the reason for this dizzying alternation between rigidity and fluidity relates to the core identity issue with borderline personalities: They just don't feel like whole, substantial people, so they rely on others to mold and support their own self-identities. This accounts for their characteristic dread of being alone. Without external social support, they are unable to modulate their own feelings of emptiness and disintegration and may resort to substance abuse, marathon sex, binge eating, or self-injury to provide some kind of external stimulation, some bodily anchor to temporarily stabilize the drifting vessel of their psyche.

Anger is another core feature of the borderline personality. Frequently capable of superficial cordiality and charm, borderlines may fly into rages—privately smoldering or openly aflame—that seem inextinguishably all consuming. Much of this anger relates to the fear of being abandoned by overly idealized others: "I loved you, I trusted you! How dare you not fulfill my each and every emotional need: I hate you, I'll kill you!" As employees, they may overidentify with their work role or supervisors to the extent that a threatened job loss is equated with death of self. Except perhaps for paranoid personalities, borderlines are the types most likely to hold a grudge. They can be destructively vindictive and relentlessly stalk their targets, or they can bide their time and wait for the right moment to strike back. Outward-directed anger may alternate with inward-directed self-loathing in the form of suicidal gestures. On a less extreme level, borderlines are often the classic injustice collectors who always seem to carry around a voluminously catalogued and cross-referenced mental file of hurts, slights, and betrayals that they can flawlessly recall and recount at a moment's notice; in this way, they share similarities with the passive-aggressive personality.

The Borderline Boss

Hold on to your seats, keep your arms and legs inside the vehicle at all times, and hang on for the ride. Severe borderline personalities rarely maintain a sufficient level of interpersonal stability or sustained work productivity to attain lasting positions of responsibility, but milder forms of this personality type may function adequately, even superbly, on the job, reserving their most flagrant disturbances for their long-suffering families, close friends, or intimate work associates.

The watchword is *unpredictability*. Your borderline boss may send you off to do a project, which you complete and turn in only to be told it wasn't what she wanted at all. You swear it was and you have her written confirmation to prove it. "Well, that might be what it says, but you knew that's not what I meant." She's not bamboozling you. She really believes that because she changed her mind on the project, you should have somehow become aware of the changes. The past is irrelevant; what she believes and says now is reality.

Another difficulty in dealing with borderline bosses is their use of idealization and devaluation. Say you've managed to complete a few tasks satisfactorily and made your boss look good. Now you're the golden boy or gal; you can do no wrong. You continue to pile success upon success, basking in the glow of profuse supervisory praise. Then you drop the ball. Once. Hard. All past triumphs and accolades are instantly and irretrievably forgotten and you're on the shit list. How long you stay on that list is determined by your boss's moods and circumstances. After reaming you mercilessly and humiliating you in front of your colleagues, she will come back an hour, a day, or a week later sweet as can be, all past unpleasantness now dispelled, and expect you to respond in kind. If you continue to pout, she'll berate *you* for holding a grudge and lecture you about how unprofessional it is to let personal feelings interfere with business.

If there is some advancement, bonus, or promotional advantage to gain by sticking with your borderline boss, you may be able to do so—and keep your sanity in the process—if you learn to predict her moods and antics and can steel yourself to the emotional pyrotechnics and inconsistencies that come with the job. Some obsessive-compulsive workers make very good assistants to borderline bosses because their basic orderliness of mind and tight organization of work operate as a kind of psychic glue that holds the crumbly ego of the borderline together. More practically, obsessive-compulsive employees may be singularly able to actualize the creative ideas of their more impulsive and scattered borderline boss. Dependent personalities may latch on to borderline bosses because the latter's stormy moods and erratic behavior give the dependent employee a vicarious taste of passion and excitement. In addition, dependent workers may relish the idealization that borderlines ladle out—as long as things go their way.

CASE STUDY. Hilda's employees at the finance company had all sorts of pet names for her. "Hilda the Horrible" was one. "Hitler" was another. Some of the others are unprintable. However, she was known for running a tight ship and being a meticulous and hard worker, so her employees treated her with a kind of respectful disdain, even as they felt themselves going crazy from the daily pressures of working for her.

What had earned Hilda this special opprobrium? If you asked any of her employees, they'd probably say something like, "You can't trust her. She's a big phony. She'll reel you in by acting all compassionate and concerned and then use what you told her against you. If you do a hundred good things that reflect credit on her, you're her fair-haired child, but then screw up just once and you're in the dog pile." Add to that the occasional rages with which Hilda would lambaste the entire office and then storm off only to reappear hours or days later acting like nothing had ever happened.

The staff noticed that these mood swings seemed to occur in cycles. There'd be a run of several days where Hilda would be if not actually pleasant then at least civil, and the office would hum along efficiently enough. But then, there would begin a phase of edgy, crackling irritability, almost as if some kind of brain static were stretching and twisting Hilda's proverbial last nerve. "She'll be talking to you and you'll get the feeling that she's holding back all this anger, but she won't tell you what you supposedly did wrong to deserve it." Soon this smoldering ire would begin erupting into the little tirades for which Hilda cum Hitler was known. Finally, she would virtually disappear for a day or so, either sequestering herself in her office, or calling in sick. Then, she'd reappear and the cycle would start again.

Despite the overall good productivity record, there was considerable turnover in the department during the year since Hilda took over. The one holdout was Terrence, who never seemed to be fazed by Hilda's antics, and the other employees marveled at this, even as they scratched their heads about what his secret was. So somebody just flat out asked him. Terrence shrugged. "It's simple," he said. "I don't take it personally—that's just her baggage, not mine."

The stunning simplicity of this revelation sunk in for at least some of the other employees. Hilda was not going to change, so the people who wanted to keep working in her department would have to learn to detach and compartmentalize their emotional reactions to her episodic nuttiness while continuing to work with her efficiently. In addition, the successful remaining employees learned to keep their conversations with Hilda polite but not emotionally involved and to be careful not to say anything that might be used against them later. Although some just couldn't take the drama and quit, most stayed and learned to function within Horrible Hilda's world.

The Borderline Employee

"It's an honor working for you. Anything you need—anything!—I'm there."

Sure, that's how it starts. The borderline employee's tendency to overidealize may initially make her the most devoted of employees. But watch out if you cross her—which usually means doing something to suggest that you are really not the all-protective, lovingly supportive authority figure she had built you up to be. Remember, nothing rattles the borderline's shaky ego stability and fills her with panic and rage more than the threat of abandonment and betrayal. Then you're dirt. This period of loathing may last until she perceives that you "love" her again, in which case she'll be back to Mary Sunshine. Until the next time. And on it goes.

Another problem with borderline employees may have little to do with the job per se. Their chaotic personal lives—stormy romances, ongoing family feuds, suicidal depressions and mood swings, impulsive spending, substance abuse, and other health problems—may result in the overuse of sick days; disturbing calls at the office from disgruntled mates and paramours; and fluctuating work quality due to fatigue, anxiety, depression, or poor health.

On the other hand, many borderlines actually find work to be their one dependable haven of sanity and stability, and they will fight mightily to insulate this environment from the personal flotsam that otherwise swirls around them. These so-called high-functioning borderlines may seem to be almost superhumanly competent and reliable employees because their jobs are literally what hold them together. Friends and workmates who come to know this person may be stunned by the contrast between the individual's masterly efficiency and productivity at work and a personal life wracked with chaos and despair.

And therein lies one key to dealing with your borderline employee. As much as possible, try to provide her with a model of stability and reliability. Reward accomplishment appropriately, but set limits firmly (if gently). Give constructive criticism in as positive a context as possible: "You're doing great so far on the acquisitions project. Here are some ways to make even better use of your skills." To borrow a concept from psychodynamic theory, if you provide the right kind of *holding environment,* your borderline employee will probably try to do her best for you. Indeed, by acting like a true leader (see Chapter 12), you may come to be one of the few people in this person's life she can count on, and as this track record sinks in, the employee may respond over time with increasing loyalty and trust. Just be prepared for storms along the way.

> ⠿ *CASE STUDY.* Starting with next to nothing, Rafael had struggled for many years to build his medium-size air-conditioning and appliance-contracting company into a successful business, and he never forgot where he came from. So, he made a special point of treating all of his employees with courtesy and consideration as long as they were willing to do an honest job for the company. In that spirit, he expressed his concern to Sara when she came to work one morning with a bruise on her face. "I fell," was her clipped response.
>
> Sara had been a quietly efficient office manager for the past nine months, but since joining the company, her personal life had remained an enigma. The staff knew she wasn't married and lived with her eight-year-old son, but beyond that, she avoided conversations about her activities outside work. She seemed to have a pattern of coming in Mondays in a distraught and exhausted state, as if she had spent the whole weekend in

a pitched battle for her life. She often came to work early and stayed late, as if she didn't want to go home. Her mood would improve during the middle of the week, then begin to sour again as the weekend approached. But she did her job well answering phones, finalizing contracts, and filling out daily work schedules, so that everybody else's job was easier—so, hey, no complaints.

Then, one Monday morning, Rafael and the staff were surprised to see that Sara had arrived at the office earlier than anyone else. She appeared even more disheveled than usual and Rafael thought he could detect the faint smell of alcohol on her breath. Keeping true to his philosophy of respecting employees and desiring to salvage an otherwise excellent worker, Rafael called Sara into his office, sat her down, and asked what was going on. At first, she tried to stonewall him again, so he gently but firmly informed her that although her personal life was her own business, when it affected her health, appearance, or behavior on the job, it became a work and risk management issue. She could either tell him what was going on or get help from the company EAP, but there couldn't be a repeat of this the next Monday.

Sara hesitated for a few moments, then out spilled a tale of woe that surprised even the worldly Rafael. Sara lived a secret double life. Her evenings and weekends were spent in classic *Looking for Mr. Goodbar* mode, cruising bars, picking up men, and getting herself into desperately dysfunctional relationships. She would fall in love with a guy, and then either he'd cheat or she would, leading to battles and rejections, which would send her into despondent drinking binges. A few of these brawls had been physical and Sara confessed that the two sick days she took a few months ago were really to go to court to get a restraining order on some barfly who was stalking her. She started to cry: "I don't want to lose this job. This is the only place I feel safe, that I feel sane, that I don't feel like I'm dissolving into nothing."

Rafael listened quietly, then made the following proposal. He felt for Sara, he really did, but this was still a business. All of his

employees knew that he expected them to behave profession-
ally while at work, whether it was a technician out on a repair
job or an office staff member speaking to a client. He would like
Sara to begin seeing a mental health professional, either
through the company EAP, or privately through her insurance.
He couldn't *order* her to do this, but he was prepared to enforce
his rules about workplace conduct and decorum. One thing that
had to stop immediately was coming to work in an intoxicated
and disheveled state. Sara was actually relieved and reassured
by Rafael's combination of firmness and compassion and
agreed to make an appointment with a counselor that week.

If *You* Are a Borderline Personality

If You Are a Borderline Boss

I don't mean this in a flippant way, but it's probably no fun being you. For
whatever reason, you have a tough time dealing with your own self and
the people around you, and you probably feel you've been disappointed,
let down, and betrayed by a number of people in the past and present. Your
emotions often seem to run away with you and you find yourself impulsively doing things that you're later sorry for. Much of the time, you feel
out of control and that scares you. Other times, you feel angry and resentful
that other people seem to have such an easy time of it. Yet, you must have
done something right because here you are as a manager or supervisor
trying not to take out your crap on the people who work for you. Here are
some recommendations for making this domain a little more comfortable.

Don't suffer needlessly. If you're feeling emotionally overwhelmed, get
professional help. If nothing else, there are medications that can keep the
destabilizing mood swings from wrecking your life and your career. And
the right kind of psychotherapy can help you deal more effectively with
people in both your personal and work life. I'm not talking about mind
control here; in fact, getting the right kind of treatment will actually give
you *more* control over your own life.

Give people the benefit of the doubt. Unlike the paranoid personality, your
mistrust of people is not as neuropsychologically fixed in stone. Through a

series of lifelong vicious cycles, you've been emotionally knocked around so long that people have become a source of aversion to you. At the same time, you may desperately want to trust someone but fear the person will betray you in the end. The problem is that if you act this way toward your employees, it soon will become a self-fulfilling prophecy. So when starting to work with people, try to assume they'll do a good job. I'm not saying to be a fool or a patsy, but start out on the right foot and people will usually reciprocate.

If You Are a Borderline Employee

The expression "out of control" is your catchphrase, whether you apply it to yourself or others pin it on you. So, in your work life or personal life, here are some recommendations for taking some of that control back.

Don't go it alone. Get professional help. Although this advice applies for virtually all the people described in this book, for borderline personalities in particular, a stable, supportive, and professional therapeutic relationship can have a unique long-term healing effect. Don't discount this resource.

Use the Emotional Red Flag (ERF). Be very cautious if you find yourself liking or hating someone too much—"ERF alert!" Ask yourself if there's a reason for this or if this is part of your overreaction pattern. Try to get out of all-or-nothing thinking: Even if you don't like someone, you may still be able to work with that person constructively.

Utilize work as a refuge. Your job may be the one place you feel relatively competent and in control. This doesn't mean you should move into your office or change your name to the company logo, but try to examine the personal characteristics that make you function well at work and then see if you can apply them to other aspects of your life, for example, family communication styles. Modeling your own mature, stable behavior at work may enable you to apply these characteristics to your life in general.

CHAPTER 4

Preeners and Predators
Narcissistic and Antisocial Employees

In graduate school, I came across an article in a psychology journal that somewhat whimsically, but insightfully, divided personality disorders into "onion" and "garlic" types. Onion personalities are the internalizers; as with eating too many onions, these individuals give themselves mental indigestion. They may secondarily disturb others around them (phew—onions!), but most of their suffering is unto themselves. However, the externalizers—the garlic personalities—feel just fine; there's no bellyache or psyche-ache and the distress they cause is only for those around them (phew—garlic!).

Most of the personalities we've discussed so far are of the onion variety: They suffer as we suffer and that, at least, gives them some motivation to change. However, in this chapter, you'll learn how to deal with the garlic people who think that they're just fine the way they are—that if we can't deal with them, then hey, that's *our* problem. And your problem is that you may be working with one or more of these people right now.

Narcissistic Personality

What They're Thinking
"Rules are for the little people, not for me. Only I see things the way they really are. I'm always right, because I'm smarter. It's my way or the high-

way. Good things should come to me because I deserve them. I'm entitled to success, no matter what, because I'm special. People who criticize my performance are just jealous of my talent. Why don't other people acknowledge and appreciate me like they should? As long as people recognize my brilliance and power, I treat them right."

What They're Like

A *narcissistic personality* shows a pattern of grandiosity; entitlement; a need for admiration; and a lack of empathy for other people's ideas, feelings, or opinions. In other words, these are the classic "egotists" or "narcissists" who are largely indifferent to the feelings and reactions of others and expect unearned high praise regardless of their actual effort or accomplishment. The general response of others to obvious narcissists is some version of "Get over yourself." With their sense of entitlement and grandiosity, narcissistic personalities may not get it that others don't share their own inflated view of their competencies and worth, or they may simply not care about the meaningless opinions of inferior beings. Many narcissists are into thrills that make them feel good about themselves, so dysfunctional behavior associated with such personalities may include substance abuse, pathological gambling, sexual exploits, and other dubious adventures. The narcissistic personality often shades into and is commingled with elements of the antisocial and paranoid styles.

When people already believe that they are highly talented and accomplished, they're not likely to direct much effort toward self-improvement, because how can you improve on perfection? In mild cases, the narcissist may perceive that others don't share his inflated self-image but may "forgive" them because, after all, how can such intellectually shortsighted people possibly hope to understand his greatness. In more severe cases, the narcissist may have difficulty differentiating self from other and wish from reality, and so may idiosyncratically construe events on the basis of his own desired outcomes rather than on actual reality or sensitivity to the feelings and reactions of others. In such cases, this personality style may blend into the paranoid one.

Yet under the surface of many a narcissist's superficially bloated ego lies a core of fragile self-esteem and intense feelings of shame and inadequacy. In such cases, the expansive, hand-shaking, backslapping narcissist who's getting the adulation he thinks he deserves may suddenly turn on an emotional dime and transmogrify into a sullen, nasty, and vengeful enemy when the thin skin of his good fellowship is scratched by a critique or jibe. In other cases, the narcissistic hide is so thick and tough that even the worst insult hurled at him hardly makes a dimple—he *knows* that others merely resent him for his greatness and, like an elephant scoffing at a gnat, indulgently takes their petulant buzzings in stride.

The Narcissistic Boss

Like many other personalities, this kind of boss carries dual best case–worst case scenarios. In many business and political settings, narcissistic personalities may be enthusiastic, charismatic leaders who are eminently able to articulate the department's or company's mission (typically their own) and to inspire their employees to express that mission with cultlike dedication and zeal. Similar to histrionic personalities, as long as they feel their egos are being stroked, narcissists can be expansively generous to their underlings, regarding these noble servants as extensions of their own personas: "What's good for me is good for the company." Also like histrionics, narcissists are often possessed of keen interpersonal intelligence and are capable of flashes of brilliant insight and creativity—the executive idea generators of the company—but they usually need considerable assistance in the nitty-gritty details of bringing their plans to fruition.

Unlike histrionic personalities, however, the narcissistic boss who feels betrayed by an erstwhile acolyte will not likely just go off and sulk dejectedly but may become enraged and vindictive toward the traitor. Narcissists also tend to have much longer memories for injustice than histrionics (who usually just want to go back to having fun as quickly as possible), but they usually don't have as deeply detailed and cross-referenced an injustice file as the borderline or paranoid. If, for some reason, you have to disagree with your narcissistic boss, be sure to make it very clear how your alternative course of action will reflect positively on him and how if things get better because of your plan then . . . er . . . ah . . . maybe it might really have been his idea all along. Yes, this is one type of boss with whom the exquisite art of sucking up will serve you well if pursued with tact and backed by competent service.

If you do get your narcissistic boss mad at you, all is not lost. Remember, unlike many borderline or paranoid personalities who seem to actually get off on fuming with martyred outrage, narcissists—again, like histrionics—

fundamentally want to feel good about themselves. They enjoy the adulation of others, and if you can survive their initial firestorm over your perceived infraction, they will usually afford you an excuse to get back in their good graces. Be deferential and diplomatic and know at least that one compensation for your butt kissing will be a boss whose beneficent noblesse oblige you can rely on, as long as you know your place and play your role.

The main problem that arises in this context is when the narcissist consistently fails to put his money where his mouth is and the productivity of the whole department or company begins to suffer. If the underlings are unable or unwilling to keep picking up the slack, they may have to band together to complain higher up the ladder, thus risking the narcissistic boss's wrath. Still, such palace coups are far less bloody than what might occur when going up against an antisocial or paranoid boss.

CASE STUDY. Paul seemed the natural choice for executive director of New Lights, a faith-based support and advocacy group that raised money for medical and educational causes. "You have to be part preacher and part CEO to do this kind of work," Paul confidently told the hiring board, "and I'm just the man for the job." He justified his high-end salary demand by telling the board, "Wait till you see what I can do." Bowled over by his enthusiasm and charisma, the board hired Paul right away.

A few board members became suspicious when the first thing that Paul did was reorganize his personal staff, requesting three more assistants "to handle the increased business we're going to see." But Paul seemed so sure of himself and full of novel and innovative fund-raising ideas that the board figured it would justify the budget. The budget, however, kept expanding and now included expensive lunches with prospective donors: "You have to spend money to raise money," Paul explained. A few of these contacts actually did yield some substantial donations, but not enough to justify Paul's ever-ballooning budget.

Part of the problem was that Paul seemed to be in too many places at once. Overbooked on meetings, twenty different projects all going at once, Paul churned out one brilliant fund-raising plan after another. But his neglect of the follow-up meant that many donation pledges remained unrecorded and uncollected. Everybody knew Paul had good ideas and good contacts, but the money just wasn't coming in like it should.

The board members came to a decision: If Paul wanted to stay on, he would have to submit a monthly budget proposal to be approved by the board, would have to downsize his personal staff to two, and one of those assistants would have to be Dinesh, who was known as an excellent business manager and organizer. Paul wouldn't have to stop doing what he did best, chatting up prospective donors, but there would have to be some fiscal accountability and it would be Dinesh's job to keep things on track. Initially, Paul grumbled about "having to take orders from bean counters to do God's work," but Dinesh knew how to keep a low profile and let Paul hog the fund-raising limelight. Eventually, they worked out a respectful, if cool, working relationship.

The Narcissistic Employee

As might be expected, the narcissistic personality can make for a difficult employee because he feels chronically underappreciated. At the beginning of his employment, he'll seem flushed with enthusiasm over being able to impress everyone at his new job with his skill and brilliance. However, as it dawns on him that he is not the special star but just one of the troops, and as he realizes that his bosses and coworkers want him to do things in the regular way and expect a certain level and type of output, the mood of the narcissistic worker may sour and his motivation may flag. Supervisors may notice that as time goes by, their bright, new, creative team member seems to be more talk than action. Coaching, counseling, and mentoring (see Chapter 10) are all difficult with the narcissistic employee, because his self-inflated view and sense of entitlement cause him to dismiss out of hand any advice or direction he feels is coming from people who are, after all, beneath him.

If the narcissistic employee is doing an acceptable job, and there is genuine room for improvement, a collaborative, hand-on-the-shoulder, "we're in this together" coaching style may be effective, especially from someone the employee respects. The narcissistic worker may welcome the attention from the higher-up, especially if the coaching session includes soliciting the employee's input and advice: "You see the problem, don't you, Ralph? You've usually got some good ideas about these things—how do *you* think we can use your work to make our department more productive?"

Remember, the narcissist may actually have some useful ideas, even if he's not too good about carrying them to completion. Of course, if the narcissistic employee spouts forth unrealistic, nonsensical, and purely self-aggrandizing schemes, at least you'll be able to decide if you want to waste any more time with him. Again, the problem is rarely a lack of brilliant ideas; it's the narcissistic employee's lapses on the follow-through ("Why should I have to do all the scut work?") that cause the project to crash prematurely or rot on the vine.

A more malignant kind of narcissistic employee is the one whose sense of entitlement expands to include his natural right to manipulate and exploit others for his own purposes; this type often has features of the antisocial and paranoid personality styles as well. Often these individuals can be found at middle-management levels, where they have carved out their own little underground fiefdoms, intimidating their subordinates and sweet-talking (but resenting it) their superiors to keep the lid on. After a corporate shake-up, subsequent investigations may lead to the discovery of all kinds of unfair, corrupt, and illegal practices having occurred for years under the direction of these managers.

Even if not frankly dishonest, narcissists can develop intense personal investments in their job roles, and this is one type of personality that may likely resort to aggressive litigation or even violence when sanctioned or terminated. Thus, disciplining and, if necessary, firing these workers must be done carefully, tactfully, and be well documented (see Chapters 10 and 11).

> ::::: *CASE STUDY.* Considering that he was obviously smarter than most of the other applicants, Angelo couldn't believe that it had taken him three tries to pass the qualifying exams for the county firefighter-paramedic service. But he was overjoyed to finally become part of Station 33 and threw himself into the task. Generally acknowledged as a skilled and hard worker, he soon began to grate on his workmates with his constant corrections and advice about everything they were doing, whether it was

routine maintenance around the station, prep drills, or actual fire or emergency medical calls. Coming from the new kid on the block, this quickly fostered a "who-died-and-made-you-the-damn-fire-chief?" attitude on the part of his station mates.

Still, as long as Angelo did his job and pulled his weight on calls, the grumbling was kept low key. But then other things started happening. One morning over coffee, the station captain was surprised to see a letter to the editor of the local newspaper scathingly criticizing the Board of County Commissioners for its underfunding of emergency services. The letter was signed by Angelo, with the tagline, "Firefighter-Paramedic, Station 33." On his next shift, Angelo was promptly summoned to the station captain's office and reminded of the department's policy forbidding any employee to make a public statement about departmental activities without prior approval from the public information officer. It was clear from his expression that Angelo wasn't happy about this policy, but, for the sake of his job, he agreed to comply, muttering to himself about his free speech rights.

Things went well for a number of weeks until one evening there was a general call out involving several county police and fire stations to respond to a major traffic collision with fatalities involving an allegedly drunk driver and a tanker rollover. All of the paramedics dove into their work and lives were saved that night. But, as the crisis was winding down and the personnel were reporting in, there was Angelo standing in front of the news cameras holding forth about the state drunk-driving laws and the insufficient resources allocated by the county for traffic control and emergency response services.

The next morning, the captain of Station 33 received a stinging call from the county commissioner's office. Angelo's antics not only had violated the rules on public statements by county employees but may have compromised the legal case against the allegedly drunk driver. What was the captain going to do about this?

Although it was Angelo's day off, the captain summoned him in for an emergency meeting. Angelo obviously knew what the meeting was about because, as soon as he arrived, he launched into a speech about how he was proud to be a firefighter and how he had a right to express his views. The captain contained himself while he listened. Then he said, "Angelo, this is the second time you've disregarded county and departmental policy about public statements by county employees. As a result, there may be all kinds of administrative and legal implications for this department. You have an otherwise excellent work record, so here are your choices. You can go on disciplinary suspension without pay for two weeks. You can send a written apology to the Board of County Commissioners detailing what steps you're taking to prevent this from happening again. You can take a continuing education training course on county rules and by-laws at the local fire academy. Or you can resign. Think about it and get back to me by your next shift."

Angelo left the meeting feeling stunned and outraged. After all he'd done for that department—how dare they treat him this way! Maybe those other drones had to follow the stupid gag rules, but Angelo had so much to offer, it would be a crime to keep his superior ideas to himself. After a sleepless night, he sent a long, detailed e-mail to the captain of Station 33 and to the Board of County Commissioners explaining that he was not prepared to be silenced in his good-faith efforts to improve county services to its citizens. He was thereby tending his resignation and would seek employment at an agency and in a jurisdiction that was prepared to appreciate him. When last heard of, he had joined the military and was shipping out to the Persian Gulf as an army medic trainer. Perhaps in this role, his former captain mused, he might find a productive niche as the all-wise teacher and mentor to young army medics and might thus actually contribute to saving American lives.

If *You* Are a Narcissistic Personality

If You Are a Narcissistic Boss

You'll probably be surprised to hear me say this, but you may be (at least partly) right about your high opinion of yourself. No, I'm not patronizing

you. Many people of high talent who have scored legitimate accomplishments feel no compulsion to be overly modest about them. The problem
is finding the right audience. Most people won't want to hear you blow
your own horn, even about real victories, because it implies an invidious
comparison with their own imputed lack of achievement. So, to maintain
peaceful relations with the mortals, you may often have to self-congratulate
in silence.

The problem arises where it's a matter of blowing your horn without a
backup band. Then, you have to be careful about trumpeting your *future*
successes or *potential* big deals, or you'll end up being perceived as a tuneless
blowhard. Even where your achievements are more substantial, a separate
problem is expecting other people to rise to your standards. Assuming your
talent, energy, and drive have propelled you to the top (or on your way to
the top) of your game, most of the people who work for you won't have
your level of motivation or ability. Therefore, to get the best from the
people you have, you can't give them the impression that you think they're
a bunch of slackers, or their motivation will disintegrate completely. Here
are some recommendations for maintaining your authority as a competent
and confident manager.

Document your credentials. Whether it's your resume or the diplomas on
your wall, don't be afraid to use concrete reminders of what you've accomplished. Even if others remain unimpressed, this will help assuage your ego
when people take you for granted. I'm not saying to marinate in your own
accollades, but when you're feeling down and disrespected, it sometimes
helps to remind yourself that you *have* accomplished some important
things—even if no one around you recognizes it at the moment. Use your
past and present achievements to give yourself hope for better days.

Separate the sizzle from the steak. Be realistic about what you can be
proud of and tout. Try to separate your great ideas for someday from what
you've actually done up to today. In fact, the more you accomplish in the
here and now, the more credibility your future plans will have.

Know your audience. The mechanics at the auto body shop don't really
give a flying lug nut that you graduated at the top of your business college
class. The other CPAs in the financial firm will be unmoved by the Ama-

teur Mr. Galaxy bodybuilding trophy on your desk. When you tell your friends at the Christmas party that your book on Southeast Asian economic policy won a United Nations scholarship award, don't be surprised if they ask you why you didn't make a million bucks and go on *Oprah*. Not everybody appreciates everything; share your accomplishments with those who can relate.

Treat all employees with respect. One area where your high-status recognition can make a difference is in how you treat those who work for you. Your attitude and behavior toward the troops may have more meaning to them when they know it comes from a special person. Whenever possible, act with nobility. Don't look down on, or talk down to, employees or you'll sap their motivation and make them angry and spiteful, no matter how great you think you are.

If You Are a Narcissistic Employee
You probably walk around in a continual state of frustration, irritated by feeling stuck in a job that's beneath you and working for people you know you're better than. In what kind of unfair universe could this possibly have happened? Here are some ways to break this cycle of unproductive rumination.

Take an honest self-inventory. This is probably the hardest thing to do because you've become so accustomed to seeing your lack of success as everyone else's fault. But I'd like you to sit back, take a deep breath, and ask yourself: "If I possess a range of talents and abilities that should be getting me ahead, what am I doing or not doing that's standing in the way of my success? And what are those other more successful people doing or not doing that's enabling them, even with less talent than I have, to get ahead?" Use the answers to these questions as a source of strategy, not sour grapes.

Emulate the successful. This is a corollary of the previous recommendation. You can't be a carbon copy of someone else, but you can learn the basic elements of success in your field by observing, analyzing, and creatively replicating what others are doing right.

Present your ideas appropriately. Often, it's not that others don't want to hear your ideas; it's just that they don't want to feel like you're putting them down by acting like a self-important asshole. Learn diplomacy. Again, observe how others get their good ideas across successfully and emulate those positive aspects of their style that jive with your own personality.

Antisocial Personality

What They're Thinking

"It's a dog-eat-dog world. Look out for number one. Rules are for losers. I'm smarter than all these suckers. Their way of doing things is too boring—I need excitement. Don't think too much—shoot from the hip. No guts, no glory. My needs come first. I can get over on anyone. Though I walk through the valley of the shadow of death, I will fear no evil because I'm the baddest son of a bitch in the valley. Live fast, die young, and leave a good-looking corpse."

What They're Like

An *antisocial personality* shows a pattern of consistent disregard for, and violation of, the rules of civilized behavior and the rights of others. In its extreme form, this pattern is associated with destructive impulsivity, criminal behavior, sexual promiscuity, substance abuse, and an exploitive, parasitic, and predatory lifestyle. Not the kind of person you want working in your company, but, all too often, the kind you get.

In their most severe form, antisocial personalities show a flagrant disregard for the rights and feelings of others. They seem to have literally been born without a conscience and without the ability to empathize; other people are simply sources of gratification for them. Ironically, in a business culture that seems more and more to endorse a style of Machiavellian management and winning through intimidation, the antisocial personality has become a paradigm of the cutthroat, chainsaw-type entrepreneur. In their less extreme forms, antisocial personalities may show a keen predatory intelligence and be quite intuitive about the needs and desires of different people, which they then use to manipulate others to their own ends. Many an employer has been sucked in by the glib, superficial charm of the well-groomed interviewee with an impressive but probably phony resume.

And yet, many antisocial personalities do possess genuine mechanical and technical skills that, at least initially, allow them to ingratiate themselves to their employers. Fundamentally, however, antisocial personalities live for the game. The thrill of putting one over on the suckers—that is, all the rest of us—and reinforcing their own sense of cleverness and powerfulness becomes an end in itself. For this reason, a few of them manage to rise to positions of corporate or political power where they are in a position to do great harm.

Usually not before they have left a trail of mayhem behind them, something eventually manages to trip these characters up. Their continued partying or sexual harassing or cheating or embezzling finally can't be covered up or explained away. Often, observers are surprised at the paltriness of the reward for which these individuals may risk their whole careers, not realizing that the antisocial personality can't resist the temptation to score one more con, no matter how seemingly inconsequential. The thrill of the hunt must be fulfilled. Reasoning, pleas to conscience, punishment, psychotherapy, even appeals to simple self-interest all have little effect: The antisocial personality feels entitled by his superior strength and cleverness to use other people for his own ends and to take advantage of those sorry chumps and suckers who play by the rules.

There actually seem to be two, albeit related, species of antisocial personality. The first, characterized primarily by the cunning-conning dimension, is often very intelligent in a devious kind of way, can mask or project emotions at will, and is preternaturally clever at manipulating other people. This kind of antisocial personality is better able to suppress his impulsivity in the service of a bigger scheme—the classic "smooth operator." This character tends to slip up when the webs he has woven become too tangled even for him to keep straight; then, all kinds of plots and intrigues may start to unravel, threatening to undo the con man. Even at that point, he may show surprising resilience, projecting a sincere-sounding facade of remorse and then getting right back to mischief, as soon as the heat is off.

The second kind of antisocial personality *tries* to be just as cunning and conning but is relatively lower on the IQ scale and higher on the impulsivity dimension, and so he tends to screw up more quickly, more often, and in the form of more frankly confrontational or even violent behavior. He soon learns to live more by his fists—actual or metaphorical—than by his wits and relies on bullying and intimidation to get his way. In the worst case, this is the classic habitual criminal who is unwilling to live by society's rules, is always in one kind of trouble or another, has a long legal rap sheet going back to childhood, and forever blames bad luck or everyone else around him for his troubles.

Of course, in real life, many antisocial personalities are somewhere on the continuum between these two subtypes. For example, a successful con man may glibly ply his deceptive trade until someone exposes or challenges him, whereupon he may fly into a rage and impulsively resort to violence as "the only way out—I had no choice; the guy got in my face so I had to drop him."

The Antisocial Boss

This boss will drive and exploit his underlings as long as he can get something out of them, but don't expect any real gratitude or loyalty: Once your usefulness is over, out you go without a second thought. Nevertheless, as long as you serve his purposes, you may be a pampered and well-treated right-hand employee. If you can stand the uncertainty and can tolerate the disingenuousness, hang on for the ride. Many people actually get a kick out of working for an antisocial boss, vicariously basking in the sense of power that can come from allying oneself with a ruthless corporate carnivore at the top of the proverbial food chain. You may even be in a position to help your boss moderate some of his excesses, and thereby aid him in achieving even greater success. And to keep you in his pocket, he may praise and reward you profusely, but don't believe any of it. He knows it was really his own strength and cleverness that got him to the top; you're just a disposable functionary, temporarily along for the ride.

And what a thrilling ride it may be—until the antisocial boss's sins catch up with him, in which case you'll probably be dragged down by whatever scandal or catastrophe finally undoes him. Worse, he will have no compunction about throwing you to the wolves, lying about how all this mess was *your* idea, how he was merely duped into your web of wrongdoing, an innocent victim of circumstance. On a more everyday level, the antisocial boss will blithely steal credit for his employee's work and lie and change his story when it suits him, blaming others to cover his butt. And when the smoke clears, don't be surprised if he turns around, slaps you on the back with a collegial guffaw, and expects you to forget the whole thing, to let bygones be bygones—until the next time, repeating this cycle of betrayal and rapprochement until you're fed up enough to leave.

Overall, seriously antisocial bosses tend to be notoriously bad in the management department. Their impulsivity and lack of reflection may lead them to issue and alter instructions at whim, resulting in the derailment of projects, which they will then blame on their supervisors, associates, or employees—anyone but themselves. The one consolation is that truly anti-social bosses usually don't last long; sooner or later they screw up and get canned, but sometimes not before they've done a great deal of damage to relationships and careers. One need only think of the corporate and political scandals in recent years to understand my own variation of a well-known principle: Power corrupts and absolute power corrupts absolutely—but only if someone is absolutely corruptible.

CASE STUDY. "You didn't get to the top of the medical management game by being a pussy," Carl told himself. Like any business, it was eat or be eaten. He always knew he was a smart operator: He had brains and knew how to use them to get ahead. He sailed through college and medical school—partly because of his native intelligence, partly because of devising new and more clever ways to cheat on exams. In fact, entrepreneur that he was, in college he ran a clandestine online term-paper mill with another student for several years and when it finally looked like the operation was going to be busted, Carl managed to bail and pin the whole thing on his unsuspecting partner.

In medical school, he was almost expelled twice for questionable academic activities, but he managed to fast-talk his way out of the jams. While in med school, he ran an online travel agency and some other businesses that were eventually shut down by authorities. Although bright, he was involved in so many outside activities that he graduated med school with only average grades. He took his residency in orthopedics, already with an eye to setting up a chain of rehab clinics.

He opened his first clinic with a bank loan. With his charm and enthusiasm, he was soon attracting a steady stream of patients, many from attorneys representing workers compensation and other insurance cases who were seeking quick disability determinations for their clients so they could collect cash settlements. This quickly evolved into an illegal kickback scheme with several disreputable attorneys. It wasn't long before Carl's clinic garnered underground reputation as the go-to place for doctored disability reports.

The money was pouring in, and Carl soon opened a second, then a third clinic, expanding his insurance fraud operation, even while doing a fair share of legitimate, good-quality rehabilitation, largely through the efforts of his dedicated physical therapy staff. Cracks in the operation started appearing when Carl told his staff that he expected their clinical notes to be written a "certain way." Staff who balked at this record-tampering scheme were either bribed to comply or asked to resign.

But why stop with insurance profits? Medication management was an important part of rehabilitation, and Carl soon had a lucrative side business as a "candy man" to a steady stream of selectively referred chronic pain patients. With all his profits, licit and illicit, Carl invested in real estate and securities and was quickly becoming a wealthy man. He was poised to open several more clinics when the hammer fell.

One of his pain-pill patients died of an overdose and the family sued. One investigation led to another, and within a matter of weeks, Carl was the subject of several criminal charges and additional civil lawsuits. With characteristic cunning and aplomb, Carl and his lawyers managed to work out a deal whereby he would avoid jail time and pay a combined settlement in exchange for surrendering his state medical license and divesting his stake in his clinics, which were sold off to a huge national medical management chain.

Which gave Carl another idea. Even without a medical license, he still understood the business of health care and, through a combination of intelligence and guile, quickly fast-tracked himself an online master of healthcare business administration degree. He then pitched himself to the board of another major medical management company, a rival of the one that had bought his clinics. He got himself hired as a district manager, and it wasn't long before he rose to the rank of executive vice president of the corporation. He proved to be especially good at acquiring and expanding existing facilities and opening up new ones. The awards, bonuses, and accolades poured in.

What his backslapping corporate comrades didn't know, however, was that Carl was operating another string of insurance scam and pill-pushing clinics under a pseudonymous company name in another state. When this latest deception was discovered, it all came crashing down. Carl had simply spread himself too thin and no amount of cleverness or money could get him out of this one. Carl is now serving a prison term and, not surprisingly, continues to operate several, albeit more modest, businesses from his jail cell.

The Antisocial Employee

You may have encountered a number of otherwise competent employees who never seem to make the most of their skills, instead drifting from job to job, staying a while before either messing up or abruptly walking off, and never achieving anything of substance, all the time believing that they're smarter than everyone else, and that it's just a matter of time until their cleverness pays off in a big score. Shady or outright criminal activity will alternate with ordinary chump work, and while temporarily on such a straight job (usually only because they have no other choice at the moment), they may bend every rule and exploit every angle until they finally get fired.

Your antisocial employee will do the absolute minimum amount of work he can get away with, take advantage of every benefit and privilege, antagonize your good employees, drive business away, and finally sue you or attack you when you try to discipline or fire him. What do you do?

The best measure is prevention. Take your hiring responsibilities seriously, screen carefully, and check all references. The best predictor of future behavior is past behavior, so study the applicant's work record. A one-time jail stint early in life may represent a young-and-dumb mistake by an otherwise decent individual, but be wary of a string of such brushes with the law or an inconsistent or suspiciously rosy work record.

If you're already stuck with an antisocial employee, try to make the most of him by giving clear directions and monitoring his performance. For short, simple tasks, such as seasonal retail work or a temporary construction job, his skills may allow him to do an adequate job. And with his high energy level and boundless craving for thrills and action, he may throw himself enthusiastically into a particularly stimulating job. But this character also bores quickly, so don't expect a long-term commitment un-less he's using your company for his own purposes. Finally, have a well-thought-out and carefully documented system of discipline, so if you have to fire him, you minimize the risk of a huge legal stink for spite and profit.

CASE STUDY. "Forget 'em if they can't take a joke," had al-ways been Chico's motto. Hey, he had no beef with any-body—as long as no one got in his way. He enjoyed getting high but wasn't "one of those suckers who gets hooked," whom he viewed with contempt. He'd done a little jail time when he was "punk enough to get caught" but managed to keep most of his illegal activity from the cops and even took straight jobs—cook, store clerk, construction worker—when he was between hustles and needed money.

This was one of those times. In a hurricane-ravaged part of the country, a government contractor was looking for able-bodied young men to help clear debris to prepare building sites for new homes. Chico signed on and was attached to a work crew. At first, the on-site supervisors were impressed by how intensely Chico threw himself into the physically demanding work; he seemed to take genuine pleasure in flexing his muscles and breaking a sweat, and he soon was promoted to crew boss, overseeing the work of about a dozen other workers. Again, this started well, Chico relishing his role as the alpha dog but man-aging to avoid turning it into an overt power trip. If anything, the crew members felt there was too little supervision, often won-dering where their boss was and having to figure out the day's work orders themselves.

Within a few weeks, things started to unravel further. Chico showed up later and later for his shift. A number of times, his crew noticed that he looked stoned or hungover. He went from being a tireless worker to a worker who always seemed tired. As crew boss, he had access to the toolshed and the area su-pervisor noticed that certain items seemed to be walking away. Increasingly, Chico prevailed upon his crew members to do his jobs for him or to lend him money that he kept promising to pay back. He was quick to take advantage of the fact that many of the workers were undocumented and scared of drawing attention to themselves by filing a complaint. What his supervisors didn't know, however, was that Chico was doing a substantial side business selling drugs to workers and residents up and down the hurricane-affected region.

One morning, the area supervisor called him into the field office and told him he would have to reassign Chico to another work crew—and as a regular worker, not as a boss. In that moment, Chico felt the double sting of being generally disrespected and, furthermore, seeing his lucrative drug hustle evaporate. The supervisor was startled by what he perceived to be a look of pure, boiling rage on Chico's face; he was sure Chico was about to clock him. Through superhuman self-restraint, however, Chico managed to control himself—no way was he going back to jail for this piece of crap.

The supervisor offered to let him finish out the week as crew boss before his reassignment. Chico just stormed out of the office. The next day, he didn't show up for work. Attempts to reach him by phone failed. The day after that, it was discovered that a variety of tools and electronic equipment were missing and several company vehicles had been vandalized.

If *You* Are an Antisocial Personality

If You Are an Antisocial Boss

Let's be straight. Probably the only reason you're reading a book like this is to get the goods on other people, to make you a better exploiter. But as long as I have your attention, let me tell you something I know you won't believe: sooner or later, you *will* outsmart your damn self. So if you enjoy getting over on people for the thrill of it, at least act in your own self-interest by noting the following recommendations.

Play by (at least some of) the rules. Nothing says you can't be an aggressive entrepreneur, but try to keep it safe and legal—if only not to see everything you've worked for blow up in your face. When tempted to push the limit, ask yourself this simple question: "If it all goes to shit because of this, will it have been worth it?" Only you can answer that question.

Don't burn your bridges. One reason for treating your employees decently is that they're more likely to do what you want if they like you than if they hate your guts. So try to keep your power trips under control or you may find one day that the power has been yanked away from you. Again, only you know if you have enough good sense to do this.

If You Are an Antisocial Employee

You picked up this book out of curiosity, but, in your opinion, this whole psychology hustle is for suckers—you don't need any help understanding people; you've been playing with their heads your whole life. You're only working at your present job (maybe a clerk in a bookstore) for what you can temporarily get out of it. Okay, so here are some recommendations for doing just that.

What goes around comes around. If someone were deliberately screwing you, laughing at you the whole time, and you found out about it, what would you do? Right. And that's probably what *they'll* do when they discover you've been screwing them. So save yourself some payback and steer clear of messing with people who may later mess you up—physically, legally, or economically.

Think ahead. I know long-term consequences aren't typically on your radar, but think about how to use the job you're in now to your own legitimate advantage later—which will probably be more beneficial to you if you do things the right way instead of the hard way.

Get smarter. This applies to everyone, but especially to you. You're often tempted to take illicit shortcuts because you don't know how to do it the straight way. You're a smart cookie—learn something.

CHAPTER 5

Detailers and Vigilantes

Obsessive-Compulsive and Paranoid Employees

Focus is a good thing, right? Especially in the business world, the ability to concentrate on a project, stay on task, and screen out distractions is prized as a productivity-enhancing cognitive skill. But, as Aristotle said, a virtue is situated between two vices. Too little focus, and our efforts become aimless and scattered; too much, and we start grinding our mental gears, gumming up the engine of creativity with dollops of trivia. Or we squint so hard that we start to see shapes and patterns that aren't really there, make connections in our heads that aren't connected in real life. The personality patterns in this chapter can be said to involve too much of a (sometimes) good thing, extreme variations that impair, rather than enhance, productivity at work.

Obsessive-Compulsive Personality

What They're Thinking

"I've got to get it 100 percent perfect. God is in the details. Haste makes waste. Leave nothing to chance. Look before you leap. If you want something done right, do it yourself. Keep tabs on everything at all times."

What They're Like

This worker can be your best dream or your worst nightmare. The *obsessive-compulsive personality* is preoccupied with orderliness, perfectionism, and control. In milder forms, these types make excellent detail wonks who can be relied on to know everything about everything and to carry out instructions to the letter and beyond. At worst, they can become so immersed in minutiae that they miss the proverbial forest for the trees: Projects may be done perfectly, but they are completed too late to do any good.

These are your classic, card-carrying workaholics, so slavishly devoted to their jobs that they may neglect family, friends, and all other extracurricular activities. Their minds are exquisitely tuned to detail and they tend to excel in jobs that require exactitude and precision, even seeming to relish the kinds of repetitive checking tasks that would numb the brain cells of most other employees. Obsessive-compulsive employees used to be seen carrying slide rules; now they wield Palm Pilots. It's no coincidence that they gravitate toward jobs that make the best use of their high-level cognitive skills and devotion to detail—engineering, economics, accounting, editing, and so forth. At the same time, they are much less likely to have the intuitive flashes of insight or to possess the glib social adroitness of the histrionic or narcissistic personality.

Obsessive-compulsive personalities are not necessarily asocial or even particularly shy, as we've seen with avoidant personalities; indeed, they can be socially adept, even formally cordial, when the situation calls for it. But overall, they'd rather get back to the work on their desk than schmooze at the watercooler. Interpersonal interactions for them are just another type of tool for getting the job done.

The main psychological dynamic is *control*. Obsessive-compulsive personalities are extremely uncomfortable with imprecision, ambiguity, or lack of clarity. The greater the intellectual grasp they have on a situation, the better—they are scientists, not artists; planners, not dreamers; astronomers, not astronauts. In fact, the modern U.S. work culture appears to reward those who "give 110 percent" and "go the extra mile," and in these settings, an element of obsessive preoccupation and compulsive striving may well be an asset.

It's a matter of degree. Problems arise when this cognitive style intrudes into work situations where spontaneity and sociability are more appropriate. If not sure what to do, these individuals may be paralyzed with indecisiveness. They will squirm uncomfortably at a marketing luncheon to woo a new client, but then they'll head straight back to the office and grind out a meticulously researched, polished, and professional-looking prospectus that clinches the deal. At best, they derive their satisfaction from a job well done; at worst, there is no such thing as good enough and they will make themselves sick—and drive everyone around them crazy—trying to be better than perfect.

The Obsessive-Compulsive Boss

Be prepared to work hard, but if you're able to meet the exacting demands of your obsessive-compulsive boss, you will be respected and rewarded. Remember, for these managers, it's the job that counts, so if you measure up to the task, your obsessive-compulsive boss will be more than happy to give credit where it is due—unlike the narcissistic, antisocial, or sometimes histrionic boss who'll be delighted to let you do all the work and then jump in and steal the credit. Also, unlike these other types, the obsessive-compulsive boss gives as good as he gets: You know he's working just as hard, if not harder, than you are and he's not putting any demands on you that he wouldn't be prepared to shoulder himself. In fact, he might try to horn in and actually do your job himself; micromanagement is an occupational hazard with these types.

On the other hand, the demands might well be excessive. In many cases, the boss really may not realize that everyone around him doesn't have the same drive or passion for perfection that he does, and therefore they simply cannot keep up with his grueling pace or exacting standards. In other cases he may not care, rationalizing that "a job worth doing is worth doing right," and expecting his employees to meet his standards or else. Dependent personalities typically make good subordinates to obsessive-compulsive bosses: Their overwhelming eagerness to please and their penchant for following precise directives gives them the motivation to exert the sometimes superhuman effort needed to satisfy their demanding boss—at least with him they always know what they're supposed to do.

The key to avoiding this kind of stress may be prevention—assuming you have a choice. Don't sign on for projects with an obsessive-compulsive boss unless you're prepared to keep up the pace. If you don't have that option, or if the project is too important a career move to pass up, try to obtain as clear an idea as possible of what the expectations are at every step of the way, and then take a deep breath, dive in, and do your absolute best. You'll probably find that your obsessive-compulsive boss actually appreciates your asking for direction and may be very obliging in spelling out exactly what he expects you to do—unlike the histrionic or borderline boss, who will send you off on any number of half-baked projects and wild-goose chases.

Also, obsessive-compulsive personalities usually have fewer personal axes to grind than other types, and any criticism you get will probably be directed at the work, not at you. He may be blunt, but he is rarely cruel or vindictive, unlike many antisocial, narcissistic, or paranoid bosses, who will relish the reaming they give you. And remember, if you demonstrate true commitment and competence at your job, the appreciation of your obsessive-compulsive boss will be genuine and long remembered, filed away in his meticulously organized and cross-referenced memory banks.

CASE STUDY. Richard was brought on board specifically to "tighten up the ship" of the accounts receivable department of a successful e-tail and mail-order company that was growing so fast that it had gotten out of control of its start-up owners. Richard had a reputation as the "Mr. Fixit for accounts problems." With impeccable accounting and finance credentials, Richard lost no time in diving into the paperwork and computer database and discovered that he had his work cut out for him: He had to revamp the whole system to bring it up to date. Employees were impressed to see Richard still at his workstation when they left for the day and back again when they came in the next morning. It only took a few days for Richard to diagnose the system's problems and he then called a meeting to discuss it with the staff.

Not knowing what to expect from their new boss, the accounts receivable employees were impressed by Richard's clear, organized presentation, accompanied by full-color printouts with graphs and pie charts. Admiration soon turned to trepidation, as the presentation wore on and on, laying out detail after detail about exactly what had to be done, exactly who was to do it, and exactly when it had to be done by. If the employees were leaving this introductory meeting exhausted, imagine what the upcoming work schedule would be like.

At first, it was hard to complain about the workload because no one worked harder or longer than Richard himself. It soon became apparent, however, that Richard had bit off more for his employees than they could chew. The amount of work to be done by each deadline was unwieldy at best, inhuman at worst. As employees approached Richard to request modifications of the workload, they were met with polite but firm rebuttals: "We have to follow the schedule. I'm sorry, there are no exceptions." Staff found themselves putting in extra hours and taking work home with them. The work that got in on time was often sloppy and contained errors, which Richard coolly met with instructions to "correct it." A vicious cycle developed. The grueling pace led to more and more errors, which meant pushing back the deadlines, which meant more pressure to get the corrections done fast, which meant more errors, and so on. The situation was headed for a meltdown.

A self-appointed subcommittee of workers decided to meet with Richard to see if they could work things out. Always polite, Richard listened carefully to their complaints. They were surprised when Richard, so bright in other areas, just couldn't seem to comprehend that the other staff didn't share his indefatigable devotion to work and ability to put in Herculean work schedules. Finally, Sheryl, a bookkeeper who had been with the company since way back, took a different approach with her new boss. Whatever the staff's motivations or abilities, she reasoned, the work just wasn't being done according to Richard's schedule. For the sake of the project as a whole, could she and Richard sit down and see if they could come up with a more workable way to work?

Reluctant at first to change anything, Richard was finally persuaded by the brutal logic of the situation. For the rest of the afternoon, he and Sheryl tweaked the work schedule so that the tasks were distributed in more manageable doses. At the end of his meeting with Sheryl, Richard said he would prepare the necessary materials that night and scheduled a follow-up meeting for early the next morning.

"Oh, no, not another meeting!" the employees wailed when Sheryl told them the news. Yet there they were, bright eyed and bushy tailed the next morning, hoping for some kind of reprieve from their well-meaning, but overzealous taskmaster. They winced as more graphs and pie charts flew up onto the projector screen. But this time, the work assignments seemed to reflect human reality. In fact, what Richard seemed to lack in empathy, he more than made up for in efficiency. The new schedule was more workable, and the staff was able to complete it with far fewer errors, if maybe a couple of weeks later.

The best part was that Richard was a quick study and adapted the lessons from this assignment to his future supervisory activities. Make no mistake, once he "discerned the parameters of the performance tempo of our department," as his classically Richardian-phrased memo put it, he worked his staff hard, but never to the point of overwhelming them, and always commended them for a job well done.

The Obsessive-Compulsive Employee

This is the detail person you want working on your complex projects. Histrionic or narcissistic bosses often intuitively select obsessive-compulsive assistants because they are able to translate the boss's grandiose schemes into practical, workable plans: They are the ultimate reality checkers. An obsessive-compulsive boss and obsessive-compulsive employee may work well together, each complementing the other's feverish pace; however, there is a danger of competition developing between them for the highest degree of perfection. And if you're a more laid-back type, you will probably find your obsessive-compulsive employee grating with her constant fussing and nit-picking, useful though it may be to the overall quality and organization of the work.

So give your obsessive-compulsive employee a break. She's doing her absolute best for you at all times—how many employees can you say that about? Her errors are likely to be those of commission: Too much attention to detail risks delaying and suffocating the project. Now it's your turn to give her some direction. Let her know in what areas she can ease up and streamline the project, and on what elements of the task you want her to focus her laser-beam concentration. And she's not immune to honest praise, so don't forget to thank her for a job well done.

⸬ *CASE STUDY.* Tamika agonized over the presentation. No matter how many times she went over it, she found minor errors of grammar or thought of better ways she could express her boss's ideas. For his part, the boss was growing impatient. He had to make the presentation at Friday's seminar, and it was already Wednesday. As it was, there would be precious little time to practice and rehearse.

Tamika's job was to take the random notes and ideas of the professional presenters at a prominent sales seminar and motivational speaker's bureau and turn them into tight, pithy speeches, perfectly worded and timed for the specific audience requesting the seminar, as well as for transcription to tapes and CDs that the company would market. Tamika had always been brilliant at verbal organization and expression and loved to read and write. Her personal library at home was carefully organized by subject matter and her books all stood neatly upright on the shelves like little literary soldiers. Her career dream was to break into the selective field of political speechwriting. Happy to stay out of the limelight, Tamika got sublime satisfaction from making order out of chaos and basking in the accolades of her grateful bosses.

But lately, her work had been getting "too perfect." The quality of Tamika's seminars continued to shine but she found herself becoming caught up in details that no one but she could notice: a tiny turn of a phrase here, a grammatical pause there. The speakers told her to lighten up; she was doing fine, the presentations were excellent. Furthermore, the speakers often made their own last-minute changes in text, based on what they intuitively felt their audiences wanted to hear. But now Tamika's job was in danger because, as one speaker put it, "Perfect and late is perfectly zero."

Finally, Todd, one of the company's best presenters, came into Tamika's punctiliously groomed cubicle to have a talk. Todd shared that he had for a long time been a slave to his own perfectionism in speaking. He couldn't rehearse enough and would often go hoarse from overpreparation. Then, going out there and getting the least little feeling that the performance wasn't going perfectly, he'd start to choke up; this would make him even more anxious, leading to a vicious cycle that almost made him quit the public-speaking business.

Then, a friend introduced Todd to, of all things, Japanese garden horticulture, along with the Eastern philosophy that "even a perfect garden is never finished." "People who achieve excellence can always improve," Todd told Tamika. "There's no such thing as an end to perfection. But for one's work to have an impact in the real world, a person has to make a decision to give forth the product of his or her labor, to decide it's time to take a break from planting and pruning and show the garden." In Todd's case, he decided that he would stop rewriting and rehearsing when he felt that his speeches were perfect *enough*; as a side benefit, he found that leaving just a little to chance allowed for a healthy dose of spontaneity that audiences really loved.

Strangely, for someone with such a stratified mind, this shared insight had a positive effect on Tamika. She could pursue the overall goal of perfection in her craft without having to imbue each particular presentation with life-or-death importance. She decided she could pass on the gardening, however. Although she continued to be stuck every now and then, she was able to increase her seminar output efficiency and came to enjoy her job even more.

If *You* Are an Obsessive-Compulsive Personality

If You Are an Obsessive-Compulsive Boss

You've spent a lifetime at work feeling frustrated at the failure of those who work for you to meet your exacting standards that you know are right. You're the kind of person who takes responsibilities seriously and you can't fathom why your employees don't as well. But one of the things you've hopefully learned from this book so far is that there are all different kinds of people in the world of work and not everyone will share your dedication and commitment to excellence. So, instead of unproductively demoralizing your workforce by making your employees feel like they're always letting you down, try these practical recommendations.

Quietly set the example you want your people to emulate. Probably one thing your employees will never accuse you of is not giving as good as you get. They know you work hard. Although they may grumble about the demands you put on them, they respect your commitment, even if they may never admit it. So let your example be their guide without throwing it in their faces.

Set realistic objectives. I know this is harder for you than it sounds because your idea of "realistic" isn't necessarily everyone else's. However, you've probably worked with your people a while and you have a pretty good idea of what they can and can't do. So scale back your demands to accommodate the human reality around you. Note that I am *not* saying you should accept lazy or slovenly work. But, in court, when there is no law or precedent to cover a particular decision, the judge often invokes the principle of "standard of the community." That is, what is the average or usual level of this behavior for the environment we currently live in. Use the same principle to determine what the average or 50 percent level of performance is for this kind of job with these kinds of workers. Then, tweak it up to 75–85 percent of maximum to generate some positive momentum. But don't push for 99 percent of maximum all the time or you'll burn out your workforce and the project will crash.

Critique with care. Make sure you couch constructive criticism in the context of what's also going right. Again, I'm not asking you to praise shoddy work, but use what's good as a springboard for improving what's not so good.

If You Are an Obsessive-Compulsive Employee

At work, you probably have one of two main problems, sometimes both. Either you walk around feeling terribly underappreciated for the excellent work that you do (why do so many of your colleagues get away with doing a slipshod job and reap just as much credit as your spit-and-polish performance?), or your technically perfect work is itself underappreciated because of either the miss-the-forest-for-the-trees syndrome or the too-much-too-late syndrome. That is, you're so focused on the details that you lose sight of the broader purpose of the task or assignment, or you take so long to perfect your work of art that it's turned in too late to be of practical use. To break the logjam, consider these recommendations.

Pick your battles. Every now and then, there may be a major project that demands your ferocious concentration and attention to detail. However, most daily work tasks just have to be done well—and "well" doesn't have to mean perfect. Again, don't get me wrong; I'm hardly criticizing anyone for wanting to do his or her best—I wish more people had that attitude. But if always striving for the absolute best burns you out, what have you accomplished? Furthermore, if you kill yourself over each assignment and your supervisors don't appreciate it, aren't you wasting your efforts? So do your usual excellent work every day and save your 110 percent turbocharge for those situations that truly call for it.

Lighten up. Sure, easy for me to say. I know you can't change your whole personality and you don't have to. But people are more likely to listen to people they feel familiar and comfortable with, so try to insert some of your human side into your interactions with supervisors and coworkers.

Paranoid Personality

What They're Thinking
"It's a dog-eat-dog world. Watch your back. Stay one step ahead of the enemy. Do it to them before they do it to you. If you're really special, people will hate you and envy you. People can't be trusted. Don't let on that you're on to them. Keep your friends close and your enemies closer. I know they're out to get me, but I'll beat them at their own game. Business is combat."

What They're Like

A *paranoid personality* displays a pattern of pervasive distrust and suspicious-ness, so other people's actions and motives are invariably interpreted as deceptive, persecutory, or malevolent. The true paranoid never met a mo-tive that wasn't ulterior. Their radar is supersensitive in picking up verbal and nonverbal cues of duplicity, hostility, and betrayal. Actually, their per-ceptions may be quite accurate; it's their interpretations that are skewed. Like skilled psychologists, paranoid personalities often show keen insight into human motives and actions, but unlike trained professionals who rec-ognize a range of motivations for people's behavior, paranoid personalities have only one all-fitting interpretation: People are mean, duplicitous, selfish creatures who will smile in your face and then turn around and screw you the first chance they get.

Which, in fact, pretty much describes the paranoid personality himself, since *projection*—the attributing to others of internal motives most distasteful to oneself—is the primary psychological defense mechanism of the para-noid personality. These individuals can't help being suspicious and always have to keep their guard up; what else can they do, surrounded by a sea of enemies? In addition to projection, paranoid personalities tend to external-ize blame generally; nothing is ever their fault. And why should it be, since underlying the paranoid cognitive style is often a sense of narcissistic grandiosity: They're so talented and special that people naturally hate them and want to take them down a peg. Of course, this is typically their own projected view of others in positions of authority, whose power and status they bitterly envy and covet.

In that sense, there are similarities between paranoid and narcissistic personalities. But whereas the narcissist might self-servingly accept certain sycophants into his inner circle of trusted admirers, the paranoid trusts no one. When your willingness to serve has reached its limit and you want to leave or rebel, the narcissist will merely discard you. The paranoid will hunt you down like a dog and punish you for your betrayal. In this, the paranoid resembles the borderline personality. But the latter's shifting moods and malleable perceptions leave room for possible eventual exculpa-tion of your sins and mitigation of your sentence—if you can somehow earn your way back into the borderline's good graces. The paranoid's ven-dettas, however, are carved in stone: Once on the hit list, your fate is sealed.

Because, like obsessive–compulsives, paranoid personalities frequently have a talent for technical details and are able to channel considerable energy into pursuing their goals, they may actually achieve considerable success at work. Thus, in highly competitive industries and jobs that call for complex strategic combativeness against well-defined corporate enemies, paranoid personalities may be quite successful and may even emerge as leaders.

However, a war-room mentality that is not kept in check, or outward-directed suspicion that is blown back toward coworkers and subordinates, can result in a lot of negative fallout. Thus emerges a vicious cycle of mistrust and hostility as coworkers come to shun their persistently obnoxious paranoid associate, only confirming his suspicions of plots and intrigue, leading to more outright avoidance and hostility and perhaps even preemptively defensive moves on the part of others. Eventually, as the saying goes, "Just because you're paranoid, it doesn't mean they're *not* out to get you."

The Paranoid Boss

With some degree of ambition and natural talent, a number of these personalities can rise to positions of power and authority. In fact, a cultish charisma may characterize a paranoid boss's relationship with his subordinates, and many actual high-profile cult leaders in the news have probably been paranoid personalities tinged with narcissism. Even in less extreme cases, the paranoid boss sees enemies—or at least rivals—all around him and you'd better be on his side, 100 percent, or else.

There is a subculture in the corporate world that actually admires and encourages this kind of Machiavellian, us-versus-them business ethic. As an employee, be prepared to have every aspect of your work, and sometimes your personal life, painstakingly questioned and investigated until your credentials as a true believer are established. However, if you buy into your paranoid boss's conspiracy theories, and show devotion to the cause (or give a convincing appearance of doing so), your fealty may be reciprocated by fierce, protective loyalty toward you for "defending the faith."

The danger, of course, is that this perception can change in a flash, especially if your paranoid boss thinks you're trying to put one over on him. If you are perceived to have betrayed or abandoned the cause, you will come under increased scrutiny and nothing you do or say will ever be trusted again. Allies become enemies in the blink of a jaundiced eye. Of all the personality types, the paranoid (with the borderline a close second) has the longest memory for real or imagined treachery. And unlike the border-line, whose impulsivity usually impels her to take immediate and dramatic action, the paranoid often broods and bides his time. Weeks, months, or years may go by and you may think all is forgotten, but the paranoid is just waiting for the right opportunity to serve you your just desserts.

The best way to deal with a paranoid boss is to make no promises you can't keep, ask for as clear a job description as you can get, and then be scrupulously honest and meticulous in carrying out your assigned tasks. That way, by not trying to elevate yourself to the level of trusted confi-dante, you won't set yourself up for the fall from grace when the relation-ship turns sour. Of course, if expressions of butt-kissing loyalty are necessary for advancement under a paranoid regime, you may have to ask yourself how much of your soul you're willing to sell to get ahead. How-ever, it may be some small comfort to realize that with their keen percep-tion into the motives of others, paranoid bosses often sniff out the insincere sycophants who are merely sucking up for their own ends, and they may actually come to trust and even grudgingly respect the employee who doesn't necessarily agree with everything the boss says, but at least can be relied on to tell it like it is.

> ::::: *CASE STUDY.* Along with the rest of the staff at the Holy Grace Church, Sharon was quite taken by the new Pastor Brown's demeanor of quiet benevolence mixed with strength of purpose. So she was especially honored when he asked her to be his personal assistant upon the launching of his new mem-bership drive and community outreach program. This was a growing suburban community and new congregations were springing up and vying for members. Unlike some of the previ-ous clergy they had worked with, Pastor Brown apparently took his mission very seriously. His fiery sermons trumpeted the im-portance of the house of God as an instrument of social justice and the importance of self-sacrifice to noble causes. He was especially good at forging complexly woven interfaith connec-tions among seemingly disparate congregations and other or-ganizations for collaborative activities involving important social causes.
>
> Then one day, Pastor Brown announced that they would no

longer be affiliating with the Divine Light Church, even though it was the same denomination. Pastor Brown cited "political reasons." Some of the staff pointed out that the Divine Light Church was the biggest cosponsor of fund-raising activities and that this separation would mean a huge dent in their own congregation's activities. In addition, because Divine Light had a large minority population among its flock, it would be losing a valuable liaison with a significant portion of the community. "We have to be true to our mission," was Pastor Brown's curt reply.

A few days later, Pastor Brown asked Sharon to approach a long-standing church donor and tell the person that the Divine Light Church would no longer be sponsoring the Thanksgiving meal program for the homeless and that Holy Grace would be taking over the project. "But that's not true," said Sharon. Pastor Brown replied, "To serve God, sometimes we must do what's necessary," and added an appropriate-sounding Biblical quote, although Sharon was pretty sure that's not what the Good Book meant. Pastor Brown also asked Sharon and another church staffer to go online and search financial and court records to dig up any incriminating information about the Divine Light Church and its leaders and members. When the staff members balked, Pastor Brown asked them straight out, "Whose side are you on?" Then, he thought for a moment, and said, "Okay, I'll do it myself."

Over the next couple of weeks, the Holy Grace staff found Pastor Brown increasingly preoccupied with phone calls and e-mails and less concerned with work out in the community. He still delivered powerful and inspiring sermons on Sunday, but at times they seemed to ramble into idiosyncratic tangents. Then, one day, to the church staff's surprise, two police officers showed up at the door. They told the staff that Divine Light Church had received suspicious and threatening phone calls and e-mails traced to this address. It turned out that nothing specifically illegal was said in those messages, but this news made the staff extremely uncomfortable. When they asked Pastor Brown about the police visit, he said he was only trying to "protect" their own church.

To keep the situation from escalating, Sharon offered to run interference for Pastor Brown in researching the Divine Light Church's activities and that of other congregations and organizations, to make sure they weren't trying to interfere with Holy Grace's activities. This worked for a while, as long as Sharon was able to document daily her investigative efforts. Soon, however, even this wasn't enough to quell Pastor Brown's growing suspicions. Over the next few weeks, productive fund-raising activities virtually ground to a halt as the pastor preoccupied himself with preemptive attempts to alienate the Divine Light Church and a growing list of coconspirators from prospective donors. Finally, the Divine Light's staff and the donors themselves complained to Holy Grace's executive board and Pastor Brown was asked to resign. The pastor immediately filed a lawsuit against both Divine Light and Holy Grace.

The Paranoid Employee

Since a feeling of entitlement and superiority, often in compensation for inferiority feelings, typically drives the paranoid psyche (as with the narcissist), being in positions of perceived powerlessness, or being afforded less authority than they feel they deserve, may intensify the paranoid dynamic in employees. Interestingly, the paranoid employee may outwardly bow and scrape like the worst office toady, but secretly he seethes with resentment at having to serve a boss whom he *knows* is less capable and qualified and deserving of the job than he is, and who, besides, probably got to his position through some sort of nepotistic politics or trickery. And because many paranoids possess sharp intuitive skills, this perception may not be completely off base. It's the intensity of the reaction that's the problem, as well as the narcissistic-like intolerance of having to pay one's dues and earn one's way up in the corporate hierarchy like a mere mortal.

If you supervise a paranoid employee, watch your back. This is not to suggest that you become paranoid yourself, but like the antisocial employee, the paranoid will have no compunction about sticking it to you to get what he feels he deserves. The motivational difference is that the antisocial employee takes advantage of people for the sheer predatory thrill of ripping off unearned goodies, whereas the paranoid employee actually feels morally justified in using any means necessary to take what he feels he deserves by dint of his inherent superiority or subjection to past inequities. The practical difference is that the antisocial employee's impulsivity will often impel him to make rash power grabs that may backfire and spell his doom, whereas the more cunning paranoid employee can afford to wait and carefully spin his web.

In managing the paranoid personality, take care to keep workplace assignments rational and straightforward. Expect suspicious questioning of other people's motives and of the reasons for assignments, and be prepared for "helpful" information about the incompetence or malfeasance of fellow workers. As much as possible, offer calm, rational explanations for work tasks and provide forthright but nonconfrontational reality checks for paranoid misperceptions or misinterpretations, especially under conditions of stress when conspiracy theories most often tend to spin out of control.

In general, paranoid employees respond better to tight logic than to loose assurances and also tend to accede (if grudgingly) to legitimate authority, so don't be afraid to stand your ground as the boss and make it clear that you expect policies to be followed. Overall, if you can convince your paranoid employee that there is a direct connection between him doing his job properly and his chances of realistic advancement up the corporate food chain, he may become one of your most assiduous workers—although always and forever looking for the next angle.

> **CASE STUDY.** If Tyrell were able to have a sense of humor about it, he might have chuckled at his fellow officers' teasing him about being "a disgruntled postal worker working for the police department." As it was, however, Tyrell took his alleged discriminatory and abusive treatment by the Municipal Public Safety Agency with grim seriousness. Almost from the day he began working there four years ago, he believed he was the object of a ceaseless campaign of harassment and racial discrimination. He had filed numerous grievances, had several hearings held, and had written the police commissioner and the mayor, all, in his opinion, with insufficient action.
>
> The problems began when Tyrell failed to make his pay grades, which were tied to each officer's twice-yearly performance evaluations (PEs). His PEs tended to be in the unsatisfactory to acceptable range and he felt that he was being judged

more harshly as a minority than were the other officers. When his captain pointed out to him that several other African-American and Latino officers had achieved satisfactory to outstanding PEs, Tyrell just grumbled something about "playing the game."

His reputation and performance as a patrol officer were basically competent and there were no serious reports of misconduct on his record, but many of the citizens on his beat knew to "not look that cop in the eye or give him any crap" when he talked to them, because any kind of even mildly challenging engagement could trigger a round of rigorous questioning and searches that might take hours. But what Tyrell really wanted was to be in the detective division; however, his consistently low performance ratings kept him from consideration for that unit and consigned him to the street—more evidence of discrimination, in his view.

As his turndowns for the detective position became more frequent and his promotions and pay raises lagged, Tyrell became more and more confrontational with departmental brass, his fellow officers, and the citizens he patrolled. He grew increasingly convinced of a departmental conspiracy against him. He even started avoiding Jerry, a white officer whom he had genuinely liked in the beginning because they shared a love of football and cars. A major departmental storm was brewing that could involve a civil rights complaint, an employment discrimination lawsuit, and media involvement.

That's when Captain Williams stepped in. A senior African-American police officer who had come up through the ranks, Williams had pretty much seen it all and was respected and liked by all the officers in the department. He had a particularly good reputation as a field training officer, introducing the departmental rookies to the realities of patrol policing. He sat Tyrell down and asked him to go over his whole complaint. At first, Tyrell was characteristically suspicious. Wasn't this just another front brother who didn't know if he was black or blue? But with few others willing to listen, Tyrell unburdened himself on the senior officer. After he was done, Captain Williams did the talking.

The first thing Williams did was commiserate with the younger man. Yes, being an African-American police officer did have unique challenges that outsiders could only dimly understand, including the "black-and-blue" issues of divided loyalties, response to authority figures, and reaction of the community. But if it were all about departmental discrimination and keeping the brothers down, Williams said, there'd be no black cops left, much less any in higher positions, including several African-American police chiefs around the country. Williams himself had dealt with some of the most blatant racism in his early days in the department, from both citizens and his fellow officers.

"But," said Williams, "I looked at your PEs and I talked to your captain and the problems have nothing to do with your race; they have to do with your performance." It was clear from the write-ups, Williams went on, that there were certain skills that Tyrell had mastered poorly, including equipment maintenance, completing paperwork, and using effective communication and conflict-resolution skills while on patrol.

Williams offered the following: He'd help Tyrell sharpen his skills in the deficient areas and pointed out that the department even gave pay increments for completing continuing education credits at the local community college police academy. If Tyrell bumped up his PE ratings over the next two performance periods and he was *still* being turned down for detective work, then Williams would go to bat for him with the department and, if it came down to it, help him pursue his discrimination complaint. For the time being, the lawsuit was dropped and Tyrell, under Captain Williams's firm mentorship, began working on the skills that would prepare him for the position he wanted.

If *You* Are a Paranoid Personality

If You Are a Paranoid Boss

You're using a lot of energy in always being on the defensive, but you feel you have no choice. And, let's face it, sometimes the proverb I cited earlier is true: "Just because you're paranoid doesn't mean they're *not* out to get you." So I'm not going to tell you to just relax and let your guard down if you truly feel that baring your flanks will just get you shived. But at least try to allocate your vigilance wisely. Otherwise, the suspicions will grow and grow and pretty soon you won't trust anyone and nobody will trust you: the epitome of the self-fulfilling prophecy and the vicious cycle. Here are some recommendations to help you feel more secure without spreading yourself too thin.

Know your enemies. And this means knowing who's *not* your enemy and being careful not to make them into one. If you're truly facing a threatening person or situation, the last thing you want to do is alienate potential allies. So use your native intelligence and analytic ability to discern who is really against you, whom you can trust, and who is basically neutral and can just be dealt with on that basis.

Beware of dichotomies and extremes. You know that neutral middle group I just mentioned? Sometimes people may criticize or disagree with you without it meaning they hate you or want to hurt you. Remember what President Reagan used to say: "Trust but verify." Evaluate before acting. You don't have to be a dewy-eyed Pollyanna, but it can be draining to be on red alert all the time if you don't have to be.

If You Are a Paranoid Employee

You've probably never had an easy job. Almost everywhere you've worked, somebody's tried to wear you down or tear you down. Sometimes there was a good reason for it. For example, you tried to fight for the right thing, but corrupt special interests were against you. Sometimes, there just seemed to be no good reason for everybody ganging up on you. So to help your work life go a little smoother, here are some recommendations.

Be honest with yourself. Yes, some people may have it in for you, but are you sure you're not doing anything to aggravate the situation? In workplace relationships—and all relationships, really—vicious cycles are all too easy to develop. You're suspicious that some people are against you, so you act suspicious, which ticks them off, so they act meaner to you, which only convinces you of their malevolence, and so on. Without overly relaxing your guard, try to give people the benefit of the doubt and see what happens. Which brings me to the next recommendation.

Learn to be a politician . . . or a godfather. Remember that famous line from *The Godfather*? "Keep your friends close and your enemies closer." The best way to observe someone closely is to draw the person into your confidence. Be careful of foregone conclusions and self-fulfilling prophecies. If you're wrong and these people prove to be just harmless, if annoying, coworkers, then there's one less hassle to worry about. But if you're right, and they really have evil intent, then by getting close, you'll have given them enough rope to hang themselves, and you'll be able to present a credible case against their wrongdoing without seeming, well, paranoid.

. . . .

CHAPTER 6

Oddballs and Spoilers

Schizoid and Passive-Aggressive Employees

Could some of the people you work with be described as eccentric? Not necessarily unpleasant, but just a little weird? If so, you may be tempted to overlook their potential to become productive employees once you can get past their off-putting personas. Other workers may be harder to understand because they seem to run down the road of life throwing bricks in their own path and then complaining about their stumbles—all the while sneaking and sniping at other people and biting the hands that feed them. In this chapter, you'll learn the best strategies for working with these types of employees.

Schizoid and Schizotypal Personalities

What They're Thinking

"I'm here to do my job; just leave me alone. I see things my own way and I have my own way of doing things. People don't understand me, but that's okay. Success isn't important; it's just *being* that counts. This is my work self, not my true self. It's important to keep the forces of the universe in balance and I can't do work that will give me bad karma. If I don't like the vibes here, I'll just quit."

What They're Like

The central characteristics of both schizoid and schizotypal personalities are avoidance of others; severe deficiencies in social skills; general withdrawal from life; and abnormalities in perception, thought, and emotion. The *schizoid personality* shows a pattern of aloof detachment from social interaction, with a restricted range of emotional expression. These are people who don't need people, and they are perfectly happy being left to themselves. A *schizotypal personality* additionally includes more serious disturbances of thinking, more bizarre behavior, and possibly delusional ideas. It is thought that these two personality disorders really represent points on a continuum from schizoid to schizotypal to outright schizophrenia, the latter characterized by severe distortions of thought, perception, and action, including delusions and hallucinations (see Chapter 7). In fact, schizoid and schizotypal personality disorders may episodically deteriorate into psychosis under conditions of stress, and there is evidence that an early history of poor work adjustment may be associated with greater likelihood of later schizophrenic breakdown.

Due to their impulsivity, poor socialization, impaired contact with reality, bizarre behavior, and general inconsistency, untreated individuals with more severe expressions of this spectrum—schizotypal personality disorder or outright schizophrenia—are not likely to last very long in any kind of normal employment environment, and any work they do is likely to be in the context of a supported or accommodated work setting.

However, many milder schizoid personalities function adequately in a variety of employment settings. They will be the so-called oddballs or space cadets who keep to themselves, never really causing any trouble but never forming any kind of substantial bond with their workmates. Coworkers will notice a distinct lack of interpersonal relatedness, a lack of "presence" in social interactions: "It's like I'm talking to him, and he answers, but he's not really in the room." Absent are the normal little sociable pleasantries and banter that characterize contact between people who spend many hours a day together. The schizoid employee doesn't share jokes, declines office gossip, prefers to eat lunch alone, and keeps workplace conversation on work-related topics. Again, not necessarily unpleasant, just blah.

Some similarities may be noted between the schizoid personality and the avoidant personality, in that both tend to shun social interaction, but for opposite reasons. Avoidant personalities fear people; more specifically, they fear rejection by other people, so they protect their tender emotional flanks by not exposing themselves to possible criticism, real or imagined. Schizoid personalities just don't need people. They could care less what other people think of them, so they make no effort to impress or ingratiate themselves with others. For them, people are just objects in the environment, like office furniture, tools, telephones, or computers.

Many schizoid personalities may be well suited to isolated, low-level jobs of limited complexity. In the office or on the shop floor, they will keep to themselves but may be among the most reliable of workers, having few interpersonal entanglements to interfere with their schedules. They will come in on time, follow orders, and accommodate shift changes, all without complaint, unless their job interferes with something more important, like a religious group meeting or personal ritual. Then they may abruptly quit, because the job no longer "fits" them. A fair number of schizoid personalities are actually quite intelligent and may possess superlative technical skills. These may be the classic technogeeks, content to live twenty-four/seven by a computer screen and keyboard, preferring the company of images and icons to real flesh-and-blood people.

The Schizoid Boss

Their aversion to human interaction makes it quite unlikely that schizoid personalities will aspire to positions of power and authority. Nevertheless, occasionally, by virtue of their demonstrated skill and reliability, they may be promoted or conscripted to head up a technical department and thereby have to supervise the work of others. If you work for a schizoid boss, you'll be treated with benign neglect. She will provide hardly any direction and you'll have to ask for instructions if the task is not clear. However, once engaged in a neutral and nonthreatening way, you may find her quite patient and helpful in unraveling some technical snag.

Also, because schizoid personalities aren't usually into power for its own sake, your boss is less likely to ride you or abuse you, although she may be a stickler for detail if she wants a job completed just so. In this regard, she may resemble the obsessive-compulsive boss, but, unlike the latter, the schizoid boss is less likely to criticize or demean you or your work; she'll just quietly send you back again and again until the job is done to her satisfaction. From the point of view of corporate career climbers, the ironic downside to the apparent egolessness of the schizoid boss is that it immunizes her to the broad spectrum of organizational suck-up strategies. If you think you can ingratiate, flatter, or cajole your way into your schizoid boss's good graces, you're wasting your charm. At best, she'll be mildly amused by your antics; at worst, she'll be annoyed that you're squandering valuable time and energy that could be used to get real work done. Probably, she'll just ignore these blandishments because she just doesn't get it.

So utilize your schizoid boss for her technical skills, enjoy the relative autonomy and freedom of your work role, do a good job, and seek your social nourishment and ego strokes elsewhere.

> **CASE STUDY.** "Sure." That was about all anybody had ever gotten out of Melanie by way of verbal comment. As the head bookkeeper of a home furnishings superstore, Melanie came in every day, did her work meticulously, and never seemed to turn down a request for an extra assignment or rush job. "Sure," was her standard comment, and she completed the task without a second thought.
>
> Because of her easygoing style, everybody sort of liked Melanie. Well, "sort of," because nobody really knew her. She came in, went straight to her cubicle, did her work, generally ate lunch alone, rarely tarried at the coffee urn longer than necessary to fill her cup with hot water for her organic tea, and then went back to work. At the weekly staff meetings, she sat silently while the other employees kibitzed, and she gave her report in a calm, matter-of-fact way. Only occasionally did other staff members observe her sitting at her desk with her eyes closed, with a serene, meditative look on her face. And she was always reading, which she preferred to do on her lunch and other breaks, rather than hang out with her coworkers. Yet, when spoken to, she was always cordial and polite, even if her tone had a somewhat flat and disengaged quality to it.
>
> Because she was so skilled and quick at her bookkeeping work, Melanie seemed the logical choice to become the division head of her department when the previous occupant retired. When offered this position by the store manger, Melanie responded with her characteristic, "Sure." Over the first few days, when employees e-mailed questions to her, she responded in a

brief, logical, matter-of-fact, and technically correct way. The only thing that seemed to get her rattled was when employees would come to her cubicle. Then, she seemed to take on the demeanor of a trapped animal, squirming and bouncing in her seat as she tried to get the interaction over with as fast as possible. The employees were only trying to be friendly, so they couldn't figure out Melanie's reaction. Yet, she never actually told her employees to stay away.

The employees soon figured out that the normal workplace face time and repartee were only a source of stress to Melanie. Fortunately, 99 percent of the work exchanges in the department could be done through the intranet, so it soon got to the point where days would go by without the employees even seeing Melanie, despite the busy online billing and bookkeeping traffic. Although they initially felt uncomfortable deliberately avoiding personal interaction with their new supervisor, the employees came to understand that this was the way Melanie liked it. Intriguingly, the detachment of a computer screen actually allowed Melanie to be a little less stiff and formal in her communications and something approaching a normal human dialog began to evolve between her and one or two of the workers. One day, one of these employees took a leap and invited Melanie out to lunch. "Sure," she replied.

The Schizoid Employee

The counterpart to the hands-off schizoid boss is the hands-off schizoid employee. Actually, the less you see of this employee, the better, since he will typically require both interpersonal distance and quiet, nonthreatening support to do his job well. Positions in which monitoring can be impersonal—for example, memos and e-management—and in which there is some structure and pacing inherent in the work itself, may be especially suitable for this worker.

Again, don't expect your schizoid assistant to laugh at your jokes, commiserate with your personal troubles, or respond to carrot-and-stick approaches to motivation and discipline. Let him know what you want done, how you want him to do it, when it's expected to be completed, and then let him alone. However, to compensate for the sometimes–observed schizoid tendency to get off track, periodic supportive supervision sessions may be necessary to monitor and productively focus his progress.

CASE STUDY. Jason was born to fix things. Even as a kid, his schoolmates called him "the cyborg" because he seemed to be half human, half machine. At one point, his parents brought him to a psychologist because "he has no interests outside his basement." But he caused no trouble, did reasonably well in school, and eventually entered college, where he never managed to complete more than a few courses, always being sidetracked with "special projects." Eventually, he got a job in the tech support department of a major retail electronics chain and quickly became the top service tech of that store, where he was perfectly content to stay in the back at his workstation. He became the go-to person for solving complex computer and electronics repair problems, saving the store a lot of money because customers knew they could get their gadgets fixed properly and didn't have to return them.

He was so good, in fact, that he was selected to be part of a new elite program team of "Service Commandos" that the company was launching. This program would send specially trained technicians out to homes and businesses to service their machines. Team membership would entail an increase in pay and status, and the branch manager felt that no one deserved this promotion more than Jason did. So the manager was surprised when Jason responded to this generous offer with, "Do I have to accept it?" "Why would you *not* accept it Jason?" the manager queried. "This job would be perfect for you."

It soon became apparent that what Jason feared most was the fact that he'd have to move out of the comfort zone of his store workstation. Stability, predictability, and sameness were so important to him that the prospect of traveling to different work sites on different days and dealing with all different kinds of people filled Jason with dread. Where most of the other techs would jump at the chance to get out of the cooped-up repair shop, Jason regarded this as being cast adrift at sea.

However, so convinced was the manager that Jason would grow into this role that he continued to urge and cajole Jason to try it. In fact, the manager told him that many of the store's tech clients had received such good service from Jason in the past that, as soon as they heard about the Service Commando program, they specifically requested Jason at their sites, and—here was the serious business angle—the branch manager didn't want to alienate good customers. So, torn between his fear of leaving the workshop and reluctance to disappoint his boss, Jason went off on his new assignment.

It wasn't long before the meltdown began. For the first time in three years, Jason started calling in sick. He often got lost on repair calls and had to be talked in to his location by cell phone. At the sites, he seemed so hurried about getting out of there that the quality of his work began to decline, spurring complaints from previously satisfied customers who now also began remarking on his "weird attitude," something they had never noticed back at the store. A few clients became alarmed when Jason appeared to be talking to himself.

After a couple of more weeks of this, the store manager conceded defeat and put Jason back in the store. The one positive compromise was that Jason would be available to consult by phone or e-mail with the on-site techs if they hit a snag. Things went back to normal and Jason continued to be the top fix-it person at the store.

If *You* Are a Schizoid Personality

If You Are a Schizoid Boss

You're probably insightful enough to know that most people don't see things your way, yet you wish your employees could just do their jobs without bothering you about every little thing. You accept that other people like to waste time socializing, but this kind of empty banter just makes you uncomfortable. You have a right to your own space—physically and mentally—but if you want to keep your job, some minimal degree of interaction with people will be necessary. Here are some recommendations to make this a little easier.

Have a schedule for people time. You probably do this already for other activities, but to minimize unexpected intrusions, institute regular times to meet with your employees to discuss whatever issues are relevant. That way, at least you know when the conversations are coming and can prepare for them.

Use alternative forms of communication. As noted previously, a lot of communication can be done by intranet or Internet e-mail. If you're more comfortable with this medium, and your employees don't mind, then do it.

Practice minimal social skills. No matter how technically efficient you are behind your computer, employees will do their work more effectively if they feel they know you as a person, even a little bit. So come out of your cave occasionally, even briefly, to get a cup of coffee, say hello, and so forth. If necessary, get a personal coach to help you master these rudimentary social skills.

If You Are a Schizoid Employee

You want to do your job and be left alone. Once again, that's fine, but sometimes even the most solitary job requires some interpersonal interaction, so heed these recommendations.

Prepare for encounters. If you know in advance you're going to meet with a coworker, supervisor, or customer, try to have as clear an idea as possible of what they want from you and what you want to say. Not every situation can be anticipated in every detail, of course, but the less you're caught off guard, the less uncomfortable you'll feel.

Rehearse social communication. By rehearse, I don't mean repeating a mechanical rendition that has you performing like a programmed cyberbot, but practicing such fundamental human verbal stroking as discussing the news, asking about a coworker's family vacation, and so on. Again, the intent is not to turn you into a social butterfly, but just to round out some of your square edges so you'll get along better with the people you work with.

Passive-Aggressive Personality

What They're Thinking

"Life isn't fair. I try to be good, yet bad things keep happening to me. You try to be straight with people and they just screw you. Other people always seem to have all the unfair advantages. Why should I play by the rules when the game is rigged against me? I have no choice but to get what I deserve any way I can. Why am I always the victim? Why does this keep happening on every job? I do everything they tell me, and I still get in trouble. It's not fair! It's not my fault! I'll show them they can't do this to me—but I don't want to get caught."

What They're Like

Controversy still exists as to whether the *passive-aggressive personality* is a separate personality type or a combination of traits and attitudes that spans several of the other personality styles. However, the consensus is that many individuals exhibit patterns of behavior that can certainly appear passive-aggressive and that this behavioral type is seen frequently in many work-places.

The essential dynamic of the passive-aggressive personality is superficial compliance that masks opposition and rebellion against authority. In the workplace, passive-aggressive personalities will shirk responsibilities while complaining about the unfairness of their workload. Unlike the brash, con-frontational challenges to managerial authority that may characterize the antisocial, narcissistic, borderline, or paranoid personality, the passive-aggressive personality's sniping is almost always indirect and under the table. Indeed, the very term *passive-aggressive* denotes the intention to do ill while appearing to do good.

Sabotage is a favorite ploy, and this includes self-sabotage. Projects and assignments will be completed late, incompletely, or incorrectly, always for purportedly external, unavoidable, "perfectly explainable" reasons. These perennial foul-ups will always be framed by the passive-aggressive worker appearing to bend over backward to be compliant and diligent, often ac-companied by martyred mewling. In some cases, especially where the worker is becoming desperate, he or she may resort to more overtly mali-cious acts, such as *real* sabotage of files or equipment, tampering with other employees' work, corporate espionage, malicious whistle-blowing, and so on.

Because passive-aggressive workers are experts at deflecting blame, they may succeed in covering up their more covert forms of negligence or troublemaking for some time, particularly if they are employed by a large, bureaucratic organization that overlooks low levels of performance or mild degrees of finagling. In most productive workplaces, however, there is generally little tolerance for persistent passive-aggressive behavior, which can be insidiously destructive to team morale and tends to generate animosity among coworkers and supervisors alike. Thus, a history of periodic job changes is typical. A common theme of the passive-aggressive employee's resume consists of rising to a certain level in a company, and then abruptly leaving or being terminated, usually for reasons that are difficult to pin down: "It just wasn't working out." "They really didn't have the right place for me there." "I'd gone as far as I could in that firm." "When the crap hit the fan, they needed someone to hang the whole thing on, so I got nailed—but it wasn't my fault!"

Motivationally, the passive-aggressive personality typically feels incompetent to get what he wants through his own efforts, so he becomes a master of procrastination and a tactic called *self-handicapping:* "If I'm not really trying so hard, then I don't have to feel so bad if I fail. But I'll look like I'm really, really, really working at it so others will admire me for my struggle." An interesting parallel occurs in clinical treatment and rehabilitation settings, where one sometimes sees *pseudocompliant* patients. In the clinic, these patients make a grand, glorious display of doing everything they're supposed to, following exercise instructions to the letter, going the extra mile, and so on—they just don't get better. They'd rather be perceived as struggling but helpless to overcome the forces (oh, so unfairly) arrayed against them, rather than make the transition into true health and independence because then they'd have the same responsibilities as everyone else and not be able to claim special privileges as a martyred victim. In the workplace, these personalities often represent the classic wrecked-by-success syndrome: individuals who seem to be on the threshold of achieving their self-stated career goal, when—alas—forces beyond their control conspire once again to bring them crashing down.

The Passive-Aggressive Boss

Given the fact that the passive-aggressive style is often a hedge against preordained failure, rarely do these individuals rise to positions of high corporate power. Many, however, are able to manipulate themselves into middle management and, if this is your manager, be prepared for frustrating inconsistency and to have your work criticized and used to absorb the blame for the passive-aggressive boss's own foul-ups. How can he be expected to get anything accomplished with the shoddy workforce he's saddled with? If you happen to point out to him that you've done everything he's told you to do, even against your own better judgment, and the project still tanked, he'll deny he ever told you anything of the sort and call you paranoid for doubting him. He'll blame you for his failures in order to continue projecting the image of trying so hard but being let down at every turn by the people around him.

His slipperiness makes the passive-aggressive supervisor so maddening to deal with. It may help if you can assist your boss in attaining some real accomplishments for which he—and by extension, you—can get legitimate credit. But to the extent that this shows you in a positive, competent light, he will resent you. Remember, too, that for this personality, success implies expectation, expectation breeds fear, fear elicits self-loathing, and this self-loathing is then projected onto others, including his employees. So ultimately, he'll hate you for helping him because ultimately it demeans him. The logic may be twisted and the psychodynamics perverse, but the practical upshot is that this type of boss will be virtually impossible to please. You may need to keep an accurate log of your actions and communications to protect yourself. Be very direct in asking for clarification and try to get witnesses. Even then, if things go wrong, be prepared for this master of deflection to try to pin the rap on you.

> ▦ *CASE STUDY.* One thing Sam's employees at the real estate agency could agree on was that nobody liked him. Indeed, "Sam the Sham" was infamous for assigning sales territories based on incomplete listings and then either stealing them himself or reassigning them to other agents, forcing them to split the commissions with him. He got away with this because of the company's sponsor clause by which a manager could cosign a listing with new agents, ostensibly to help the newbies develop their own contacts, but after the mandatory probationary period, agents were supposed to have the right to utilize this device or decline it at their own discretion.
>
> Sam claimed to run his real estate office as the place where

"every agent is a top producer" but then would always seem to secretly undermine the success of the sales agents who didn't sign him onto their listings, whether this entailed lost paperwork or computer files or failure to respond to phone calls or convey phone or e-mail messages. When a large and profitable property was sold, Sam always managed to get himself on the listing and push the paperwork through, but when it was clearly someone else's sale, he'd drag his feet. Although they couldn't prove it, some of the agents were convinced that Sam was hacking into and stealing or deleting their e-mails.

Because Sam was still bringing in the numbers for the real estate firm without doing anything frankly illegal (that anybody could pin down), it was hard for upper management to do much about his antics. When questioned about his actions, Sam always looked incredulous and couldn't believe his agents' lack of gratitude for his "helping" them by putting his name and resources behind their listings.

Some of the real estate agents in his department decided to take their own measures. In an "active-defensive" (rather than passive-aggressive) action, they banded together to mutually list their properties, thereby pointedly excluding Sam from being on the listings. That way, even though they were sharing commissions with one another, they at least had a choice in the matter, instead of Sam extorting a portion of their income. In addition, by all participating in this arrangement (except for a few holdouts who were profiting from Sam's scam or just too afraid of him), the agents precluded Sam from playing divide and conquer.

When Sam caught on to this mutiny, his campaign shifted into high gear, which now included clearly illicit actions. He began altering listing information and routing top properties to the few agents who were still willing to play ball with him. He was always all smiles: "I'm just trying the get the numbers up for the whole office, so everyone can share the credit. Remember, I want every agent to be a top producer." The entire office was on the verge of total war when upper management got wind of the matter. Unfortunately, their solution was to make it someone else's problem and Sam was transferred to another branch office.

The Passive-Aggressive Employee

Even worse than some of the other types of workers that can merely drive you nuts, the passive-aggressive employee can literally sink your career—all the time acting like the injured party. Often, her pseudocompliant behavior makes her acts of resistance and sabotage difficult to clearly identify and document. She is an expert at following the letter of the law while completely violating its spirit. She will make her ten required marketing contacts per day—no, twelve!—yet manage to ruin the deal on each one by her snippy attitude during the sales pitch or by misplacing or messing up the paperwork. When coached, counseled, or disciplined, she will gape at you with wounded incredulity: Can't you see she's trying to give 110 percent? And you're criticizing her? Indeed, more than for almost any other personality type, the words, "But I'm *trying*," comprise the passive-aggressive's plaintive refrain, right up there with, "It's not my fault!"

When they feel they've endured enough, some passive-aggressive employees may up the ante. She just happens to trip over that office chair and files a workers compensation claim. She overhears an innocuous remark and lodges an employee discrimination suit. Based on her self-collected evidence of egregious wrongdoing by your company, she is compelled by high conscience to blow the whistle on you to the regulatory authorities. When her consistently substandard work results in her dismissal, she files a sexual harassment or wrongful termination lawsuit.

In supervising such employees, informal coaching and counseling sessions will have little impact. Either you'll be yessed to death and then she'll march right out and go back to business as usual, or you'll be met with denial, deflection, and projection of blame—"It's not my fault!" In such cases, you'll need to use direct confrontation, written instructions, and strict accountability to enforce work standards, and be prepared to deal with the inevitably ensuing attitude problems. It may help if you can find ways to help your passive-aggressive employee take credit for her real accomplishments. But again, this will likely make her feel patronized and resentful because it puts pressure on her to continue producing, leading to the classic case of biting the hand that feeds her.

Ultimately, you will probably have to let your passive-aggressive employee go. Be careful to meticulously document and communicate the reasons for this decision, and, if possible, offer her a face-saving way of leaving the company with as few fireworks as possible. Unfortunately, she will inevitably move on to become someone else's problem, so be careful about references and recommendations.

CASE STUDY. Sherrie's patients loved her and she almost always got the highest patient-satisfaction survey scores of any of the nurses on her hospital cardiology unit. She would breeze into the patients' rooms, all smiles, and chat with them while she did her rounds; she seemed to take a real interest in their care and show genuine enthusiasm for her work—nursing wasn't just a job for her; it was a calling. The doctors, too, enjoyed working with Sherrie because she was able to project just the right attitude of take-charge competence combined with I-know-you're-the-boss deference to the doctors. In fact, her skill with patients and good working relationship with physicians put her on the short list of candidates for an opening charge nurse position.

But her colleagues could tell a different story. During report, when nurses on the outgoing shift shared patient information with incoming nurses, Sherrie's notes were always sloppy and fragmentary and she seemed to be impatient with the reporting process. Unbeknownst to the patients and most of the doctors, Sherrie had been making careless mistakes in medication, IV procedures, and charting, leaving many of the other nurses to go back and correct her mistakes. When several near mishaps came to the head nurse's attention, Sherrie blew them off as the fault of bad equipment or a nurse from some other shift. In fact, there always seemed to be an alternative explanation that implicated anyone and anything except Sherrie herself.

Then one day, small doses of narcotics were found missing from the locked medication dispensary. Although an investigation was unable to reveal who had taken the pills, all the other nurses and the head nurse knew who it was. When she was questioned by the head nurse, the director of nursing, and the hospital administrator, Sherrie threatened to sue. Unfortunately for her, though, she had (inadvertently? deliberately?) left enough of an evidence trail to implicate her in several misdeeds, which was sufficient to justify firing her at the hospital's discretion.

Because no patients had yet been harmed by her actions, Sherrie was given the option of resigning or of taking remedial continuing education courses and working under close supervision for the next year while on probation and enrolled in the Impaired Medical Professional's Program. She didn't want to lose her job so she grudgingly took the second option, but those staff who knew her could not bring themselves to be optimistic for the long term and many of her fellow nurses griped among themselves that if the doctors and administrators knew the whole story, Sherrie would have been fired long ago.

If *You* Are a Passive-Aggressive Personality

If You Are a Passive-Aggressive Boss

Even though you won't admit it to me, to anyone else, or even to yourself, chances are that part of you feels like an imposter in the supervisory position you're in, that somehow the world is too complex or hostile for you to have achieved your measure of success legitimately, so you basically had to fake it or steal it, and you now have to maintain the clever subterfuge to keep it up. You're also aware on some level that you frequently get in your own way and sabotage yourself, but you don't know what to do about it and don't know if you can change. The following points may give you a push in the right direction.

Payback is a bitch. If you think you have to undermine your employees to highlight your own success, don't be surprised if they start to fight fire with fire. All they have to do is the same thing you do, and ultimately they'll win because your success depends on their success and there's more of them than you. You simply can't be an effective manager unless you change your backbiting style. I know that's difficult, which is the reason for the next recommendation.

Get professional help. Although this is a general recommendation for many of the people described in this book, it's especially trenchant for you because, unlike the blindly self-inflated narcissistic or paranoid manager, deep down don't you really wish you didn't have to be this way? A skilled therapist or life coach can help you learn to trust your own abilities so that you can take pride in earning, not stealing, credit for what you do. Therapy may be especially helpful in addressing the corrosive self-handicapping that has been hobbling your success.

If You Are a Passive-Aggressive Employee

Maybe the only way you feel like you can grab a little power is to sabotage the success of other people, especially those above you. But let's be blunt: Do you really want to walk around feeling like a loser your whole life? If not, pay attention to the following recommendations.

Excel at something. Find something you can be good at without trickery or subterfuge, such as a sport or a hobby. When you feel resentful toward those above you because you don't think they deserve to be there, remind yourself of your special skill. This may also give you the confidence to stop sabotaging yourself so much.

Find out how others do it. Despite what you've led yourself to believe, most people earn their way into the positions they're in by dint of their talent and hard work. If you're willing to do the heavy lifting, you can too. But maybe you never learned to do things the straight way. So do some research and try to figure out how others have achieved their success. Learn from them and emulate their constructive behaviors. Sure, there's always a little luck involved, but as Thomas Edison famously said, "Chance favors the prepared mind." Prepare yours.

Get professional help. As with the boss, make up your mind if you're tired of living this way and get professional guidance. At least, a professional will have no ax to grind and will be objective in listening to you, figuring out what's going on, and making suggestions as to what to do about the self-inflicted missteps that keep you forever slipping and sliding down the muddy road to nowhere. Find someone to help you get some traction.

CHAPTER 7

Working Wounded
Mental Disorders on the Job

The previous five chapters discussed workers with a variety of personality styles and disorders that, although they may cause significant problems, are generally perceived to be part of the individuals' selves, as the core of who they are. The next three chapters describe syndromes that are usually classified as *mental disorders*. That is, they are typically regarded as syndromes the individual *has*, as opposed to core characteristics that define who he or she *is*, although, in the real human world, the dividing line between personality and psychopathology is never neatly drawn.

It's also important to understand that these disorders span a wide range of severity levels and the people described in these chapters are not necessarily "worse" than those discussed previously. In fact, you may well be working right now with someone who experiences bouts of anxiety and depression, who worries over imaginary illnesses, who's sustained a concussion in a car accident or football game, or who has wrestled with substance abuse or bipolar disorder or schizophrenia, but you wouldn't know it because they're being effectively treated, their symptoms don't show, they do their jobs, so it's none of your beeswax.

Like the personality styles and disorders just discussed, it's only when these syndromes become more serious and disruptive that business managers have to confront difficult and disturbed behavior on the job. In the most severe cases, your direct role in dealing with these workers will cede to that of mental health clinicians and your most important contribution will be to refer your employee to proper professional help. As noted previously, many of these individuals may already be in some form of treatment during their tenure with your company.

However, clinicians aside, you as a manager still play an important role in the lives of these employees and there is much you can do to influence their productivity and well-being at work. These chapters will guide you. In addition, you may have to deal with occasional crises and emergencies and no book can take the place of formal training in crisis intervention. But you have to start somewhere and, as long as you understand the limitations, the nuts-and-bolts practical recommendations provided in these pages will help you deal constructively with a crisis, should one occur on your watch.

Anxiety Disorders

Most people's normal mood isn't especially happy or sad, angry or loving, agitated or calm, but just a steady sense of what I call *provisional well-being:* the overall feeling that life has its difficulties but everything is basically okay and we hope for better days. It's like the feeling between meals when we are neither hungry nor full, when, in fact, we're too preoccupied with what we're presently doing to pay conscious attention to our gastrological—or emotional—states at all. All healthy people show a range of moods, getting periodically happier, sadder, angrier, or calmer in response to various life circumstances, and some otherwise normal people seem to be innately predisposed to either the cheerier or more dour side of the mood spectrum: glass-half-full people as opposed to glass-half-empty types. Like any trait or syndrome, the *extremes* of mood characterize a disorder, especially when these mood disturbances impair healthy life functioning or produce unreasonable conflict with others.

What They're Like
Anxiety disorders are characterized by heightened worry, fear, and arousal. *Generalized anxiety disorder* (GAD) involves a pervasive feeling of anxiety that is not necessarily tied to any specific event or circumstance, sometimes referred to as free-floating anxiety. These employees always seem nervous

about something, although the level of anxiety may wax and wane in response to different circumstances. Other people may perceive these individuals as never being able to relax or be at peace. In extreme form, these individuals may be virtually paralyzed into frozen inactivity by high levels of anxiety that interfere with work productivity. They may describe a state of "going blank."

Some individuals, with or without GAD, may suffer from *panic disorder,* which involves brief episodes of extremely elevated physiological arousal and fear. The individual may experience a racing, pounding heart; profuse sweating; rapid, shallow breathing; numbness and tingling in the face and extremities; and faintness or light-headedness—all the hallmarks of sheer terror. Many employees fear they will pass out at their desk or on their way to work during an attack, although this is exceedingly rare. The attacks may occur in response to certain triggering events, or they may happen randomly out of the blue. Panic attacks are also likely to occur in the context of depression, often in response to perceived abandonment or loss of support. Coworkers who observe these attacks may think the employee is having a heart attack, an epileptic fit, or a fainting spell.

If the anxiety and panic are associated with particular places or situations, the individual may develop one or more *phobias,* which are irrational extreme fears of particular persons, places, or things. Note that these are not delusions, because the person often recognizes that the fear is irrational, yet he or she feels powerless to control it and must avoid the feared situation to forestall panic. Thus, sufferers often feel demoralized and out of control at not being able to will themselves out of these seemingly ridiculous fears. Phobias may be generalized, involving a wide variety of people, places, or things (usually with some elements in common), or they may be quite specific—for example, a particular room, type of object, or certain kind of person. Employees who have been victimized by sexual assault or workplace violence may develop phobias to certain people and work sites, or they may develop a more complex syndrome called PTSD.

Posttraumatic stress disorder (PTSD) is a distinct syndrome of emotional and behavioral disturbances following exposure to a traumatic stressor that injures or threatens oneself or others, and that involves the experience of intense fear, helplessness, or horror. In the workplace, this typically follows some type of injurious accident, violent assault, or other serious threat such as a fire or bomb scare; it may also result from a more prolonged pattern of bullying and harassment at work. Employees with PTSD experience a range of symptoms that may abate quickly over a few days to weeks or persist for months or longer. Symptoms may include (1) a heightened state of physiological arousal; (2) pervasive anxiety and hypervigilance, as if the employee is constantly on red alert; (3) intrusive thoughts and images about the traumatic event alternating with avoidance and numbing to blot out reminders of the trauma; (4) repetitive nightmares; (5) irritability, impatience, and loss of humor; (6) impaired concentration and memory, making it difficult for the employee to focus on work or on daily tasks; and (7) general restriction and avoidance of life activities as the person withdraws into his or her shell to keep from being overwhelmed.

Anxiety disorders usually co-occur with some of the personality styles discussed in Chapters 2 to 6. Avoidant personalities are prone to develop phobias of situations or people, including social phobia, while dependent personalities may experience generalized anxiety, especially when they feel unsupported. Dependent as well as histrionic and borderline personalities may experience panic attacks at the perceived threat of abandonment. Obsessive-compulsive personalities become anxious when their orderly routine is disrupted by unforeseen disturbances, and such disruptions may propel a wholesale mental breakdown in certain schizoid and schizotypal personalities. Antisocial personalities are characterized by a distinct lack of anxiety, which goes along with their lack of a conscience, while the anxiety of narcissistic, paranoid, and some borderline personalities is often masked by anger.

Managing the Anxious Employee

If you know or suspect that one of your employees suffers from an anxiety disorder, the best thing you can do is to provide a firm, calm, and supportive presence. This doesn't mean you have to mollycoddle the employee or treat her like a baby; just frame your directives and constructive criticisms in terms of support and respect.

> ::::: CASE STUDY. Always skittish by nature, Christie generally
> kept to herself at work and completed her typing, filing, and
> data entry work quietly but efficiently. Luckily for her, her office
> was only on the third floor of a twelve-story office building in
> downtown Atlanta, because Christie almost never took the ele-
> vator, especially when there were more than a few people on

board. To curious workmates, she explained her daily trudges up and down the stairwell as "trying to keep fit."

On the morning of September 11, 2001, Christie was at her desk at work when a coworker ran through the offices spreading the word about the terrorist attacks in Washington and New York, many miles away. While most of the office watched the unfolding events on TV with horror and disbelief, Christie appeared to be especially stricken, literally immobilized by events unfolding on the TV screen. Over the next several days, the office got back to its regular work, but Christie appeared spacey and distracted and made numerous mistakes in her clerical and computer work.

Then, about a week later, Christie was involved in a minor fender-bender on her way home from the office. For the next two days, she called in sick. On the third day, Steve, her manager, asked her to come in "just to talk." He noticed that she seemed to have lost weight and appeared exhausted from a lack of sleep. He reassured Christie that this was not a disciplinary meeting; he just wanted to know how she was doing.

Christie related that for the past several days, she had been virtually unable to get out of bed yet could barely stay asleep for more than a few minutes at a time. She was having nightmares and dizzy spells and thought she was going to die. She couldn't even turn on the radio or TV because of the continual 9/11 coverage. After the accident, the prospect of getting in her car and driving to work terrified her—she only came in today because she feared losing her job. She started to cry.

Steve listened and then offered to give Christie a week's leave of absence on the condition that she seek professional help either from the company employee assistance program (EAP) or through her private insurance. When she returned to work, Steve let her be a little flexible with her schedule so she could avoid rush-hour traffic. As the nation regrouped from its collective tragedy, Christie and the rest of the office got back to their regular business.

If You Are an Anxious Employee

You're accustomed to living your life in a constant state of unease and you probably can't remember the last time you felt relaxed; you may not even know what that means. If work is a safe, secure place for you, you probably look forward to going there every day; if it's a place of fear and stress, each day must seem like running a gauntlet of terror. Here are some recommendations for trimming the trepidations from your daily work life.

Know what to expect. Of course, you can't predict every event of every day, but the more you have a sense of what your daily itinerary will be, the less often things will be totally unexpected and the better you'll be able to handle the occasional real surprises that pop up. So, on your way to work or as soon as you get to your desk, review that day's activities and get some mental control over the day.

Learn to relax. I know—easy for me to say. But there are a plethora of courses, tapes, CDs, and online instruction modules available. The goal is not to have you floating through the clouds, but to take just enough of the rasping edge off your fear so you can glide more smoothly through your day.

Get professional help. Medication and psychotherapy in combination have proven to be a powerful treatment for anxiety. Professional or life coaching can help reinforce the behavioral skills that accompany the insights gleaned in psychotherapy.

Mood Disorders

What They're Like

Mood disorders are generally classified as unipolar and bipolar types, depending on whether the extreme changes in mood are mainly in one direction (down-depressed) or both directions (down-depressed and up-elated or up-angry). *Major depressive disorder* is characterized by episodes of depressed mood that may last for days, weeks, or months at a time. In severe cases, the individual may be literally immobilized. More characteristically, these individuals feel dejected, demoralized, helpless, and hopeless. Sleep and appetite may be impaired; alternatively, some individuals become hypersomnic (sleep virtually all the time) or may binge eat. Concentration and memory may be affected to the point where individuals feel they are becoming demented. Gone is any motivation or enthusiasm for work, play, or family activities. Accompanying emotions may include anxiety, panic, irritability, or anger. The biggest risk factor is suicide. The disorder usually occurs in cycles over a person's lifespan and, in most cases, is very responsive to the right kind of treatment.

Dysthymic disorder is a less severe but more persistent mood disorder. Individuals with this disorder mentally limp through their daily activities, able to get by at work or at home, but experience little pleasure or excitement from life—the "walking wounded," leading a drab, joyless existence. Although many of these individuals will deny being depressed, they will report that they've never known what it's like to really feel happy. Some individuals with major depression will recover from their severe episodes only to settle into a bland baseline state of dysthymia, rarely experiencing anything that could be called a happy or even normal mood.

Bipolar disorder, also known as *manic-depressive illness,* is characterized by extreme shifts in mood, from elation to depression, usually with an absence of normal mood in between. For such individuals, there are no mediums, only highs and lows. The manic phase typically begins with the individual feeling energized and overly confident—"pumped." He becomes hyperactive and grandiose, spinning all kinds of half-baked unrealistic plans, but acting increasingly impulsive and distractible. Thinking and speech become rapid and forced. The need for sleep decreases and the individual may be hypersexual; all appetites are on sensory overdrive. The overall impression is of someone on stimulant drugs, and indeed, such individuals may abuse amphetamines, cocaine, or alcohol to enhance the natural high and try to keep it going.

Observed at work, the employee at the beginning of the manic phase may seem like a dynamo of creative productivity. He may be engaging and entertaining in a stand-up-comic kind of way, but as the mania progresses, he becomes increasingly short-tempered, irritable, anxious, and paranoid. Inevitably, the crash comes as the individual cycles into the depressed phase. At this point, he may use prescribed or illicit stimulant drugs in an effort to prolong the high, but eventually even this isn't enough to stave off the depressive avalanche. Suicide is a distinct risk at this stage. In other bipolar individuals, the manic episodes do not involve much elation at all but are characterized mainly by irritability, anger, and paranoia, and may be misdiagnosed as schizophrenia. Over time, this employee's work pattern will have an erratic up-and-down quality.

Bipolar disorder frequently co-occurs in individuals with narcissistic and borderline personality styles, while major depressive disorder may frequently be seen in avoidant, dependent, histrionic, and borderline personalities.

Managing the Depressed or Bipolar Employee

There are two basic steps to dealing with an employee with a mood disorder. First, you as a manager have to recognize it and, second, you have to get the employee to recognize it. Even if the employee appears to be in pain but is doing his job and tells you to butt out, you may have no choice but to offer your help and then back off. But if the mood disorder is affecting the employee's job performance, it may be your responsibility to intervene more rigorously. The employee is more likely to accept help if you approach him with a sincere attitude of concern.

> *CASE STUDY.* When he was "up," nobody at the insurance company could top Brian in new corporate policy sales. Whether by phone or on-site appointment, Brian had a knack for hooking a client's interest and nailing the deal. He seemed to have boundless energy and enthusiasm for his work and was generous to a fault in sharing credit and commissions with agents who had helped him out.
>
> But then the whole office would wait for the other emotional shoe to drop. After a few days, Brian's energy and enthusiasm would seem to lag. He'd make fewer cold calls and go on fewer site visits. Then some days he would just sit at his desk doing nothing in particular. The next few days he might not show up at all. But, on average, he was still among the highest producers, so nobody made too big a deal.
>
> As time went on, the cycles became more extreme and the ups became too up. Clients began to complain to the firm that Brian was overly aggressive in his sales pitches, sometimes becoming testy and not taking no for an answer or forcefully pushing coverage that the client companies clearly didn't need. Sometimes he made inappropriate sexual or ethnic comments. The downs became too down. Some days Brian didn't even bother to call in sick. Other times, he traipsed in late, looking slovenly and bedraggled. Luis, his sales manager, suspected Brian had been drinking and who knows what else.

The next time Brian came to work, Luis called him into his office. He told Brian he valued his work but he had to get a handle on his mood swings because they were starting to affect the insurance company's reputation. At first Brian denied any problem. Luis just looked at him for several tense moments. Finally, Brian said, "What can I do?"—which was all the opening Luis needed to reach into his drawer and hand Brian the company provider book of medical and mental health clinicians.

"Welcome back," Luis smiled.

Handling the Suicidal Employee

The most serious workplace crisis intervention situation for a depressed employee is potential suicide. Although rarely will you as a manager have to intervene in a suicidal crisis, some basic guidelines adapted from the work of crisis counselors Burl Gilliland and Richard James will prevent you from feeling completely helpless if an emergency ever occurs. In addition, having a plan and a protocol for taking constructive action may reduce your liability in a workplace crisis (see also Chapter 11). As with all crisis intervention recommendations in this book, these should be supplemented by proper training and practice.

If an employee is actively suicidal and threatening to kill himself immediately, call 911 and try to stabilize the situation until help arrives. More commonly, however, the employee may not actually be about to kill himself but is experiencing a downward emotional spiral in which he feels he's running out of reasons to go on. Then you have to make a judgment call as to whether to call for help or try to resolve the situation more quietly. The general rule for businesses is basically the same as for law enforcement and emergency services: When in doubt, call for backup. But until help arrives, you may have to step in.

No matter how it's handled, the first priority is always safety. Assess for suicidal intent and emphasize the employee's well-being, especially where the depressive episode has been precipitated by a work site conflict or confrontation:

> "We're going to put our business discussion on hold, Bob. Right now, we want to make sure you're okay and get you any help you need."

Crisis intervention specialists have identified several steps or stages to successful intervention with suicidal persons. These don't always have to follow in exact order, so use your judgment based on the situation.

Define the problem. Some employees' crises may relate to a specific personal or workplace event. Often, however, a crisis state will evolve cumulatively as the result of a number of overlapping stressors—work, family, finances—until the pressure hits the breaking point. In such cases, the employee himself may be unclear as to what exactly led to the present crisis state, which may further increase his feelings of confusion and loss of control. Thus, one immediate crisis-intervention goal is to help the employee clarify in his or her mind what exactly has led to the present crisis state by means of focusing and clarifying questions.

> **Employee:** I can't stand it anymore. My life is out of control. I don't see any way out.
> **Manager:** What's out of control?
> **Employee:** Everything, everything. My job, my family, everything.
> **Manager:** [Focuses] What's going on with the job?
> **Employee:** I work like a slave all year, put in for extra overtime, and now payroll tells us there's no budget for raises—after I just put the down payment on the new house. So my wife and I are fighting about money.
> **Manager:** [Clarifies] So you got caught by surprise with the no-raise thing and now all the family plans are jacked up. And everybody's walking around like a raw nerve.

Ensure safety. Of course, you're not going to solve all of the employee's problems in this one encounter. What you want to do is make sure he survives this crisis so he can avail himself of appropriate follow-up psychological services after the acute emergency has passed. For now, you want to encourage the employee to put even a few short steps between the thought of a self-destructive action and carrying it out.

> **Manager:** Is there anything here in the office or at home that could hurt you?

Employee: At home, I have an old target-shooting .22 locked up somewhere and I think I have a bottle of leftover Percocets from my surgery last year in my office desk drawer.

Manager: How about giving me the pills to hold and calling your wife and asking her to hide the gun away for the next few days?

Provide hope and support. Remember, you don't necessarily have to agree with your distressed employee's point of view, but a little empathy and commiseration can go a long way in establishing trust and encouraging a safe resolution to the incident.

Manager: Work and family hassles—they all just piled up, huh?

Employee: What a pile; yeah, that's a good way to put it. It seems my whole life, no matter what I do, nothing ever works out.

Manager: You sound like a guy who's tried to make it work, but sometimes too many things get in the way. I'm not going to pretend I have a precooked answer for you, but sometimes looking at things in a different way, trying things out you didn't do before—things like that can help you figure out new ideas. But right now, all I'm saying is I hear where you're coming from and I'm hoping you can get things together for yourself.

Employee: I don't know, but hey, thanks anyway.

Examine alternatives. Typically, individuals in crisis are so fixated on their pain and hopelessness that their cognitive tunnel vision prevents them from seeing any way out. You can try to gently expand the range of safe options for resolving the crisis situation. Typically, this takes one of two forms: *accessing practical supports* and *utilizing coping mechanisms.* In the first, try to identify any persons, institutions, or agencies that are immediately available to help the employee through the crisis until he or she can obtain follow-up care. This can consist of mental health professionals, clergy, or trusted family members. The second approach to examining alternatives is accessing and utilizing coping mechanisms. These can take the form of cognitive strategies, religious faith, distracting activities, positive images, memories of family, and so on. You can appeal to both present and past coping mechanisms. For employees who are feeling hopeless, it is often useful to recall past crises that were resolved without harm. This highlights that it's at least *possible* to get through crises like the present one.

> **Manager:** You said something earlier about how you've had bad stuff happen before. Can you give me an example?
>
> **Employee:** Well, about ten years ago, I got fired for something I didn't do; manipulation of client funds they called it. Some other guy did it, then pinned it on me, then disappeared. I didn't want to admit to something I didn't do, but they threatened to put me in prison if I didn't confess and return the money.
>
> **Manager:** What did you do?
>
> **Employee:** I basically went broke hiring a hot-shot employment lawyer who was able to track down the missing accounts and clear me. But it took a lot of time and money and sweat and blood.
>
> **Manager:** So when you put your mind to something, you're able to work it out.

Make a plan. This again involves a combination of both practical supports and coping mechanisms to get through the crisis and the days ahead.

> **Manager:** Okay, I want to make sure I have everything straight. You're going to give me the pills and have your wife get rid of the gun for now. You and I are going to walk down the hall to the EAP office and get you seen by a mental health professional right away. That person will determine if you can go home or need to be hospitalized. Whatever it takes to get you back to health, we'll cover for you here at work until you get things straightened out. Okay?

Obtain commitment. Finally, make sure the employee understands the plan and is reasonably committed to following it.

> **Manager:** Okay, are we on the same page?
>
> **Employee:** Yeah, okay.
>
> **Manager:** All right, just so I'm clear, tell me what we agreed on. [Employee repeats the plan]

Manager: I'm proud of you. After you see the clinician, check back in with me and we'll discuss the next step, okay?

Employee: Yeah, yeah, whatever.

Manager: *Okay??*

Employee: Okay, okay [laughs]. Jeez, what a pain in the ass.

Of course, this is a condensed version to illustrate the basics of crisis intervention. Because human beings are complex, none of this is a foolproof formula. However, applying the basic principles of crisis intervention in an atmosphere of sincere concern and respect can not only save a life in the short term but also preserve the career of a valued employee.

If You Are a Depressed or Bipolar Employee

You know your moods are out of control and probably wish you could do something about it. Well, you can. Here are some recommendations.

Know your pattern. Some people's mood disorders have a life of their own: They seem to occur in cycles, independent of anything that's going on in the person's life. For some, the cycles are predictable; for others, they change over time. If you can feel a depressive episode coming on, be proactive in getting help and slowing down on activities that might be affected. It's usually easier to do these things at an earlier stage of the depressive episode, because once you're deep in the throes of the "black dog" (Winston Churchill's term for his depression), you tend to lose insight and perspective and start regarding everything as hopeless. Manic phases are harder to stave off, because, at the beginning, you don't feel sick—you feel pumped; only later does the mood cycle morph into edgy irritability and finally depression. However, there are still ways to take control.

Know your triggers. For some people, their mood episodes are triggered by specific types of life events. Although it would be fatuously unrealistic to tell you to "avoid stress," if you know that there are certain situations that get you particularly upset, and if you can sidestep those situations without significant consequence to your career or personal life, then there is great wisdom in the concept of picking your battles. At the same time, for many situations, you can train yourself to be more stress resilient through appropriate courses, programs, personal training, and cognitive-behavioral psychotherapy.

Seek professional help. As with anxiety disorders, a combination of medication and psychotherapy usually proves to be the most effective course of treatment for mood disorders. Consult a qualified mental health professional and start living more of the life you really want.

Schizophrenia and Psychotic Disorders

What They're Like

Schizophrenia denotes a group of serious mental disorders characterized by severe disturbances of mood, thought, and goal-directed action. Schizophrenia is a progressive syndrome, usually first presenting in adolescence or early adulthood (although childhood forms occur), and often characterized by *delusions* (disturbances of belief) and *hallucinations* (disturbances of perception). In schizophrenia, hallucinations are typically auditory (hearing voices), and more rarely, visual (seeing things). Untreated schizophrenic individuals may suffer episodic bouts of delusional and hallucinatory psychosis, between which they may appear simply odd or weird, unable to maintain any consistent work or other activity.

Diagnostically, schizophrenia is divided into several types, although overlap is common. The primarily *paranoid* type is characterized mainly by delusions of persecution and accusatory hallucinations; this may be the most highly functioning type of schizophrenia. The *disorganized* type is characterized by general aimlessness and impaired contact with reality. The *catatonic* type is more commonly seen in institutional settings, because of the individuals' near immobility. Finally, the *undifferentiated* type may comprise features of the other three classifications or show additional symptoms. In the most severe forms, many schizophrenic individuals make up the ranks of street people and are unlikely to be encountered in most workplaces. However, some higher-functioning schizophrenic employees, especially if under proper treatment, may be able to hold certain jobs and some of them may be working for you.

Delusional disorders are distinguished clinically from schizophrenia by the fact that the affected individuals may function adequately in most life areas, despite the presence of isolated, fixed ideas that are sufficiently out of sync with reality to qualify as delusions. Thus, at work, a junior secretary convinced that the company CEO is in love with her would (if factually untrue) have an *erotomanic* type of delusional disorder. A *grandiose* type of delusion might describe the data entry tech who believes that he possesses the true secret for company domination of the industry if only he could get before the corporate board of directors and share his insight. *Persecutory* delusional disorder would characterize the individual who believes that shadowy operatives both within and outside his own company are after him (often for the purpose of stealing or silencing his grandiose ideas). The *jealous* type of delusional disorder would apply to the manager who is absolutely convinced that his wife is having an affair with one of his employees, despite no shred of hard evidence. Finally, a worker who believes that his body is being contaminated by deadly toxic mold or microwaves in the workplace might be suffering from the *somatic* type of delusional disorder.

Managing the Schizophrenic Employee

It's unlikely that you would hire anyone whose behavior appeared patently bizarre at the outset, so usually this worker will be hired for a particular skill while she is in a period of remission or simply because your company needs bodies in a low-level, high-turnover type of job, such as janitorial, restaurant, or seasonal work. Only later does the employee's condition come to your attention, either because of her own actions or coworkers' reports.

The most common workplace symptom of schizophrenia is simply not showing up, as the behavior of these individuals tends to be extremely unreliable and inconsistent. In these cases, you'll probably just let the person go. More rarely, a schizophrenic employee will annoy, harass, or even assault fellow employees or customers, or others may just be "weirded out" by the employee's behavior. In such cases, you'll have several options.

If the employee's disorder meets the criteria for a disability under the Americans with Disabilities Act (ADA), you may have to accommodate it unless doing so would present undue hardship for the company; consult your company manual and an employment law attorney, if necessary.

If inappropriate work behavior seems potentially correctible, use the techniques of coaching, counseling, and discipline described in Chapter

10. Especially important in these cases is encouraging and supporting the employee in obtaining proper mental health treatment, including medication. Although rare, if the employee becomes violent, use the violence response strategies described in Chapter 11.

> ▦ *CASE STUDY.* It was the Christmas rush and the hotel needed people to fill its housekeeping and service staff to cope with the anticipated capacity crowds. Therefore, when the housekeeping supervisor noticed that Maria acted a little strange during the brief intake interview, she brushed it aside. For the first week, Maria did her job adequately, cleaning and preparing the rooms for guests. Then one day, her coworkers were surprised when she refused to get into the service elevator unless she could stand on the right side, next to the floor buttons. She seemed to rush through cleaning some rooms but lingered overly long in others. When asked why she was doing so, she replied that some of the rooms were "wrong."
>
> Although rushed during the holiday season, the housekeeping supervisor and the hotel manager took time from their busy schedules to sit down with Maria and make sure she understood the rules of her job. They noted that she seemed a little distracted and internally preoccupied and her speech sounded a little disjointed, but she was able to express that she understood the rules and would comply.
>
> A couple of days later, a few of the other housekeepers noticed through a partially opened door that Maria was speaking and gesturing angrily while in one of the rooms. Fearing that this was a confrontation with one of the guests, they called the housekeeping supervisor, who entered the room to discover Maria heatedly conversing with a newscaster on the television. Maria was given the rest of the day off and told to "pull herself together" for her next shift. She never showed up for work and all efforts to reach her by phone failed. Her final paycheck was sent to her last known address.
>
> A few weeks later, the hotel manager was alerted by alarmed employees to find Maria sleeping in one of the unoccupied rooms. When the manager asked her to leave, she began shout-

ing and crying, and hotel security called police and paramedics,
who took her to a local hospital.

Handling a Psychotic Episode

Although most problems with schizophrenic workers will be quiet sins of
omission, managers may occasionally encounter an employee in the throes
of a psychotic crisis. In such cases, you should observe a few basic rules of
engagement. First, if possible, assess the nature of the employee's psychotic
state and overall behavior before approaching. This is to prevent either a
lapse of precaution or an unnecessarily confrontational response. Approach
the employee as slowly and as nonthreateningly as possible. If more than
one manager is present, keep the sensory overload to a minimum by having
only one person speak at a time. Try to determine if the employee can be
verbally engaged. Always speak and act slowly, firmly, and deliberatively—
remember the difference between *authoritative* (Sheriff Andy Taylor) and
authoritarian (Deputy Barney Fife).

If the employee is willing to talk, encourage venting, but not ranting. If
he expresses delusional ideas and beliefs, neither argue nor agree with the
delusions. Through their painful life experiences, most schizophrenic individuals have learned that other people don't believe their delusional ideas,
so pretending to do so may only serve to alienate or enrage a disturbed
psychotic employee further. Conversely, it is highly unlikely that trying to
"talk sense" into a delusional person is going to make him suddenly see
things more rationally. Instead, acknowledge the content of the delusion
and try to ally yourself with the employee's perspective and perception of
the situation while keeping the focus on present reality.

> "Let me try to understand this. The criminals have been sending
> you downloads and text messages through your office computer and
> cell phone telling you they're going to kill your family, and you're
> trying to fend them off. Do I have that right? That must be pretty
> frightening."

Listen carefully and speak slowly with the goal of calming the situation
as much as possible. Remember that psychotic individuals can be very unpredictable—sitting and mumbling distractedly one moment, thrashing and
kicking violently the next. If it looks like physical restraint may be required,

call for security or law enforcement backup: Don't put yourself, the employee, or bystanders in danger by trying to physically intervene personally unless you are specifically trained to do so. The employee may have to be secured and taken to a medical facility by responding authorities. If so, continue showing your concern by following up with the employee later.

If You Are a Schizophrenic Employee

For as long as you can remember, the world has been a confusing and frightening place. During the times you're feeling more stable, you may seek employment to keep yourself going financially or because you want to function like a regular person. Here are some recommendations for keeping things on an even keel.

Take care of your physical and mental health. If you've been prescribed medication, take it. If you have scheduled meetings with a doctor or other mental health clinician, keep them. Numerous people with schizophrenia live productive lives if they can keep their most disturbing symptoms under control.

Choose your job carefully. You may not have many job options open to you, but, if you have a choice, pick a type of work that's least likely to trigger your symptoms or stress you out.

Know your cycles. As with many of the other syndromes described in this book, they sometimes occur in predictable cycles. Understand your pattern and if you feel an episode coming on, take a leave of absence to recover—understanding, of course, that your job may or may not be accommodating. That leads to the next recommendation.

Know your rights. Contact local and regional authorities, support and advocacy groups, legal aid societies, and so on. If you have trouble getting organized, ask someone to look up this information for you.

Alcohol and Drug Abuse

Even without serious personality disorders or psychopathology, by far the most common problem affecting the behavior and work performance of your employees will involve drugs and alcohol.

Studies show that substance-abusing employees function at about two thirds their capacity. They are more than twice as likely as nonusing employees to request time off or to just not show up for work, and three times as likely to be late. They are more than three and a half times as likely to be involved in a workplace accident, five times more likely to file a workers compensation claim, and they cost their employers about twice as much in medical claims. Finally, there is the fact that many of the personality disorders and psychopathological syndromes already described have substance abuse as a complicating factor.

What They're Like

There is such a variety of substances and range of reactions that the effects of individual substances can only be summarized here. Basically, there are two aspects of alcohol and drug use that can affect work: acute intoxication and long-term lifestyle effects. You'll usually not see actual intoxication at work until later or in more severe stages of the alcohol or drug abuse. However, the effects of these substances on the employee's work and overall life may be noticeable early on.

Intoxication and Withdrawal: Signs, Symptoms, and Syndromes

Signs of *alcohol intoxication* are familiar to anyone who has ever been at a New Year's Eve party: slurred speech, impaired coordination, silly behavior, and so on. It is possible, however, for many drinkers who are legally intoxicated at work to act relatively normally, especially if they have been long-term but low-level users of alcohol. Alcohol has varying effects, depending on the particular drinker, with some inebriated individuals becoming mellow and tractable, others angry and agitated. In general, alcohol and most other drugs lower inhibitions and self-control, so any intoxicated person has to be approached with caution.

Less common, but potentially more serious, are signs and symptoms of *alcohol withdrawal* in individuals who are physiologically dependent on alcohol. This usually presents as an agitated state with tremors ("the shakes"). In severe cases, this can be accompanied by hallucinations and/or seizures. A distinctive state of agitated delirium, characterized by intense fear and tactile and visual hallucinations of vermin crawling on the skin, is called *delirium tremens* ("the DTs"). Typically, such individuals will be so clearly impaired that the need for immediate medical attention is obvious. Years of long-term heavy abuse of alcohol can also lead to *alcoholic dementia,* but these individuals are likely to be confined to institutions and not typically encountered in the workplace, although some old-timers in low-demand, routine jobs who are nearing retirement may skirt through their workday in a cognitively impaired state.

An even rarer, but more dangerous, syndrome is *pathological intoxication,* where small amounts of alcohol trigger violent rages in susceptible individuals, which is thought to be due to an electrophysiological disturbance in sensitive limbic areas of the brain. Witnesses will describe an explosion of rage in which the person appears to be on automatic or "like a runaway train," fueled by adrenaline and capable of inflicting severe damage to anyone who gets in his way. These episodes typically last only a few seconds to minutes, and there is usually at least some recall of the incident by the individual, who may also subsequently express regret at losing control. During these brief episodes, it is useless to try to talk the person out of his aggressive actions. The only effective strategy is to call for help to employ appropriate physical restraint to keep the individual from harming others.

Other substances of abuse have different effects on behavior, depending on their biochemical action within the user's brain. *Stimulants* ("uppers"), such as cocaine and amphetamines, produce a racing kind of high, with rapid thought and speech, erratic and impulsive behavior, and a hyped-up energy level. Such individuals may occasionally become violent, but more commonly, they will be simply annoying and raucous, quite similar to the manic state described earlier in this chapter; in fact, many manic individuals deliberately use stimulants to enhance and extend their natural high. Danger on the job may arise when their overconfidence and impulsivity lead to temper flare-ups provoked by confrontations with supervisors or co-workers.

Central nervous system *depressants* ("downers"), such as barbiturates (e.g., quaaludes) or benzodiazepines (e.g., Xanax, Valium), have effects similar to alcohol, which include a calming effect and loosening of inhibitions, which may lead to impulsive and dangerous actions. Alternatively, these employees may be observed to be literally sleeping on the job or at least be so drowsy and out of it that they pose a danger while driving or operating equipment.

The effects of *hallucinogens,* such as marijuana, LSD, or angel dust, may range from mellow goofiness to violent delirium. *Organic hydrocarbons,* such as the glue and paint thinner enjoyed by sniffers or "huffers," tend to produce a toxic delirious state; these latter substances are also extremely injurious to nerve tissue and can produce brain damage with persisting cognitive impairment.

Handling Intoxicated Employees

Because a behaviorally deteriorated state can be caused by a variety of factors, it is first important to distinguish drug or alcohol intoxication from other medical or psychiatric conditions. Remember, several syndromes may go together. For example, the delusions of a paranoid schizophrenic employee may be fueled by this morning's cocaine, so he smokes some pot in the bathroom to calm down and begins hallucinating, so then he chugs a beer in his cubicle to quiet the voices, and this interacts with the postconcussive effects of a recent head injury he sustained in a car accident. Now you're faced with a fearful, angry, and confused person whose behavior is erratic and unpredictable.

In most cases of alcohol use, the person's breath will give him or her away. For other substances, you may have to rely on your knowledge and experience (observational or autobiographical) of drug-induced states. Always approach a substance-impaired employee with caution and assess for danger to self or others. Use tact, patience, and verbal intervention skills, but know when to call for help. Remember, you're dealing with a person whose powers of perception, comprehension, reasoning, and self-control have all been impaired by the substance that has been ingested. If the employee voluntarily leaves the work site, make sure he gets home safely by having someone drive him or by putting him in a cab. If there's any doubt about his safety or medical condition, call for paramedic support. Many jobs have a zero-tolerance policy about drug and alcohol use on the job. If your employee has violated such a workplace rule, he may be subject to discipline or termination (see Chapter 10).

Lifestyle and Work Style Effects of Substances

More common than actual intoxication at work is the effect that drug or alcohol use may have on the lifestyle and work style of employees. Some substance-abusing employees keep it together for years, and, without a random drug test, you'd never know about their evening or weekend extracurricular activities. Other employees show erratic work histories that may be the result of the substance use itself or associated with one or more co-occurring psychological syndromes, the two factors often exacerbating each other in a vicious cycle.

Managing Substance Abuse in the Workplace

As noted previously, different businesses often have widely varying levels of tolerance for employees who use drugs and alcohol, from "don't ask, don't tell" to zero tolerance. Much of the difference relates to safety and liability; for example, the rules for a fire department or construction company are likely to be stricter than those for an entertainment promoter or ad agency. The first step is to understand your own company policy thoroughly and enforce it.

Aside from the safety and liability issue is the health and welfare matter. Employees diagnosed with a substance abuse disorder may actually have rights under the ADA. At a minimum, you should try to be proactive in referring these workers to your company EAP or other services for help. For employees who violate the rules, some combination of coaching, counseling, and discipline may be effective. Finally, for the sake of your other employees and the company as a whole, termination may be the only choice for a worker who clearly can't or won't straighten himself or herself out.

> *CASE STUDY.* Frank always had it all under control. As the lead afternoon news anchor at one of the region's top local TV stations, Frank had the poise, charm, and quick wit to entrance viewers and attract advertisers. He was poised to go national and his agent had several bids circulating. No one knew much about Frank's personal life, except that he was single and seemed to thoroughly enjoy the perks of being a local celebrity.
>
> But in this highly competitive business, the national network and cable offers weren't coming in as fast as he thought they should. Over the next several weeks, Frank appeared distracted at work. Never one to be fazed by a news show workday that routinely started at 4:00 A.M., now on some mornings, Frank appeared tired and unkempt. During some of his afternoon newscasts, he needed to be cued more than usual. Almost all of the station production crew suspected what was going on, but

none wanted to get on Frank's bad side—much less open the Pandora's boxes of their own lifestyles. When a few concerned coworkers probed by asking Frank if everything was all right, he shrugged off their concerns: "Hey, who's the man?" he would always reply.

Bev, the station manager, was no Pollyanna; in her long career as a media producer, she had seen this sort of thing before: bright, rising local star thinks success isn't coming fast enough and starts to white powder his sorrows. She was also not one to mince words when she called Frank in for a meeting. "Frank, you're using," Bev said bluntly. Before Frank could even open his mouth, she added, "No, if it affects this station it *is* my business. If I'm wrong, walk out, get a lawyer, and sue me. If I'm right, you can thank me later for saving your career." She added, "Think about it overnight and tell me tomorrow what you're going to do. You have the makings of a great career in media journalism, but I can't support you if you screw around with my little one-horse station. Are we clear?"

The next day, Frank came in, fresh, bright-eyed, and all smiles. He told Bev that "everything's under control." Not good enough, Bev countered; overnight, she had gotten some e-mails from the corporate owners of the station regarding Frank's performance of late. He could peruse them at his leisure when he had time, but for now, Bev needed to hear some specific steps Frank was going to take to control his drug problem. Reluctantly, he agreed to see an EAP counselor and be guided by the clinician's recommendations. Bev knew that Frank's only motivation was to further his network career, but she hoped this was enough for now. "Are we clear about this?" Bev asked at the end of their meeting. "Hey," Frank replied, "who's the man?"

If You Are a Substance-Abusing Employee

If you're using, on or off the job, chances are you've rationalized it in one of two ways:

"What I do on my own time is my own business."
"I'm just medicating myself like lots of other people."

Maybe you feel you've got it all under control. Or you might wish you knew how to stop but can't seem to get a grip. Or you'd like to quit, or at least slow down, but you don't want to get into that whole "recovery" lifestyle. I've found that one of the biggest impediments to getting clean and sober for some people is that they think this means they have to start going to meetings. While I enthusiastically endorse the twelve-step programs for many people who are battling addiction, this approach may not be appropriate for all, and there is a growing self-recovery literature to substantiate this viewpoint.

If it turns out you need to follow the twelve steps to save your health and career, then do it—it's your life we're talking about. But I'm going to offer you something to try first, an alternative mini-program that I've used with public safety and corporate personnel to help them get a handle on their alcohol use. I'm sticking to alcohol because I can't legitimately tell you what degree of *illegal* drug use is okay or not. Besides, for most of the impaired personnel I work with, alcohol is their preferred poison, if only because it's so easy to get.

Conduct an honest self-appraisal. You have to decide if you can really limit your alcohol intake or if you have to quit completely. Then you can decide if cutting down is an option for you or if you have to maintain a sober lifestyle for your own health and career.

Manage your times and places. Drinking is often a "vacuum activity"; that is, it expands to fill the empty time and space created by a lack of other activities. As with any bad habit, it's almost impossible to tell yourself, "Just don't do it." What's more effective is to "do something else." If you've got another activity that's enjoyable, use that to replace drinking time. Go bowling. Go fishing. See a movie. Find a nondrinking crowd on your off-hours and hang out with them. Spend more time with your family. Or if family stresses are part of the problem, until things get sorted out, put in more productive overtime at work—without overstressing yourself there, that is.

Drink differently. Keeping busy should take care of a good portion of the drinking-alone problem. But we all know that alcohol is part of the fabric of socialization in our culture and if you don't want to stigmatize yourself as "the dry guy" or "AA Annie" in the group, try limiting your time at alcohol-fueled gatherings. Arrive late and leave early—I'll bet you're smart enough to come up with some excuse. Drink slowly to keep the blood alcohol concentration low. Sip a beer instead of a Scotch on ice. Alternate the vodka and Coke with just a Coke. Once again, only you know if you can pull these stratagems off without losing control of your alcohol intake.

Quit successfully by quitting successively. If, in spite of these measures, you do really feel you're getting out of control, you may have to take firmer measures with yourself—and it still doesn't mean going to meetings yet. First, try this: Stop drinking for one day. Just one day, so you know you can do it. Then, expand the nondrinking time to more days of the week. Doing this will give you a feeling of control over yourself, which can be a powerful self-esteem builder and spur further control efforts. Get to the point where you're limiting your intake to just a few hours a week, then every two weeks, then a month. Then take the plunge and quit. While you're doing this, make sure to fill your time with other activities.

Get help. Now may be the time to consult with a mental health professional, but not just to help you with the alcohol problem. If the stresses of life are running you down, the therapist or counselor may help you cope more effectively. Then, you'll feel more in control of your life, and hopefully you won't need to drown yourself as much or as often. This goes for whether the problems involve the job, family, or both.

Choose life. Finally, if you need to get out the big guns—Alcoholics Anonymous or an inpatient treatment center—realize that saving your career and preserving your health and family is as damn good a set of reasons as any to get your life back on track. In many cases, however, with a little willpower and determination, you can use the self-help strategies outlined above to take back control of your life. If you can't, it takes guts to admit it and more guts to do something about it. Get yourself together.

CHAPTER 8

Brain Alert
Neuropsychological Disorders at Work

N*europsychology* is the specialized field of psychology that deals with cognitive, emotional, and behavioral disorders that relate to disturbances in brain functioning. Less common than the personality styles and psychological disorders discussed so far is a subset of behavioral syndromes that involve different perturbations of brain function and straddle the domains of psychology and medicine. It's important for managers to know about these syndromes because they may be mistaken for other behavioral disorders or even willful misconduct. In addition, to the extent that they represent true medical disabilities, employers may have to accommodate them under the Americans with Disabilities Act (ADA). Finally, some of these syndromes may be associated with unique types of workplace crises that have to be handled for safety and risk-management purposes.

Attention Deficit Hyperactivity Disorder

What They're Like
A lifelong difficulty in focusing and sustaining attention on tasks and goals; a tendency toward impulsive action; poor tolerance of frustration; heightened emotional reactivity; a desire for immediate gratification; and poor planning, judgment, and anticipation of consequences are traits that charac-

terize children, adolescents, and adults with *attention deficit hyperactivity disorder* (ADHD), which appears to be far more common in males. To complicate matters, ADHD typically co-occurs with other syndromes, such as conduct disorder, antisocial personality, mood disorders, learning disabilities, and substance abuse, which makes overall adjustment to school and work problematic for these individuals. Still, because many of these people may possess high intellectual ability and specific skills, they can earn their way into a variety of occupations.

Actually, "attention deficit" is a misnomer. These individuals don't lack attention; they just have inordinate difficulty allocating it appropriately. If they are interested in something, they can rivet their concentration to the point that you'd have to set off a bomb to distract them. However, if the task or project holds no intrinsic interest, they seem to be singularly unable to make themselves focus on the unappealing material and will be distracted by a million other things. In fact, this jumping from one thing to the next is a big part of the hyperactivity seen in these individuals.

The difficulty setting their attention-gyroscopes appropriately accounts for many of the problems of grown-up ADHD employees. Their need for stimulation may cause them to get bored very easily, which makes sustained attention to any task very difficult. They will be inattentive and distracted at meetings, to which they probably arrived late because of their terrible time management skills. They procrastinate, not necessarily because of some self-handicapping dynamic, as with the passive-aggressive personality, but because they have trouble focusing on what is important and what is extraneous and end up going in circles. At the same time, their poor frustration tolerance may cause them to fly off the handle if they perceive something you do or say as annoying or threatening. All of these problems are exacerbated by increasing fatigue.

Managing the ADHD Employee

Although some employees may tell you forthrightly about their ADHD diagnosis (and some will use it as the basis of a claim for special workplace accommodation), in most cases you'll just notice the characteristic behavior pattern. Therefore, the following recommendations apply to any employee who shows difficulty sustaining attention and concentration and focusing on work. Naturally, if an employee just can't do his or her job, you may have to dismiss that person. Nevertheless, as noted previously, if there is a formal diagnosis of ADHD, this may become an ADA issue that you need to accommodate. Or you just may want to make a well-meaning attempt to salvage an otherwise good employee. In either case, be sure to document everything you do.

Make tasks explicit. As much as possible, be very clear about what the employee has to do. Most jobs require some degree of discretion and independent decision making, but keep the simple things simple. One way of organizing a task is to break it down into a sequence of steps. Encourage the employee to do this and help where necessary. Also, help the employee to use cues and reminders. These can be Post-it notes, beepers and timers, computer clock reminders, and so forth. If feasible for your workplace, consider flexible schedules. Many ADHD employees can do a good job if they break up the workday into digestible chunks or work unconventional hours.

In meetings and supervision sessions, ADHD employees may irritate managers who are trying to engage them because they seem to be internally preoccupied and to be disregarding what the manager is saying. This is probably an expression of their difficulty focusing on what is being said; after all, the hallmark of this syndrome is impaired ability to pay attention. Keep your questions and statements clear, simple, and direct and repeat them as often as necessary. ADHD individuals may have difficulty with verbal expression, so use clear questioning and paraphrasing. They also tend to have poor memories, so what seems to be evasiveness to your questions may actually represent a true problem with remembering what you said or recalling what actually happened. Their sense of direction may also be impaired, so they may have trouble accounting for their whereabouts. If the ADHD employee starts to get agitated or upset, modulate your speech and behavior to present a model of calmness.

> **CASE STUDY.** Robby bounced into the manager's office at a medium-size computer graphics and website design company all smiles and enthusiasm. Computers were his life, he told the manager, and this job would let him do what he loved. A quick check of references and credentials and a few test runs showed that Robby indeed had the technical chops to do the job.
>
> Robby started out great and soon became one of the top designers. But then he began coming in late. The manager

didn't make a big deal about this because Robby seemed so focused and productive while he was working. In fact, if a project fascinated him, he would stick to it for hours, skipping lunch, and having to be literally chucked out of the office at closing time. However, if it was an ordinary assignment, he would become distracted or sloppy. It soon became apparent that it took far longer for Robby to do the simple, routine tasks than the more challenging, complex ones. This was the opposite pattern of the other workers, who mostly preferred the easy assignments, and soon all the tough jobs were delegated to Robby, while the other designers slacked off. At that point, even Robby began to become overwhelmed and this informal arrangement began to unravel.

The manager knew it was time to do something. He called a staff meeting and announced that from now on, design assignments would be made on a rotating basis, so whichever job came up next was assigned to the next available employee. Then he sat down with Robby. He had him allocate a set time every day for routine repair and service work so it would be more predictable and less ambiguous. He helped Robby break down the duller tasks into doable steps and to use a simple digital watch with a beeper for time pacing. The manager allowed some flextime as long as he completed his work orders, but Robby had to take lunch and arrive and leave on time like everyone else. After a while, Robby grew less antsy and got into a rhythm. He still tended to get distracted and sidetracked at times, but he was able to respond to his beeps and cues to get back on track.

Dementia

What They're Like

As the U.S. workplace ages, you can expect to see more people staying at their jobs longer. Many workers are retiring later. Others seek second and third careers. It's inevitable, then, that managers will occasionally have to deal with employees who begin to show a decline in their cognitive faculties.

The term *dementia* refers to a progressive organic brain syndrome that impairs perception, thinking, language, memory, and behavior. The main causes of dementia in the elderly are Alzheimer's disease, Parkinson's disease, and stroke. In younger individuals, dementia may occur as the result of AIDS, toxic-metabolic and medical syndromes such as kidney or liver disease, or heavy substance abuse or overdose.

Dementia typically creeps up slowly and the difficulty an employer has in dealing with a cognitively impaired worker is largely determined by how severe the disorder is. Mildly impaired employees may seem only a bit befuddled and absentminded, whereas more severely affected workers will be quite forgetful, occasionally lose track of time or where they are, and have increasing difficulty communicating or comprehending you. By that time, it will usually be apparent that something is wrong.

Symptoms of dementia include *disorientation* to time (What's today's date? When was the last election?), place (What office are we in? Where do you live?), and person (Who's your immediate supervisor? What's your name?). *Aphasia* is a disturbance of language and can involve the comprehension of speech, the expression of speech, or both. *Aprosodia* is a flattening of the emotional tonality of speech. *Agnosia* is impaired perceptual recognition, and *apraxia* is a disturbance of complex movement. Other signs and symptoms of dementia include general agitation and pacing, and *sundowning*, which is a tendency to become more active and agitated at night.

Typically, the behavior of employees with dementia will be relatively peaceful, albeit confused; however, they may become agitated and defensively aggressive if they feel threatened. Most workplace problems will involve disorganization of work or inappropriate behavior. Many of these individuals may actually function quite well for a long time in a familiar, routine, simple job but will deteriorate behaviorally if given anything novel or complex to do.

Managing Employees with Dementia

If an elderly employee suddenly seems to become confused at work, try to assess for any of the specific signs or symptoms described in this chapter, such as perceptual disturbances, difficulty completing sequences of actions, or language difficulties. If the person is confused, frightened, or agitated, use basic calming techniques, such as a slow, even tone and pacing of voice; easygoing body language; and short, simple, reassuring phrases ("It's okay, we're going to take you home"). Be gently directive—tell and show the employee what you want him or her to do; most cognitively impaired individuals will display an easy, childlike compliance if they don't feel threatened and will be reassured more by the demeanor and tone of what you say than by the content. Because of the medical implications, it's probably best to call for paramedic backup and let them determine if the employee needs to be hospitalized or can go home.

More commonly, there will be no signal event and the dementia will evolve slowly. Little lapses may be laughed off at first—"I'm just having a senior moment"—until they become more frequent and severe and start to seriously affect the employee's work. Then, the manager is faced with the dilemma of whether to retain the employee and how to modify his or her workload.

In many cases, the early phases of cognitive decline can be accommodated through a lighter workload or reduced hours. However, many employees will object to this measure because it reinforces the fact that their mental powers are waning and fewer hours may mean less pay or at least less time doing a meaningful activity. For many senior citizens, even unpaid volunteer work is the only opportunity they have to get out of the house and socialize. If that's the case, try to find other niches for the employee to fill. A store cashier can become a greeter. A field sales rep can operate the phones. Finally, if you must let the employee go, do so with grace and sensitivity, allowing the employee to retain as much dignity as possible.

CASE STUDY. "I'm gonna die standing up," Marty always said. Coming of age during the Great Depression of the last century, Marty had never been a stranger to hard work. He began with after-school jobs and following high school did a stint in the U.S. Navy, "too late for World War II and too early for Korea." After his military service, he completed college on the GI Bill, earning a degree in finance. He went on to become a successful investment broker, regularly working sixty-hour weeks, but still finding time for his family, which consisted of his wife and three sons, all of whom became successful in their own right.

He and his wife eventually retired to sunny Florida, but he soon grew bored with the daily routine of canasta games and early-bird specials. His active mind hungered for things to do. Since his business days, he had always been fascinated by the law and so he became a volunteer guardian *ad litem* for the local county court, drawing great satisfaction from helping children and their families negotiate the legal system.

Then, subtly, almost imperceptibly, Marty's behavior began to change. Always punctual, he started arriving late for family meetings and court dates. Always articulate, he now often seemed to lose his train of thought during presentations before judges. Some of the children he advocated for became frightened by his "weird" behavior and reported it to the court authorities. Everybody liked Marty, but he was told he needed to take a leave of absence and that he could return with a doctor's note.

Medical examination and a neuropsychological evaluation disclosed early dementia, but the neuropsychologist noted that Marty could continue to work as long as the demands were lighter and the schedule shorter. The court authorities assigned Marty to Intake, where he would interview the children and families at a desk in the court office, without having to make the site visits, which seemed to fatigue him. Fortunately, Marty was able to accept the reality of the situation with characteristic good cheer: "If that's what you got for me, fellas, that's what I'll take."

Epilepsy

What They're Like

Although it is unlikely that seizure disorders will be commonly encountered in the workplace, managers should know how to recognize the signs and symptoms to be able to intervene if necessary and, more important, not to confuse these symptoms with those of other disorders or with willful misconduct. Also, a little constructive knowledge is useful to dispel many of the misunderstandings and prejudices that still surround this syndrome.

Like dementia, epilepsy is actually a medical-neurological disorder, and most seizures are fairly unmistakable while they are occurring. However, there are a number of seizure types that produce disturbances primarily in thought, consciousness, and complex behavior, and these may not be readily identifiable as manifestations of a medical disorder. In addition, epilepsy may occur along with a variety of other medical and mental disorders, including substance abuse, which can exacerbate it.

Epileptic seizures are classified into a number of main subtypes. *Grand mal seizures* conform to most people's idea of a seizure: an abrupt whole-body spasm that causes the person to lose consciousness and fall to the ground, followed by several seconds of rhythmic muscular contractions that gradually abate and leave the person mentally confused and physically exhausted when he or she regains consciousness. *Focal seizures* involve only a portion of the body or one side of the body, usually an arm or leg, and are characterized by a few seconds of rapid, involuntary, stereotyped contractions for which the person typically remains aware.

In *petit mal seizures,* more common in children, there is a very brief loss of consciousness for perhaps a few seconds, but no significant disturbance of posture or muscle tone: At work, the affected employee may be observed to "blink out" for a brief spell. In untreated cases, the individual may experience anywhere from a few to several hundred such spells in the course of a day, which can disrupt the continuity of perception, learning, and memory. At work, this may result in the employee being observed to "fall asleep on the job" at his or her desk or workstation many times a day, or become briefly unresponsive during a meeting. Unlike an actual nap, however, such spells typically last for only a few seconds and the employee will usually remain upright and appear to stare blankly, sometimes accompanied by simple mouth or facial movements.

The type of epilepsy that is most often associated with behavioral disturbances at work and elsewhere, and that may sometimes lead to trouble with the law, is *psychomotor epilepsy,* also known as *temporal lobe epilepsy* (TLE), because the electrophysiological disturbance most commonly originates from the brain's temporal lobes, a region associated with emotion, motivation, and memory. During a temporal lobe seizure, awareness of the person's surroundings may be severely disturbed, and the person's behavior may or may not appear to be under his or her control. The seizure has an abrupt onset and gradual recovery and can last for several minutes or longer.

Individuals describe all manner of sensory, perceptual, cognitive, and emotional alterations heralding the onset of a TLE seizure, ranging from shapes and colors; strange sounds; religious visions and voices; sudden fear, sadness, or elation; vivid memories from the past; feelings of great profundity and mystical clarity; to stomach flutters and other physical sensations. A dreamy, partial-consciousness state of disorientation often prevails during the seizure, during which the person may not be responsive or only minimally responsive to other people's questioning or commands. After the seizure passes, the person may have spotty recall or no memory at all for the event.

The TLE symptoms most likely to get the person in trouble are collectively known as *automatisms.* These are stereotyped, repetitive actions that in themselves are normal in the proper contexts, but occur during the seizure in an inappropriate form or circumstance. Automatisms may include aimless wandering; inappropriate dressing and undressing; sexual and bathroom behavior; picking up and carrying off objects; and approaching others with short, simple, repeated vocalizations. One of my patients had several arrests for indecent exposure for taking off his clothes and walking around a supermarket and up and down the street. Another patient was arrested for gathering up objects in a barbershop while waiting for a haircut.

Violence during a TLE seizure is rare and is most often related to defensiveness caused by fear and confusion or to combativeness upon being restrained while in the confused seizure state. In a rare condition called *episodic dyscontrol syndrome* (EDS), or *intermittent explosive disorder* (IED), more severe aggressive behavior can appear as a sudden, often unprovoked, "stormlike" outburst, primitive and poorly organized—flailing, spitting, scratching, punching, throwing—and usually directed at the nearest available person or object. The act itself can be quite destructive to objects or people who happen to get in the way, but serious injury to bystanders is usually the result of misguided efforts by observers to subdue the person during an episode that, like other seizure phenomena, tends to pass quickly on its own.

In between seizures, many TLE patients display what clinicians call an *interictal TLE personality,* with a characteristic set of symptoms, including heightened emotional intensity, interpersonal clinginess (*viscosity*), obsessive-compulsive preoccupations and behavior, excessive writing and note taking (*hypergraphia*), and sometimes bizarre sexual interests (*fetishisms*). It is thought that this personality style develops from the frequent and repeated abnormal excitation of the brain's temporal lobe limbic system by frequent TLE seizures in childhood and adolescence. Some of these signs and symptoms may be confused with schizophrenia or some of the personality disorders.

Finally, employees with TLE and other forms of epilepsy are likely to be treated with antiseizure medications, many of which have significant sedating effects that can affect mental clarity and energy level. Overwhelmingly, however, the proper use of antiseizure medication can essentially normalize the work and lifestyles of employees with epilepsy and most continue to remain productive.

Managing Employees with Epilepsy

As with any well-controlled chronic medical condition, like diabetes or high blood pressure, employees with properly treated epilepsy do not pose any significantly greater risk than the next worker. In fact, the only time your employee's condition may come to light is when the person experiences the rare seizure on the job. In such cases, this represents a medical incident, so you should call 911 immediately. However, because of the short course of such episodes, the seizure will likely be long over before the paramedics get there. Thus, there are some things you can do in the meantime to ensure safety.

Frightening though it may appear, a grand mal seizure will usually pass within a few seconds or minutes. Don't try to forcibly restrain the person during the seizure and don't put anything in the person's mouth. The only physical intervention that might help is to gently turn the employee on her side; clear away hard furniture; and try to put something soft around her head, like a seat cushion or rolled-up jacket. Otherwise, back off, observe, and let the seizure pass. When she regains consciousness, she will show physical weakness and mental confusion, which will gradually clear up over the next several minutes to hours, so stay with her until paramedics arrive.

During most focal seizures, the employee will remain conscious, so just stay with her until it passes, usually within a few seconds to a couple of minutes. Seconds also define the time course of most petit mal seizures and rarely are they dangerous in and of themselves. So, your role will simply be to ensure that the employee isn't in a dangerous situation (running a power tool, operating a vehicle) during the brief spell.

If an employee experiencing a TLE seizure begins to wander away from the work site, stay with her to avoid her stepping into danger and use the minimum amount of restraint necessary to control the situation. Employ the *sheep-dog approach*: With your simple physical presence and perhaps a light touch on the shoulder, "herd" the confused employee in the direction you want her to go. Although verbal comprehension will likely be impaired at the height of the seizure, simple, direct instructions may work with some employees: "This way; it's okay." Try not to rush or crowd the employee; remember, cases of violence during TLE episodes almost always occur when the person feels confined or threatened. When the seizure passes, stay with the employee until the paramedics arrive.

> ⬛ *CASE STUDY.* Cara was referred to my clinical practice because of her increasing anxiety and disturbed behavior at work. She had been a reliable researcher and paralegal at a law firm for several years but recently began having bizarre spells that consisted of mood swings and strange perceptions that would come and go from "out of nowhere." When these spells began becoming more and more frequent, she sought help from her company EAP, who first referred her to a psychiatrist for a medication consult. Although the physician wasn't entirely sure of the diagnosis, he started Cara on a low dose of antidepressant medication.
>
> Over the next several weeks, the symptoms persisted and Cara suspected that maybe the stresses in her life, significant but not catastrophic, were contributing to the problem, so she sought help from a psychologist (me) to "help me develop coping skills to deal with this." I listened carefully to Cara describe her symptoms, which consisted of sudden waves of strong emotion, usually fear or excitement, accompanied or quickly followed by a "clattering" sound in her ears; a sensation like "my stomach is floating up out of my mouth"; and the awful paranoid feeling of a "presence" watching her from her left side. These episodes occurred every few days and lasted only a few minutes. Otherwise, between these spells, her mental state was

normal and there was no personal or family history of psychopathology.

Cara's symptoms didn't fit any standard psychiatric diagnosis, and I hypothesized that these were temporal lobe seizures.
I referred her to a neurologist, who conducted an electroen-
cephalogram (EEG) study that confirmed the diagnosis of TLE.
Once Cara was taken off the antidepressant and started on an
anticonvulsant medication, her symptoms abated. At first she
was afraid her supervisors and coworkers would be put off by
the stigma of epilepsy, but she was surprised to find out they
were actually relieved at this diagnosis: "At least it's only a medical condition," one of Cara's work friends joked over lunch.
"We were scared you were just wacko."

Narcolepsy

What They're Like

Narcolepsy is a neurophysiological sleep-wake disorder characterized by
poor nighttime sleep and excessive daytime sleepiness. Despite the similar-
sounding names, it has nothing to do with epilepsy. The person with narcolepsy typically experiences vivid, dreamlike hallucinations that occur just
as he or she is falling asleep (*hypnogogic hallucinations*) or waking up (*hypno-
pompic hallucinations*), and these may be associated with *sleep paralysis,* the
transient inability to move while experiencing these "waking dreams."
During the day, the person may experience *sleep attacks,* causing him or her
to abruptly nod off in the middle of whatever he or she is currently doing.
These attacks may be associated with *cataplexy,* which is a sudden loss of
muscle tone that causes the person to abruptly collapse and fall. These
episodes can be triggered either by fatigue and boredom or, conversely, by
sudden strong emotion or stimulation.

Managing Employees with Narcolepsy

A likely scenario for the workplace involves an employee who always
seems to be sleepy and inattentive on the job, which is often mistaken for
depression, substance abuse, or just plain laziness. There may be actual sleep
attacks at work, but these may be distinguished from ordinary napping by

their relatively abrupt onset and short time span. Narcolepsy may also be confused with epilepsy and sometimes it may take a trained clinician to make an on-the-fly diagnosis during an acute episode. From a manager's point of view, the most important practical thing you can do if you observe a sleep attack or any other abrupt impairment of consciousness is to call 911 and then ensure the employee's safety until help arrives.

CASE STUDY. Ramon had always been good with his hands and he really liked his job at the Fix-It Depot superstore. So, his supervisor was concerned when Ramon would show up for work looking tired and drained. "You sleeping okay?" the supervisor asked. "Yeah," replied Ramon, although he knew it was a lie. In reality, for the past couple of weeks, he'd been tossing and turning at night and struggling to keep awake during the day. He'd tried a few extra cups of coffee in the morning and this had seemed to help a little, but he'd still catch himself yawning frequently throughout the day.

Because of the potentially dangerous nature of the repair work, the store had a zero-tolerance drug policy, which included random testing at the discretion of management. Although he didn't think Ramon was the doper type, his supervisor ordered a general drug screen for the workers on Ramon's shift. Ramon's report came back clean as a whistle (ironically, another, previously unsuspected employee was flagged).

Then one day a customer complained that Ramon had fallen asleep right in the middle of a conversation and the supervisor decided it was time for a talk. He told Ramon that his personal habits were his own business but that the health of the employees was related to their own safety and the store's liability. He would like Ramon to voluntarily undergo a medical exam before the supervisor had to order it.

Fortunately, the company doc was on the ball and, after listening carefully to Ramon's symptoms, he referred Ramon to a neurologist, who was able to conduct a *polysomnography* (sleep lab) test. The diagnosis was mild narcolepsy and Ramon was prescribed a low dose of psychostimulant medication to take during the day that wouldn't interfere with the company's drug policy. Although he still had an occasional bad night and felt a little tired the next day, overall, Ramon felt "200 percent better" and was able to go back to work.

Tourette's Syndrome

What They're Like

Beginning in childhood, *Tourette's syndrome* (TS) is characterized by the progressive development of multiple *tics,* which are rapid, involuntary, co-ordinated spasms of small muscle groups. Most TS tics are of the motor variety, in which case the person may appear characteristically "twitchy" and the syndrome may be mistaken for ADHD, which, to complicate the diagnosis further, it often co-occurs with. A smaller number of TS patients have vocal tics, which usually consist of throat clearing, grunting, uttering of single syllables, or other simple vocalizations. A minority of TS patients exhibit *coprolalia,* in which they emit various kinds of foul language, typically involving sexual or racial epithets, probably because most of these words contain hard consonants emitted with explosive breath—the vocal equivalent of a motor tic. Not surprisingly, these individuals may get into big trouble if they are heard uttering "fuck," "spic," or "cunt" in the workplace or other public areas.

Managing Employees with Tourette's Syndrome

Of course, people curse each other out for any number of reasons, and most don't have a brain syndrome. As a manager, you needn't make a formal diagnosis, but note if the employee seems to be in control of his utterances, and whether the verbal curses occur in the context of overall twitchy, agitated behavior. Usually, in addition to coprolalia, TS individuals manifest a number of other vocal and motor tics. If this seems to be the case, and no real harm has been done, escort the employee to a location where his involuntarily obnoxious verbiage is less likely to get him into trouble and discuss plans for managing the symptom while at work. Effective treatment typically combines medication and behavioral control strategies.

▓▓ *CASE STUDY*. Brad was self-referred to my office for what he called "work stress." Upon further examination, it turned out that this involved being relentlessly teased by his fellow sales and service reps at a South Florida swimming pool company. Brad had been diagnosed with Tourette's syndrome in grade school and, most of the time, his symptoms were controlled with medication. However, even now, in his twenties, he still experienced random twitches of his head and trunk, along with occasional grunts and throat clearings that his coworkers would mercilessly imitate and exaggerate—all under the guise of "just good fun."

Yet, Brad assured me that he was quite successful at pool sales, whether in the sales office or on a homesite visit, so, naturally, I wondered how his customers reacted to his symptoms. Brad's answer surprised me: "There's an initial reaction, I guess. I get 'the look' and some customers ask me what's up and I just tell them I have Tourette's and that it's a harmless neurological disorder, and they're usually like, 'Oh, I heard about that' and then we move on to the pool discussion. Others just give me a few glances, probably decide I'm a little weird, and move on to business. The customers are always so focused on their pools that, after a few seconds, they could care less if I had two heads as long as they think they're getting the best deal on the pool they want to build. No, the customers are great; it's the other asshole sales reps that give me the hardest time."

I recommended that Brad talk to the office manager but he said that he'd already done that and that the response was basically to suck it up and "as long as everybody does their job, we don't have time for babysitting." So, my approach to Brad's problem was to teach him some basic stress-management and communication skills for deflecting and immunizing himself against these jerks' jibes, as well as recommending he contact an employment attorney just to see if he had any legal leverage in terms of a potential disability-discrimination or hostile workplace case. Brad said he would consult the attorney but decided to wait before taking any action because he just wanted to keep his job.

Traumatic Brain Injury and Postconcussion Syndrome

What They're Like

Individuals who have sustained a blow to the head may suffer temporary or permanent brain damage producing a *postconcussion syndrome*. In physical occupations, such as construction, the injury may have occurred during work. Otherwise, the most common cause of a *traumatic brain injury* (TBI) is a motor vehicle accident, which can occur on or off the job.

Physical symptoms of a postconcussion syndrome include headache, dizziness, disturbance of equilibrium, and hypersensitivity to light and sound. Cognitive symptoms include impaired attention and concentration; poor short-term memory; and, in severe cases, general disorientation and confusion. Emotional-behavioral symptoms include increased irritability and anger, poor frustration tolerance, impaired judgment, and impulsivity.

Managing Employees with Postconcussion Syndrome

At work, these individuals may seem confused and disoriented and may be mistaken for being intoxicated. By far, the most common reason for postconcussion problems on the job is a well-meaning employee returning to work too soon after a TBI. Even in mild TBIs, it may take a few weeks for postconcussion symptoms to resolve; in more serious cases, several months may have to pass and some residual impairment may persist.

In practical terms, treat these individuals as you would any cognitively impaired, disabled employee. The major difference between TBI and the other neuropsychological syndromes in this chapter is that the postconcussion syndrome is neither progressive nor chronic—it typically improves with time. Meanwhile, see if you can accommodate the employee's working conditions and work schedule; she'll do better if she can start slow and gradually increase her work hours and workload as she continues to recover. In more serious cases, you may be able to alter the job description to accommodate the employee's residual cognitive disabilities.

> ⠿ *CASE STUDY.* "I must have driven a million miles in my life and I get nailed a block from my house," Katie said. "I don't even remember getting hit—the whole thing is still fuzzy." Katie was coming out of her neighborhood when an SUV, trying to

beat a red light, slammed into the side front end of her sedan, spinning her car around before it collided head-on with a pole. She was wearing a seat belt but, perhaps because of the angle at which she was struck, the air bag did not deploy and the double impact slammed Katie's head sideways into the driver's-side panel and forward into the steering wheel. She may have been unconscious for a few seconds. By the time she was fully aware of what was going on, paramedics were already on the scene. She was taken to a local hospital emergency room, examined, and released with instructions to follow up with her doctor.

Over the next few days, the worst consequence of the accident was neck pain due to a whiplash injury. Katie took prescribed pain and muscle-relaxing medication and wore a cervical collar for about a week, then felt well enough to return to work as a clerk at a local pharmacy. However, over the next few days, she began making "stupid mistakes," misplacing prescriptions, mixing up names and account numbers on orders, and putting phone callers on hold and forgetting to return to them. Always able to juggle several tasks at once, Katie started to feel like a "moron" when she would begin one task, stop to start another, forget about the previous one, and on and on.

After a few days, the pharmacy manager pointed out to Katie that her work was getting "erratic" ("I know he meant 'sloppy,'" Katie said, "but he didn't want to hurt my feelings") and asked if she was all right. He already knew about the accident and asked her if she wanted some time off—she still had plenty of sick days coming. Since it was already Friday, she decided to take Monday and Tuesday off for some doctors' visits. One of the appointments was with me. I explained to her the nature of the postconcussion syndrome and gave her some literature on it that she could share with her workmates. We devised a plan to pace her activities at work so that she could accomplish what she needed to do, just more slowly and deliberatively. By gradually increasing the tempo and complexity of her work tasks to keep pace with her recovering brain, in a few weeks she had worked herself up to speed.

If You *Are an Employee with a Neuropsychological Disorder*

Specific clinical recommendations will depend on the nature of your disorder and will probably come from a qualified medical professional. However, there are some general guidelines for anyone who is experiencing a neuropsychological disorder—or, for that matter, any chronic medical condition—that affects performance at work.

Get smart. Inform and educate yourself about your syndrome and its effects. Share this information with your coworkers if it will help everybody to be less put off by your condition. Be aware, however, that many of your workmates may not have so enlightened an attitude, so be cautious about your privacy when appropriate.

Get treated. There is no syndrome, disorder, or condition in this chapter—in this whole book, really—that cannot benefit from some type of medical treatment or behavioral intervention, or both. Try to find clinicians who are knowledgeable about your condition. Because some of the syndromes in this chapter are less familiar than others, remember that the first step to proper treatment is a proper diagnosis. Also, be aware that sometimes it takes several tries to establish a truly effective treatment regimen that's right for you.

Get connected. Without dwelling on your illness and becoming a "professional patient," find local and national support and advocacy groups that can help you understand your rights in the workplace and elsewhere and can afford a sometimes much-needed sense of community and solidarity so you don't feel so alone. Many of these organizations also have programs for employers and families.

Get to work. Like Brad the pool salesman said, if you can do your job, it shouldn't matter if you have two heads. Once your condition has been stabilized and your workload and schedule have been adjusted accordingly, dive in and be proud to earn your living.

. . . .

CHAPTER 9

Sick and Tired
Mind-Body Syndromes in the Workplace

Do some of your employees always seem to be sick? Like Chapter 8, this one deals with syndromes that highlight the intricacies of brain-mind-body relationships. However, whereas the behavioral problems in Chapter 8 can be shown to stem directly from alterations in brain functioning, this chapter discusses what happens when the mind itself seems to impose illness or disability on an otherwise healthy body.

Another feature of the disorders in this chapter is that they often stem from injuries that occur in the workplace itself. Psychodynamics aside, the practical implication of these syndromes involves lost worker productivity and increased fiscal outlays for employee healthcare and disability claims. Thus, it is in the interest of every manager and corporate decision maker to understand and effectively deal with these types of employees.

Somatoform Disorders

The common feature of *somatoform disorders* is the presence of subjective physical symptoms that suggest a physical illness or disability, but are not fully explained by a general medical condition, substance abuse, or other type of mental disorder. That is, these are medical syndromes that don't appear to be "real," yet the symptoms are real enough and disturbing enough to their sufferers. A thorough medical workup is necessary to rule out actual physical illness, and there is no clinical rule that says a somatizing patient can't also develop a real illness or sustain a real injury. In fact, somatizing patients will often latch on to a past injury or current mild chronic condition and turn that into the focus of their amplified distress.

Mental health clinicians distinguish among several types of somatoform disorder. Again, the purpose of this book is not to turn you into a diagnostician. But understanding the variation in the syndromes that affect your workers will make you better at identifying these conditions, speaking about them empathically to the employee, and minimizing the prospect of the employee rejecting your recommendations for help because you "just don't get it." Although the different types of somatoform disorder tend to be relatively consistent from person to person, it should be recognized that individuals may show more than one subtype, may display a combination of subtypes, or may alternate among several subtypes as a pattern of coping style.

Somatization Disorder

Somatization disorder involves a history of multiple unexplained physical symptoms and complaints, usually beginning in childhood and adolescence, and persisting into adult life. This is the poor soul who "never seems to have a well day in her life." Outbreaks of numerous and varied symptoms may occur in clusters that wax and wane over time, often in response to stresses at work or at home. Associated features may include anxiety, depression, relationship problems, and substance abuse, most commonly misuse or overuse of medication. Somatization disorder is commonly seen in individuals with histrionic or borderline personality styles. Somatization symptoms may closely mimic standard medical syndromes or they may be atypical or frankly bizarre in quality, location, or duration. The individuals often describe their symptoms in exaggerated, florid terms, and several physicians may be consulted concurrently, leading to secondary problems associated with medication abuse and unnecessary surgical treatment.

From the point of view of workplace disability claims that stem from an alleged work-related injury, examiners should first determine whether the symptoms the employee is now describing are actually related to the injury as claimed or really fall into a prior long-standing pattern and history of multiple symptoms and complaints. In many cases, an extensive past medical paper trail will make this determination easy, but in other cases, this may be a tough diagnostic call, especially when symptoms are allegedly new with little or no prior records to provide a clinical context.

Intention and motivation are important concepts that mental health clinicians use to tease apart the different types of somatoform disorders and to discern clues for treatment. *Intention* refers to whether or not the person is fully conscious of creating or magnifying the symptom. *Motivation* refers to the actual reasons—again, which may be partly or wholly unconscious—that the person is acting in a symptomatic manner. For example, in somatization disorder, intention is typically unconscious: The person genuinely believes that he or she is ill or impaired. The underlying motivation is frequently a quest for support and reassurance, or manipulation of the affection of a significant other. The psychodynamic goal is the satisfaction of dependency needs by reliance on caretakers or on the protective role of a medical authority.

> ::::: *CASE STUDY.* Kim is a forty-three-year-old female office manager who has undergone numerous diagnostic tests and treatments for headaches, dizziness, anxiety attacks, and gastrointestinal symptoms since her teens. Over the years, she has frequently voiced fears of having a brain tumor or a silent stroke, despite the lack of any medical evidence. Two years ago, she sustained a mild closed head injury in an auto accident. Since then, her headaches and dizziness have worsened and are accompanied by hypersensitivity to light and noise, tinnitus (ringing in the ears), anxiety attacks, and severe forgetfulness. Brain MRI and EEG results are within normal limits, and neuropsychological testing shows mild, equivocal findings. Kim is now concerned about permanent brain damage and continues to seek consultations. In addition, she has developed cardiac palpitations and intestinal cramps due to the stress of "these doctors not knowing what's wrong with me."

Conversion Disorder

The essential feature of *conversion disorder* is the presence of specific impairments of sensation or movement that appear to suggest a neurological or medical illness or injury. In conversion disorder, intention is almost always unconscious, the person being unshakably convinced that the impairment is real. The underlying motivation typically involves the attempted resolution of psychological conflicts, such as dependency wishes, by channeling them into a physical disability.

Typical conversion symptoms in a clinical setting include sensory impairment (visual, auditory, somesthetic), motor impairment (weakness, poor coordination, "falling spells"), genitourinary and sexual dysfunction, impaired speech or memory, pseudoseizures, or intractable chronic pain. There is often a nonphysiologic pattern to the symptoms, which correspond to the person's notion of impairment (especially in medically unsophisticated people), rather than neuromedical reality—although in this age of ubiquitous medical newsletters and websites, individuals may be quite accurate in their replications of an organic disability.

Unlike the anxious, agitated, angry, or depressed emotional state of many injured medical patients, people with conversion disorder may display *la belle indifférence,* a bland, almost nonchalant demeanor that seems to suggest that the conviction of physical impairment is of little concern—and indeed, actually strangely reassuring—to the person, despite his or her protests of catastrophic disability.

Conversion disorder gets its name from the fact that it is thought to represent the symbolic "conversion" of a particular psychological need, wish, or conflict into a representative somatic expression. Examples include psychogenic paralysis of an arm in an employee who fears acting on a hostile impulse toward a coworker or severe, incapacitating back pain in a worker who believes, "I was a *stand-up guy,* but my company didn't *back me up* when I needed them." Exacerbations are typically precipitated by psychosocial stresses related to job or family, including the stress of an accident, with resulting financial and legal hassles.

> ▦ *CASE STUDY.* Roger, a thirty-six-year-old construction fore-man, sustained a low-back injury at work resulting in a mildly herniated lumbar disk and some soft-tissue sprain-strain injury. He had always prided himself on being a very hard-working, independent, and capable man, holding two jobs and supporting his wife and children, plus his wife's mother. He was now told that his injury would necessitate his going on light-duty

work with no decrease in pay but a substantial loss of job status.

Over the course of several weeks, the low-back pain worsened and was accompanied by progressive weakness and numbness in his legs. Eventually, his right leg "gave out," and he now walks with crutches. When asked which doctor prescribed the crutches, he replies that he borrowed them from a friend "who also had an accident and understands what I'm going through." Roger remains convinced of his total incapacity for work and is claiming total permanent disability, despite the lack of medical evidence of serious injury, and even in the face of his insurance company's threatened termination of benefits because of his noncompliance with treatment. He frequently refers to company representatives as "spineless" and castigates his supervisor for "not backing me up" and "not standing up for me."

Pain Disorder and Chronic Pain

The essential feature of *pain disorder* is chronic pain that causes significant distress or impairment in social, occupational, or other important areas of functioning combined with psychological factors that play a significant role in the onset, severity, exacerbation, or maintenance of the pain. The pain is not intentionally fabricated as in malingering or factitious disorder but rather expresses, represents, or disguises an unconscious need, fear, or conflict—closer to conversion disorder. In addition, pain caused by documented physical injury can be magnified by real-life home or workplace stressors, setting up a vicious cycle, which may partly explain the etiology of such maladies as *fibromyalgia*, a syndrome of severe, persistent muscle pain often following an injury.

In many cases, the chronic pain syndrome has a characteristic evolution and course. The problem typically begins with some accident or injury—work-related or not—that causes an expectable degree of acute pain requiring medical treatment. In a certain proportion of these individuals, the pain and disability never seem to get better and, in fact, are reported by the person to worsen with time. Various treatment strategies are tried by different medical professionals, but nothing seems to work. Sleep, appetite, and mood disturbances complicate the picture and are often aggravated by the side effects of excessive and varied medication.

The person's ongoing struggle with continual pain results in depression, obsessive somatic preoccupation, and a tendency to increasingly conceptualize most life events, activities, and problems solely in terms of how much pain they will cause, leading to a vicious cycle of hopelessness, helplessness, and despair. Each new treatment or physician consult may briefly inspire hope, which is inevitably dashed when the procedure fails to cure or significantly relieve the pain. Resentment and bitterness grow toward the medical profession and this antipathy is reciprocated, as doctors come to dread visits by the "crock."

Pain now becomes the central focus of the person's life. The individual progressively withdraws from family and social activities, and interpersonal interactions are fraught with tension and anger. Sometimes the person develops a symbiotic alliance with a close family member, a sympathetic clinician, an attorney, or an online support group that becomes the person's advocate and champion, further fueling his or her sense of victimhood. Problems with medication and with alcohol and drug abuse may compound the situation by producing toxicity and addiction. Pain behavior becomes a major coping mechanism, progressively allowing the person to avoid any kind of stressful task or adult responsibility. This leads to further incapacitation and the inexorable decline toward total invalidism.

> ⁜ *CASE STUDY.* Gladys had worked at the salon only about three months but had already developed bad blood between herself and the senior hairstylist who, she felt, did everything possible to make Gladys's life miserable. When the feud was brought to the attention of the salon manager, she told them to "just work it out." Gladys grumbled to herself: "Of course, she's going to take her side." One day, Gladys was asked to get some bottles of conditioning formula from the supply room. The carton of bottles was on a high shelf, and, as Gladys stepped onto the ladder, her left foot slipped and she fell backward, landing on her tailbone and twisting her left foot beneath her.
>
> She yelled for help, but it was a few minutes before anyone came into the back room. By that time, Gladys had raised her-

self up and was limping around on the uninjured foot. A co-worker drove her to a local walk-in clinic, where an examination revealed a bruised coccyx (tailbone) and sprained ankle. The latter was bandaged and Gladys was told to keep her weight off that foot and take nonprescription pain medication as needed for the next several days.

But over the next few weeks, the pain got worse, accompanied by hot and cold sensations. Gladys went online and learned about *reflex sympathetic dystrophy* (RSD). Although she didn't meet most of the clinical criteria for this disorder (which includes color changes and reactivity to environmental stimuli), she became convinced that she had this syndrome and filed a workers compensation claim for total disability. Thus began seemingly endless rounds of doctor visits. Frustrated by the lack of progress in her case, she retained a workers compensation attorney. Soon the pain was so bad that Gladys didn't leave her house. Two years postinjury, she is on multiple medications, housebound, and the workers compensation case is dragging on. She has applied for Social Security disability.

Hypochondriasis

"Don't be such a hypochondriac," we say when we suspect someone is overly concerned about an illness or injury. In clinical practice, the conviction that one has a serious illness or injury in the face of numerous medical pronouncements to the contrary is the defining characteristic of *hypochondriasis*. Individuals are preoccupied with the fear of pathology, injury, disease, or deterioration and tend to misinterpret normal bodily sensations as signals of dire disease. Unlike the varied clinical presentations of somatization disorder, hypochondriacs tend to focus on one or just a few chosen symptoms and remain preoccupied with them, although the focus may shift over time from one symptom or disorder to another—for example, from memory impairment to dizziness to headaches to back pain—and the associated anxiety may wax and wane over time. Unlike conversion disorder, there may be no functional impairment; rather it is the *fear* of insidious disease that is the problem. Common clinical examples include fear of "stroking out" after a head injury, fear of further injury and becoming a "cripple" upon returning to work following a knee or shoulder injury, or fear of contamination and genetic damage after exposure to a supposed toxic mold or suspected radon.

The unconscious motivation in hypochondriasis typically involves a deflection of anxiety away from issues of broader psychosocial concern, such as career or relationships, to focus on a more delimited and hence controllable source of concern in the form of somatic symptoms and fear of further injury. These tortured souls search endlessly for the one enlightened medical expert or miracle diagnostic technique that will either conclusively validate or rule out their worst fears. Yet with each reassurance, more fears arise.

> ▓ *CASE STUDY.* Clarence was exposed to fumes from an accidental chemical spill at the warehouse where he worked. Although the place royally stunk for a couple of days, analysis by a county Hazmat (hazardous materials) unit yielded no evidence of harmful substances. Yet, long after the other workers seemed to have forgotten about the spill, Clarence couldn't get that smell out of his nose. He subsequently became preoccupied with self-perceived problems in breathing and underwent many tests and consulted numerous cardiologists and pulmonary specialists. Shortness of breath, painful inhalation, gasping and wheezing, hyperventilation, and other symptoms were described, all focused on the respiratory system, and all believed to have been caused by exposure to the putatively toxic gases from the spilled chemicals, despite the fact that no medical abnormalities could be determined.
>
> Clarence's history revealed that at age eleven, he had witnessed his grandfather gravely ill with congestive heart failure, and he had subsequently become obsessed with heart problems, spending a good portion of his adolescence and early adulthood fearing sudden cardiac death and undergoing many unrevealing cardiologic workups. The preoccupation with respiratory symptoms following his exposure to fumes appears to have been one form of extension and redirection of those fears.

However, he remains resistant to any psychological explanation of his symptoms.

Body Dysmorphic Disorder

We all want to look good, at work and elsewhere. However, there seem to be some people who are abnormally fixated on their appearance, beyond mere vanity, and their agonizing over how they look may disrupt their work tasks or interpersonal relationships. Diagnostically, *body dysmorphic disorder* involves a preoccupation with an imagined defect in appearance, or being overly concerned with a minor defect. This may include facial scars or asymmetries, lost athletic prowess, reduced work capacity, or weight changes due to immobility after an orthopedic injury. Alternatively, it may present itself as a form of *cognitive dysmorphic disorder* following a traumatic brain injury, in which diminished intellectual skills, interpersonal functioning, or employment status are the main sources of self-deprecation. Unconsciously, the motivation for such preoccupation with self-perceived ugliness or worthlessness may involve deep-seated and long-standing feelings of self-loathing that are now projected onto a more objectifiable physical or mental impairment that serves as the new focus of the individual's self-perceived "badness."

> **CASE STUDY.** "How do I look?" Janet's fellow faculty members had learned to cringe at those words. A high school teacher in the midst of a contentious divorce, Janet was assaulted by a student who hit her in the face with a canvas backpack. She was momentarily dazed and sustained a mild cervical sprain-strain (whiplash) injury, which subsequently resolved. However, she also received several scratches and bruises on her face, which, although long-since healed and virtually invisible to the close inspection of doctors and friends alike, continued to plague her each time she peered closely into the mirror. In addition, she became convinced that the neck injury had caused her head to tilt at an ugly angle and that she now "looked like a gimp." She was about to undergo cosmetic sur-

gery, but the plastic surgeon hesitated when he reviewed the history and subsequently requested a psychological evaluation.

Factitious Disorder

Factitious disorder is defined as the deliberate production, manipulation, or fabrication of physical or psychological signs and symptoms, not necessarily for material gain, but to satisfy unmet psychological needs or wishes. Because the intentionality of symptom production is conscious and deliberate, it is diagnostically separated from the somatoform disorders. However, unlike malingering, where a practical, utilitarian motive for the deception can usually be discerned, the motive in factitious disorder is primarily to assume the sick role and partake of the care, solicitous concern, and relief from responsibilities of normal life that this role entails, even at the price of substantial cost in money, health, or freedom—that is, the motive would be viewed by most people as senseless in terms of significant practical gain. In many cases, there also appears to be great satisfaction, perhaps only partly unconscious, derived from manipulating the medical system and "fooling the experts."

Historically referred to as *Munchausen's syndrome,* the manifestations of factitious disorder are limited only by the imagination and ingenuity of these individuals. Medically sophisticated employees, such as nurses or mental health clinicians, may be quite clever in feigning credible medical and psychiatric illnesses and impairments by the surreptitious use of chemical substances or medical apparatus, or by enacting realistic postconcussive, depressive, or posttraumatic stress disorder symptoms. Less knowledgeable workers may resort to cruder methods such as drinking nauseating concoctions, bruising or cutting themselves to simulate injuries, or acting like their imagined version of a brain-damaged or "crazy" person.

> ::::: *CASE STUDY.* Catalina ("call me Cat") seemed almost unnaturally cheerful in her job as a day-care worker at the County Youth Center. She was enthusiastic about her job and everybody loved her. The kids loved her. The parents loved her. And she loved being the center of their attention. Shortly after she started, however, she was told she had to spend more time

doing routine office work that would take her away from the adulation of the children and families for a few hours a day.

She never complained and acted quite the dutiful little soldier as she put in her several hours a day doing "ordinary" work. Then, she began coming to work sick, sniffling and coughing, but again, never complaining and never asking for time off. Her malady grew more mysterious. Coworkers overheard her hacking loudly in one of the bathroom stalls and when one of them later entered the bathroom, she was shocked to find drops of blood on the floor and sink.

For general public health reasons, her supervisor insisted she seek medical attention, but the doctors at the clinic were baffled by her signs and symptoms, which now included lower abdominal pain and blood in her urine as well. Asked why she always wore long sleeves in the warm Southern climate, Cat replied that she was subject to chills. When a friend from work called to get an update on Cat's condition, she was dismissive: "Those idiot doctors—what do they know?"

Then one day, a nurse at the clinic caught her cutting her arm and squeezing drops of blood into her urine specimen before quickly putting on a bandage and rolling her sleeve over the self-inflicted wound. Subsequent investigation disclosed that she was taking a powerful diuretic to induce excessive urination. Cat was told to seek mental health treatment as a condition of continuing her job. Instead, she disappeared and her daycare credentials and other aspects of her identity were subsequently discovered to be phony.

Malingering

I hear you saying: "All these psychological explanations—you doctors have a name for everything. Don't people ever just make up symptoms because they want something?" Well, yes they do, and we even have a name for that.

Malingering is not classified as a true psychiatric disorder but rather is defined as the conscious and intentional simulation of illness or impairment for the purpose of obtaining financial compensation or other reward; to evade duty, responsibility, or obligation; or to seek exculpation or mitigation for the consequences of criminal or other illicit behavior. In other words, there is a practical and "sensible"—albeit ill-intended—motive for the subterfuge and therefore it does not represent a true symptom of psychopathology, although malingering individuals may certainly have other psychiatric syndromes and personality disorders; for example, antisocial personalities will glibly fake illnesses to obtain drugs or to get out of legal trouble, and borderline personalities will feign symptoms to manipulate the loyalty and affections of family members.

In an employment context, frank malingering is most often seen following a workplace injury for which the worker is seeking compensation or other benefits. Especially if you're the employee assistance program or disability benefits coordinator for your company, you need to be aware of the several forms malingering can take.

1. _Fabrication._ The employee has no symptoms or impairments resulting from the injury but fraudulently represents that he has. Symptoms may be atypical, inconsistent, or bizarre, or they may be perfect textbook replicas of real syndromes. In common practice, this wholesale invention of an entire impairment syndrome from scratch is the rarest form of malingering.

> ::::: _CASE EXAMPLE._ Jack trips in the aisle of the grocery where he works, but he gets up, feels fine, and has no symptoms other than momentary embarrassment. A few days later, however, he files a false workers compensation claim, alleging memory loss due to brain damage. On neuropsychological examination, he reports multiple symptoms that he looked up online and performs ridiculously poorly on the neuropsychological tests.

2. _Exaggeration._ The employee has symptoms or impairments caused by the injury but presents them as being worse than they really are. This is probably the most common form of malingering in clinical and forensic practice.

> ::::: _CASE EXAMPLE._ While driving for the delivery company, Deena is jostled in the course of a low-speed auto collision. She

is momentarily dazed and subsequently experiences a moderate headache, some neck soreness, and transient chest irritation and shoulder soreness from the seat belt. Paramedics document that she appears alert and oriented, denies discomfort, and refuses care, claiming, "I'm all right; this'll pass—I have to get back to work." A week later, she shows up at the local clinic wearing a cervical collar and falsely reports unrelenting, excruciating headaches; crippling shoulder and arm weakness that precludes her from working; and virtual neck immobility due to severe whiplash.

3. Extension. The employee has experienced symptoms or impairments caused by the injury, and these have now recovered or improved, but he falsely presents them as continuing unabated, or even as having worsened over time—that is, he extends the symptoms beyond the normal time frame for that syndrome.

CASE EXAMPLE. After six months of physical therapy and massage, Hassan's lower-back pain symptoms caused by a mild lumbar disk bulge and radiculopathy (radiating nerve pain) he sustained while lifting paving stones at his contractor's job have virtually disappeared. But on his follow-up orthopedic examination, he falsely reports being as agonized as ever: "There's been no letup in the pain, Doc, and the pills you gave me don't seem to work anymore."

4. Misattribution. The employee has symptoms or impairments that preceded, postdated, or were otherwise unrelated to the index injury, but he fraudulently attributes them to that injury.

CASE EXAMPLE. Jesse reports that he was "just fine" at his waiter's job until six months ago when his leg was carelessly pushed into the restaurant wall by a patron rushing by. He is filing a claim for total disability because he now has difficulty standing or walking; the affected leg frequently "gives out," causing him to fall; and he has had to borrow crutches from his father just to make it to this appointment. Further historical exploration reveals a prior knee injury from a high school football mishap, as well as a second injury to the same joint in a motorcycle accident while he was intoxicated about a year prior to this examination.

Dealing with Mind-Body Disorders at Work

Some of these syndromes will occur in response to events that happen in your workplace; others will have their origin outside work or predate the employment but affect the worker in his or her job. Managers can minimize the disruption these kinds of employees can cause by heeding the following recommendations.

Remember that the best form of crisis intervention is crisis prevention. Take workplace safety seriously. This means not only having the minimum standards mandated by your industry but also maintaining a safety-conscious attitude around your place of business and encouraging your employees to do likewise. Have a user-friendly system of referral to obtain appropriate care for workers who become ill or get injured on the job.

Treat ill or injured employees with respect and consideration. Regardless of your view of the employee and his or her injury, syndromes are less likely to become chronic and disabling if you convey the impression that you are concerned about the employee's health and welfare and will do everything reasonable to help. Back that up with a referral system as noted earlier. You don't have to afford carte blanche medical care for every employee complaint, but try to avoid making access to treatment an adversarial issue.

Address the medical aspects. If an employee reports in sick, encourage him or her to seek medical care. If the person is injured on the job, have a system in place for timely treatment of work-related injuries. This is important for two reasons: It is part of conveying respect and consideration, and it reduces your liability if a worse syndrome arises out of the injury.

Follow up with the ill or injured employee. If a worker is out for more than a few days, call to inquire about how he or she is doing. Ask what you can do to cover for this person while he or she is away. If the employee is seeking attention through disability, defuse the process by showing honest concern for his or her welfare without the person having to become a chronic complainer.

Encourage a back-to-work attitude. Except in the case of clearly cata-strophic and severely disabling illness or injury, from the very first mo-ments, your attitude and behavior should convey that you confidently expect the employee to fully recover and return to work. If it becomes medically clear that only partial recovery is realistic, do whatever you can, within reason, to accommodate that employee's residual disability. As a rule, it's cheaper and easier to maintain a good employee than to train a new one.

Know how to coordinate treatment with discipline. If the effects of an illness or injury become a disciplinary problem, have a system in place to enforce workplace rules, even as you help the employee regain his or her health (see Chapter 10).

Document everything. Have a system of documentation—incident reports, a disability log, and so forth—so that every aspect of the illness or injury has a paper trail. This shows you are serious about employee welfare and also covers your behind should a disability claim or other legal case crop up.

If *You* Are an Employee with a Mind-Body Syndrome

You're sick and tired of being sick and tired but don't know how to get off the illness merry-go-round. Since this has probably been a lifelong pattern for you, it'll take more than a few recommendations to break the cycle, but here's how to get started:

Find a medical doctor you trust. In the present rarified healthcare environ-ment, I know this is easier said than done, but try to find a general physician who can communicate to you the results of your various medical evaluations and coordinate a rational and effective treatment plan for those syndromes that do exist.

Find a mental health clinician you trust. This is not because I think you're crazy or that your symptoms are "all in your head," but to help you cope with the stress of negotiating the healthcare system and putting your treatment in the context of your overall life.

Find an attorney you trust. Again, not because I want to encourage you to be unnecessarily litigious, but because a good attorney will stand up for your rights without dragging you down an overly complicated legal road.

Find a workmate or manager you trust. This may be the most difficult of all if you feel your job has let you down. But it pays to have an ally at the company you've worked for, if only to help cut through some of the red tape associated with getting your legitimate treatment and employment needs met.

Take support from family and friends you trust. One of the problems of dealing with a chronic condition is that, after a while, people get tired of hearing about it. So, if you have one or two people in your personal life who can be there for you, take advantage of their good will but don't overuse it—because if you're ever going to break free from a life of continual pain and misery, you'll need to pay attention to the next recommendation.

Get a life you trust. Ultimately, you'll need to decide if there's something in your life worth pursuing in spite of your condition. This will help you to stop being a professional patient and be able to participate in the world of the living.

. . . .

CHAPTER 10

What a Job
Managing Dysfunctional Employees

This chapter and Chapter 11 lay out a program for managing problem employees that cuts across the personality types and diagnostic categories you're already familiar with from reading this book so far. Indeed, after so many chapters on symptoms and syndromes, it may be hard to remember that people can cause trouble at work without necessarily having a formal diagnosis or psychological disorder.

Many of the ideas and applications presented in this chapter were developed through my experience working with law enforcement and public safety agencies where employee misconduct can have serious local, regional, and national repercussions in terms of expensive legal action, civil unrest, and loss of public confidence. Accordingly, these organizations tend to have a zero-tolerance policy toward such misconduct that may be stricter than what you're willing to enforce in your workplace. That's all right: You can pick and choose from the following recommendations to custom design a problem-management program that works for you. If you understand the basic concepts of supervision and discipline and know how to apply them practically to your own workplace, you'll feel generally more confident in managing your workforce in an authoritative, not authoritarian, manner.

Types of Problem Employees
and Employee Problems

The term *problem employee* encompasses an enormously wide range of behaviors, from tardiness and failure to complete paperwork to bullying, harassment, and workplace violence. Although some extreme forms of
behavior automatically preclude retaining an employee and may well incur
criminal charges, many kinds of less serious and far more common infractions or patterns of substandard performance are amenable to change with
the proper approach, informed by principles of practical psychology. Accordingly, this section outlines some common forms of employee problems.

Workplace aggression is defined as any act or threat of violence, including
assault, harassment, vandalism, or other acts of harm or intimidation. This
will be covered more fully in Chapter 11. For now, it is important to note
that overt aggression is often the end point of a downward behavioral spiral
that begins with other problem behaviors at work.

Workplace misconduct typically involves the violation of rules regarding
time schedules, conduct, workplace relationships, dishonest and corrupt
behavior, and other nonviolent infractions. Note, however, that the dividing line between this category and the previous one can be quite fluid.
For example, is "creating a hostile environment" by a male employee's
wordlessly salacious leering at a female coworker a form of misconduct,
harassment, or other category of problem behavior? Is threatening your
assistant with onerous duty to muzzle him regarding your bill-skimming
scheme a form of bullying, harassment, intimidation, or theft—or all of the
above? Again, recalling the principle of prevention being the best form of
intervention, the sooner such problems are addressed and corrected, the
less chance they have of mushrooming out of control.

Marginal performance generally refers to so-called sins of omission and
includes such infractions as tardiness and absences, failure to complete work
assignments, misuse of company equipment and property, insubordination
and problems with chain of command, passive violation of company rules
and safety guidelines, poor customer relations, unprofessional behavior, and
special infractions related to an individual job.

We might also take a moment to consider what makes a *good* employee.
For virtually all jobs, and especially for occupations that involve any kind

of independent judgment or decision making, there is a need for employees who possess good overall intelligence, especially abstract reasoning, mental flexibility, interpersonal creativity, and problem-solving skills. Other related positive traits and qualities include psychological maturity, common sense, reliability, conscientiousness, and the ability to apply discretion in an ethical and equitable manner. Leaders, supervisors, and higher-ranking managers should be mature, seasoned individuals with a well-developed sense of integrity and professionalism (see also Chapter 12). The challenge for all organizations and industries is to find or develop selection and training protocols that can accurately identify, predict, and develop these positive traits.

Bad Employee to Good Employee: Practical Solutions and Strategies

Productive solutions to workplace misconduct can be applied at several points along the process of hiring, training, and retaining employees. Indeed, for most workplaces, it is far easier and more economical to salvage a basically good employee with a few correctible blemishes than to jettison him or her and then recruit and train a replacement. The key is to separate out the more common not-so-bad employee from the minority who are truly, irredeemably, bad.

Different employees are dysfunctional for different reasons, and organizations therefore need to develop an integrated system of interventions to target different groups of employees at different phases of their careers. Interventions must address not just personality characteristics and individual behavior but also the organizational practices of the companies in which the employees work. Management can hardly model unfair or corrupt behavior and then expect its workers to behave honorably. Provide the example you want your employees to emulate.

I have developed the following step-by-step model of employee selection, training, and managing for organizations of all types, including public safety agencies, professional organizations, and private companies. The different stages should be thought of less as linear rungs on a ladder than as an array of cyclic flywheels, each phase shading into the next and drawing from the ones that precede it.

Selection and Screening

The best way to prevent employee misconduct is not to hire misconduct-prone applicants in the first place. If only it were that simple. It's surprising how few organizations outside law enforcement, public safety, and some government agencies employ any kind of formal psychological or informal behavioral screening measures of their prospective employees. Some companies contract with self-styled selection service providers who employ questionably valid and sometimes just plain goofy selection and screening measures and procedures. To cut through confusion, any hiring manager can use his or her brain and a few psychologically informed principles of common sense to weed out job candidates who have the word *trouble* scrawled across their forehead.

Basic *screening-out* red flags include drug or alcohol abuse, a serious or extensive criminal history, evidence of past repeated conflicts with authority, misconduct or poor performance in former jobs, chronic financial problems, or a spotty and inconsistent work record. A particularly important feature of the evaluation is the candidate's style of handling anger and frustration, both in the past and presently.

Screening-in protocols should assess not just behavioral styles and character traits but also the potential for both formal training and learning from experience. As noted earlier, traits to look for include good overall intelligence and problem-solving ability, emotional maturity, good communication skills, reliability, conscientiousness, and the ability to use discretion and independent thinking in a fair and ethical manner. Many of these traits, or their absence, will have emerged during a careful preemployment interview, if you have taken the time and care to conduct one.

Yet, even the best screening protocols and interviews are really only behavioral snapshots of the employee's psychological qualifications at the beginning of his or her career with your company. These assessment tools cannot necessarily anticipate emotional and psychological problems that may develop during an employee's tenure with your company. Ideally then, evaluations and reassessments should be a regular component of an employee's progress. Such reassessments should be balanced with fair and effective monitoring, training, and supervision throughout the employee's span of employment.

Education and Training

Here, I'm talking not about training for the specific job description (book-keeper, machine operator, stock manager, or medical technician), but training in the necessary people skills that make a workplace divine or hellish to work in. Certain interpersonal skills and qualities are largely innate; that is, you either have them or you don't. Many skills, however, can be taught, albeit to varying degrees that depend on the potential and willingness of the individual learner. Given the impact that interpersonal behavior has on employee satisfaction and productivity, it is surprising how many companies leave this dimension to chance. Notable exceptions include service industries, like hospitality or sales, where acting cordially is an essential part of the employee's "uniform," because it directly affects customer satisfaction and the bottom line. But why not apply these principles in all companies to make them more pleasant to work at?

For managers who are starting to groan and roll their eyes, let me point out that this type of interpersonal skills training need not be complicated or expensive. The general models employed by most trainers who consult to service-industry businesses and organizations are based on principles of adult learning that involve a combination of didactic instruction, behavioral participation, simulated scenarios, and role playing. The emphasis is on developing a range of psychosocial and communication skills that assume frequent—and potentially unpleasant—interactions between customers and employees. Such exercises focus on anticipating problems before they arise and on using a range of flexible problem-solving, conflict-resolution strategies to defuse problems before they explode into crises.

But formal training goes only so far. Much teaching, experience, and socialization of new employees occurs on the job under the guidance and influence of their immediate supervisors who transmit and model the corporate culture of that organization. Training thus has an important attitudinal component: It socializes workers into their respective organizations and inculcates organizational philosophies, values, and expectations. These seeming intangibles can have great impact on an employee's behavior, something managers should always be mindful of as they interact with their workers on a daily basis.

Coaching and Counseling

Coaching and counseling may be considered a more focused and individualized application of education and training that directly addresses a particular employee's problematic behavior in the context of a supervisory session. The program I've adapted to the needs of business managers grows out of Special Supervisory Agent Hillary Robinette's management protocol for Federal Bureau of Investigation agents and other law enforcement officers. Both coaching and counseling require constructive confrontation of the problem employee's behavior, but it is important to realize that such confrontation need not—indeed, should not—ever be gratuitously hostile, offensive, or demeaning. Professionalism and respect can characterize the interaction of a superior with a subordinate in any supervisory setting, including instruction, coaching, counseling, discipline, or even termination. The focus is on correcting the problem behavior, not bashing the employee. Supervisors should be firm but civil, preserving the dignity of all involved.

Coaching

The difference between coaching and counseling lies in their focus and emphasis. Coaching deals directly with identifying and correcting problematic behaviors. It is concerned with the operational reasons those behaviors occur and with developing specific task-related strategies for improving performance in those areas. Most of the instruction and guidance in coaching comes from the supervisor, and the main task of the supervisee is to understand and carry out the prescribed corrective actions.

For example, a quality assurance inspector who fails to complete reports on time is given specific deadlines for such paperwork as well as guidance on how to word reports so that they don't become too overwhelming. A restaurant waiter who behaves discourteously with customers is provided with specific scenarios to role-play in order to develop a repertoire of responses for maintaining his or her dignity without offending the restaurant's patrons.

Productively applied to the corporate world, the coaching protocol can be viewed as a series of six stages.

1. *Define the problem clearly.* This ensures that you and the employee are on the same page and prevents any misunderstanding from the outset.

> "There have been four customer complaints filed against you for discourteous behavior in the past six months."

2. *Identify the effect of the problem.* This objectifies the situation, providing the employee with a general rule of behavior that applies to everyone. That way, the employee can't accuse you of singling him or her out for personal reasons.

> "When customers experience our staff as being unpleasant to work with, they'll want to take their business elsewhere. In addition, they'll tell other people, which hurts our business still further. Lost business means fewer raises and bonuses and possibly staff cuts. It also makes the atmosphere generally less pleasant to work in. As you recall from our new-hire orientation, courteous speech and behavior is part of the 'uniform' we all wear when we're at work."

3. *Describe the corrective action.* Be crystal clear about what you expect the employee to do. Repeat it as many times and in as many ways as necessary to be sure he or she understands you. It's amazing how people hear what they want to hear, so leave as little as possible to chance.

> "There seem to be some common threads in these complaints. Let's review some of these situations and see if we can come up with better responses. You can use these suggestions or feel free to come up with ideas of your own, but the bottom line is that your style of interaction with customers has to change."

4. *Demonstrate and role-play as needed.* In the spirit of leaving little to chance, actually act out for the employee the behaviors you want him or her to emulate; then have the employee do it. Repeat until the skill or behavior has been mastered.

> "Let's play this out. I'll be the customer and you be you. Show me how you usually handle this kind of problem."

[Scene is played out.]

"Okay, here's what I'd like you to do differently. This time, you be the customer and I'll be you. Let's run through it again."

[Scene is played out with supervisor demonstrating correct behavior.]

"See the difference? Now I'll be the customer again and you go back to being you, only this time, let's do it the way I showed you."

[Role-play is repeated until supervisor is satisfied that employee "gets it."]

5. Motivate the employee for change. Although it may sound like a cliché, try to make the coaching sessions seem more like an opportunity and less like a punishment. Employees will take correction and stick to the program to the extent that they feel they have something to gain from doing so; therefore try to inculcate employee *buy-in.*

"We appreciate your efforts to be an aggressive, meticulous, high-producing sales rep and we know that better customer relations means more business, which is better for everyone. People like doing business with reps who make them feel comfortable and welcome. These ways we've discussed of interacting with customers should help you shoot your numbers even higher."

6. Document and summarize. Again, don't leave things to chance. If a repeat coaching session is necessary, you want written confirmation of what you and the employee already discussed and agreed on.

"Okay, I'm noting here that we reviewed this and that we both agree that you're going to make these changes."

Counseling

Counseling differs from coaching in two main ways. First, it is less task focused and more supportive, empathic, nondirective, and nonevaluative; it seeks to understand the broader reasons underlying the problematic behavior. This is especially appropriate when the difficulty lies less in a specific action or infraction and more in the area of attitudes and style of relating, where there may be a general factor accounting for a range of specific problem behaviors. Second, counseling has less of a top-down flow than coaching and puts more of the burden of change on the supervisee, encouraging the employee to creatively develop his or her own solutions to the problem. In the counseling approach, much of the feedback to the employee may occur in the form of *reflective statements*, so that a kind of Socratic dialogue emerges, moving the employee increasingly in the direction of constructive problem solving.

Supervisor: Do you know why I asked to speak with you today?

Employee: Well, I guess there have been some complaints about me.

[Discussion continues about the nature of the complaints and their consequences.]

Supervisor: I see you've been here three years with a pretty good record. What's been going on lately?

Employee: I dunno, maybe the job's getting to me. Ever since the 2005 downsizing and last February's robbery, it's like everything seems to drag. And the customers seem more of a pain in the butt than ever. There are fewer big deals these days and more of them seem to be these nickel-and-dime small-business operations. Every little thing seems to tick me off. Oh yeah, and things at home haven't been going that great, either.

[Some further discussion ensues about job and personal problems.]

Supervisor: Well, I'm glad you told me that, and I understand things have been rough the past couple of months, but I'm sure you understand that we need to maintain a certain standard of professionalism. I'm going to refer you to our EAP for some counseling to help you get your bearings. In the meantime, I'd like you to take the next few days to think of some ways you can improve how you're interacting with the customers. Jot 'em down, in fact, and we'll meet next time to discuss this further. You do your part, and we'll help you get through this, agreed?

Employee: Okay, I'll try.

Supervisor: Well, I need you to do more than try, because the situation does have to change. So get back to me with some specifics next week and we'll take it from there, okay?

Employee: Okay.

Discipline

If educative, coaching, and counseling measures have been ineffective, some sort of disciplinary action, ranging from an official reprimand to suspension to termination, may be indicated.

Just as the best form of crisis intervention is crisis prevention, good discipline begins with proactive assessment and monitoring of the employee's behavior to detect precursors and patterns of misconduct, so that interventions can be applied as early as possible. Many companies are too lax in this regard, not realizing that letting little misbehaviors slide is a perfect way of abetting and encouraging larger transgressions down the road.

The opposite problem in many organizations is an overly heavy-handed approach to discipline in an attempt to enforce zero-tolerance policies. However, zero tolerance for bad behavior doesn't mean zero humanity in dealing with the employee. Discipline should be consistent, impartial, immediate, and definitive—but not cruel or vindictive. Ideally, the goal should be to stop the misbehavior while salvaging an otherwise effective employee. To this end, interventions should be stepwise and targeted to the specific problem.

Discipline for the Real World

Again, like all categories, the boundaries between coaching, counseling, and discipline are elastic and interactive. One disciplinary protocol that I've adapted to the corporate world comes from the Lakewood, Colorado, Police Department's practical manual on police supervision, developed by Lieutenant Gerald Garner. This program specifies the following set of five basic principles of corrective action that should guide any effective disciplinary interview.

1. Have the required administrative support before taking corrective action. For discipline to be effective, you must be able to back it up. To begin with, you should be working from a standard policies-and-procedures manual that specifies fair and equal rules for all employees. You should also have the backing of *your* supervisors to use your managerial discretion and authority in handling the matter.

2. Have as much background information as possible. Few things erode the effectiveness of workplace discipline more than being uninformed and unprepared. You may never be able to know everything, but whatever you can find out about the incident or pattern in question will bolster your authority and leave the employee little wiggle room to finagle or snow you. It also shows that you're bending over backward to be thorough and fair because this is important enough for you to take the time to thoroughly investigate the matter.

3. Know the employee as well as possible. This is a corollary to the previous principle, but a little broader. As a good manager, you should always strive to know the people you work with and be able to anticipate how they'll react. But, as I hope I've made clear, this is not primarily just to analyze or psyche them out, but to know them as *people*, because then it's much easier to tailor your approach to them as individuals when you have to coach, counsel, or discipline them.

4. Frame constructive criticism in a supportive context. Remember to raise some good points, not just the bad. Some authorities suggest sandwiching any criticism between two slices of praise.

> "I know you're trying to keep your orders moving and we appreciate that, but some of our customers are feeling like you're rushing them through their meals, so we have to work on lightening up the intensity. And most of the customers appreciate your not making them have to keep asking for drink refills."

5. Try to obtain agreement, commitment, and buy-in from the employee— but don't be afraid to pull rank when you have to. In the best-case scenario, you want the final solution to feel like it's the employee's decision, too. That's why it's important to first ask if the employee has any ideas of his or her own about correcting the problem. Then work on them together to come up with the best solution. In some cases, however, the employee will just stare at you blankly or actively protest your suggestions; then you have to make it clear that, ultimately, you have the (company-backed) last say and it's the employee's responsibility to comply.

Discipline Without Punishment

For those readers who may be wondering what all this police business has to do with their own business, it may be instructive to compare the previous protocol with one that comes directly from the field of business consulting, the model of *discipline without punishment* (DWP), developed by management consultant Dick Grote. This system begins by treating each worker as a grown-up worthy of adult respect and thereby subject to adult responsibilities. Accordingly, the disciplinary procedure is conducted on a mature and professional level.

The focus of the DWP procedure is not on the "badness" of the employee but on the problem to be solved, and the bulk of the responsibility for its solution is placed on the employee. One important role for the manager or supervisor is to set an example of mature problem-solving behavior by keeping the tone of the meeting calm, professional, and focused. In this system, the discipline process, at least in the early stages, is less like punishment and more like coaching.

The DWP process consists of five basic steps:

Step one is to *identify the problem* to be solved by determining the exact nature of the job required and the specific features of the employee's current performance that deviate from this standard.

> "Fred, we understand that everyone has his moods, but keeping a neat appearance, smiling at customers, and speaking in a calm, friendly tone of voice is part of the professional uniform we all wear in a service organization. As you recall, this was discussed at your employee orientation and training sessions."

Step two is to analyze the *impact and consequences of the problem,* and then determine the *appropriate corrective actions* to be taken.

> "We've had three complaints about your work this month, which is more than three times our company average. When customers feel put off, it affects repeat business, damages us by word of mouth, and ultimately impacts our bottom line and our ability to support raises, bonuses, and other employee benefits."

Step three is to address the problem with the employee, gaining the *employee's commitment to change,* discussing alternate solutions, and deciding what *specific actions* the employee will take.

"Here's what we need you to do to bring your performance up to speed. [Discusses specific actions with the employee.] Let me know if you have any additional ideas that would be helpful. If you need some help with any personal issues, we'll be glad to refer you to our EAP."

Step four is to *document the disciplinary/coaching session* by describing the problem, the history, and the discussion that took place.

"Okay, I'm noting that we discussed the problem, that you've expressed your willingness to act in accord with our customer service policy, and that you'll let us know if you need help with anything else. We'll meet again in two weeks to review."

Step five is the *follow-up* to determine if the problem has indeed been corrected, to reinforce this improvement, and to take any additional action required.

"It's been two weeks since our last discussion and things have improved greatly. I appreciate your effort and I'm glad everything is working out."

········

You'll note that the DWP model shares many features with other coaching, counseling, and disciplinary model discussed in this chapter. That's because all successful systems for constructively remodeling employee behavior rely on making the employee a productive part of the process. Often, just being treated with respect and allowed a fair hearing—the concept of *procedural justice* from organizational psychology—can deflect an otherwise disgruntled employee from feeling like he or she has no alternative but to behave in a counterproductive way or, more ominously, as we'll see in Chapter 11, to "take the law into my own hands."

Psychological Fitness for Duty Evaluations

Where it is suspected that personal traits, disorders, or stress reactions are using or contributing to an employee's problem behavior, a formal *psy-*

chological fitness for duty (FFD) evaluation may be ordered. This evaluation can be used to determine (1) if the employee is psychologically capable of continuing to fulfill his or her job requirements; (2) if not, then what measures, if any, are recommended to make him or her more effective and able to function up to the standards of the organization; and (3) what kinds of reasonable accommodations, if any, must be in place to permit the employee to work in spite of the residual disabilities. The FFD evaluation thus combines elements of risk management, mental health intervention, labor law, and departmental discipline.

In this respect, managers who wish to refer an employee for an FFD evaluation may have to navigate some tricky terrain through legal and union territory. As a rule, under the Americans with Disabilities Act, for positions that involve public safety workers, such as police, firefighters, and emergency medical personnel, courts have generally tended to afford greater discretion to employers seeking to require a psychological FFD evaluation if there is a potential for that worker's impaired mental state to put the public at risk. This is one reason why many of the protocols I'm about to discuss were originally developed specifically for these groups by authorities on critical occupation evaluations such as Cary Rostow, Robert Davis, and Anthony Stone. However, these issues apply as well to medical personnel, transportation workers, security personnel, and those who work with children.

One primary driver of such assessments is concern for liability, such as claims of negligent hiring, negligent retention, and negligent supervision; these issues are endemic in the public and private employee sector. However, for most other jobs that do not involve critical safety issues, managers should consult with their business attorneys before ordering any kind of formal psychological examination. The following will summarize the main points that you, as a manager, need to understand about the basic components of a psychological FFD evaluation.

Identifying data. The employee's name, identifying demographics, departmental referral information, name of the evaluator, and dates of the evaluation.

Reason for evaluation. The main incidents, issues, and referral question(s) that have led the employee to the examining psychologist's office. The focus of the evaluation itself should be specific to the work-related question at hand.

Background information. The information in this section can be narrow or broad but, again, the scope and range of such background data should be defined by their relevance to the referral question(s). For example, conflicts with previous employers may be relevant; history of marital infidelity may not be.

Clinical interview and behavioral observations. As with all clinical evaluations, much useful information can be gleaned about a person from a good clinical interview. How the person answers questions and how he or she generally behaves is just as important as what he or she says.

Review of records. Depending on the individual case, the volume of pertinent records can range from a few spare sheets to literally cartons of documents. The psychologist's challenge is to distill the raw data in order to summarize the main points necessary to form a conclusion.

Psychological test findings. Not all FFD evaluations will include psychometric tests, but when they do, the measures administered should be relevant to the job-related question being asked. Usually, the basic areas covered include general intelligence, cognitive functioning (attention, concentration, memory, reasoning), personality functioning, assessment of mood (anxiety, depression), and screening for psychotic symptoms (delusions or hallucinations).

Conclusions and discussion. This section should be a succinct summary of the main points relevant to the FFD question(s), with documentation of the psychologist's reasoning on each point. For example:

> "Psychological test findings are essentially within normal limits, with the exception of a tendency to disregard rules and conventions and to respond impulsively under stress. This is supported by the employee's statement, 'If I know the policy is wrong, it's my responsibility to do it the right way.' This is further corroborated by records

indicating three prior disciplinary actions in his present department, and at least one prior suspension in his previous job.

"Overall findings are consistent with an employee of average intelligence, no major mental disorder, high ability and skill in certain job related areas (financial figures and spreadsheets), but with a long-standing tendency to disobey authority and respond impulsively, but not violently, under conditions of stress."

Recommendations. This is perhaps the most challenging section of the report, because here the psychologist has to boil down the findings to specific recommendations that the manager can understand and utilize and that may affect this employee's entire career. There are several possible outcomes to an FFD evaluation:

◇ *Unfit for Duty.* The employee is unfit for duty and is not likely to become fit in the foreseeable future, with or without psychological treatment. Examples include the effects of a traumatic brain injury, a long-standing severe personality disorder, or a substance abuse problem that continues to get worse.

◇ *Unfit but Treatable.* The employee is currently unfit but appears to be amenable to treatment that will restore him or her to fitness in a reasonable amount of time. For example, a depressed, alcoholic employee agrees to enter a twelve-step abstinence program, attend psychotherapy sessions, and take prescribed antidepressant medication as needed. Following the recommended course of treatment, the employee will usually be referred for a *posttreatment evaluation* to assess if he or she is now fit to resume his or her duties.

◇ *No Psychological Diagnosis.* There is nothing in the results of the psychological FFD evaluation to suggest that the employee's unfitness for duty is related to a mental disorder or mental heath diagnosis. In such cases, the employee will usually be referred back for administrative coaching or counseling, further education and training, or disciplinary action.

◇ *Invalid Evaluation.* The employee has failed to cooperate with the evaluation, has not been truthful, or has shown malingering or other response manipulation on interview or psychological tests. Again, he or she will usually be referred back to management for further administrative action.

Psychological Services

One of the purposes of an FFD evaluation is to make recommendations for education, retraining, counseling, or treatment. Unfortunately, the referral of employees for mental health services when their job performance has begun to deteriorate is often viewed as punishment within a disciplinary context, rather than as a proactive human resources intervention that might forestall further problems and help contribute to that employee's better job performance and overall health. This is especially likely if the referral for counseling follows a particularly unpleasant and contentious psychological FFD evaluation.

Ideally, the goal of company-referred psychological treatment should be to use the minimum depth and intensity of intervention necessary to restore the employee to adequate baseline functioning or to modify a preexisting pattern of problem behavior that interferes with the employee's work role. In some cases, when a certain level of clinical trust and comfort has been established, the employee may later opt for further, more extensive individual or family therapy to work on personal issues of special concern once the original departmentally referred issue has been resolved.

A preferable way of making the best use of psychological counseling services for employees is to recommend counseling well before the situation rises to the level of a disciplinary action. Many employees are actually glad to be afforded this option once they have been given "permission" by a manager to see the psychologist without stigma, especially if they trust that this supervisor has their best interests at heart. As with most recommendations, the more buy-in obtained by the employee, the more likely the process is to be successful. In my own clinical practice, I see far more voluntary referrals of employees for psychotherapy than mandatory referrals, and this is especially true where such services are encouraged and supported by all levels of management.

Termination

Sadly, not every dysfunctional employee can be salvaged. When all reasonable efforts at training, coaching, counseling, psychological services, and constructive discipline have been exhausted, employees who are persistently and irredeemably underperforming or misbehaving must be terminated. In some cases, such as theft, vandalism, or violence, formal legal charges may be brought. If things have progressed to this point, discipline should be consistent, impartial, immediate, and definitive. The weeding out of the few truly bad employees is a fundamental prerequisite for the ability of the many good employees to serve their companies and the public with skill and dedication. If it comes to that, here are some basic recommendations.

Some authorities believe that the best person to terminate an employee is the manager or supervisor who has had the best overall relationship with the worker. Others recommend that the actual firing be done by a more objective and interpersonally removed higher-up, while the trusted supervisor remains a source of support to ease the transition. However it's done, a termination should always include a systematic process of documentation. The key to effective termination, in both the psychological and legal senses, is to make it as clear as possible to the employee that this action is for a specific reason, rather than for general attitude problems or personal grievances. These reasons should be clearly reviewed and documented in writing.

In an uncomplicated termination, your company's own policies may dictate a variety of actions, including the opportunity for the employee to complete certain work projects, receive severance pay, or get insurance benefit protection for a specified time period. If the termination is particularly adversarial, the disturbed or disgruntled employee may have to be asked to leave immediately. The person may have to be escorted off the premises by company security or police. Don't give the terminated worker time to stew, either by delaying the inevitable or by allowing him or her to hang around and poison the workplace atmosphere with negative talk or dangerous behavior.

Termination should be done at the beginning or end of the shift. Most companies have a policy of not allowing terminated employees access to the premises without escort. Have a strict ID policy in place and enforce it. Even in this post–September 11 world, it is surprising how lax some companies are with regard to security, especially with people they've known in the past. Again, the employee should be afforded reasonable privacy and respect but should understand in no uncertain terms—by the presence of security or police if necessary—that the termination action is final and will be backed up. The employee should also be informed of any counseling or other services offered by the company for the transition period. Providing continued medical and mental health benefits to help the fired employee over the hump is not just the humane thing to do but may be an important measure in quelling revenge fantasies that could potentially lead to a tragedy (see Chapter 11).

In general, the least adversarial, embarrassing, and disruptive method for terminating the employee should be used. If you watch any of the police reality shows, you know that skilled officers can often finesse the nonviolent arrest of an otherwise dangerous suspect simply by using effective verbal communication strategies. It is amazing how much cooperation can be elicited from a seemingly hostile person just by treating him or her in the proper manner: firm but fair, no abuse but no nonsense—the difference between *authoritative* and *authoritarian* that I've discussed throughout this book. If the cops can do it, so can you. It's distressingly obvious how a clumsy, heavy-handed, gratuitously nasty, and unnecessarily humiliating approach can turn an otherwise malleable situation into a violent explosion or ruinous lawsuit.

After a termination, the remaining employees will usually want to know what happened. Check with your legal counsel first, but in general, company representatives should make themselves available to anyone who would like to sit down and discuss in general terms why the employee is no longer with the company. In particularly controversial or high-profile cases, management should issue a company-wide memo explaining the gist of what happened and why the actions were taken. It's not management's obligation to offer rationalizations or justifications as to why an employee was terminated, and the purpose of this informational debriefing is certainly not to violate basic privacy or to gossip about the terminated employee, but to use the opportunity as an educational experience to inculcate company policies and procedures. Address comments to the concerns voiced by the remaining workers about their own roles and responsibilities, and lay the groundwork for more effective communication in the future:

"You've all been oriented to our policy on workplace harassment and violence. When an employee consistently violates those policies and has not been responsive to our efforts to correct it, we have no choice but to let him or her go."

Again, managers should consult with their legal departments about how much information they can provide, but it is important that management control wild rumors and let the workers know that if they have a problem with another employee or supervisor they can bring it up without fear of recrimination from their bosses.

Administrative and Departmental Solutions

As noted earlier, to fully address the problem of employee misconduct and poor performance, it must be treated as a system-wide problem that includes departmental administrative policies as well as individual elements of the human resources system, such as selection, training, supervision, coaching, counseling, and discipline. These services should ideally be integrated into a structure that maximizes their impact on the individual employee and on the organization overall.

Consistent with the leadership literature from management psychology, integrity begins at the top. In this view, the most important factor for prevention of misconduct in an organization is a leader who is mature, seasoned, stable, utilizes cognitively flexible thinking, and has personal integrity and a strong personal ethic. This will be further elaborated in Chapter 12. For now, understand that company leaders who set a strong, positive tone for their agencies and back it up with firm and fair action should be able to expect an organization of which they can be justly proud.

CHAPTER 11

Danger Zone
Handling Workplace Violence

"A disgruntled [pick one: postal worker, law client, insurance claimant, store customer, hospital patient, factory worker] *stormed into his place of business yesterday, killing six people before turning the gun on himself. Film at eleven."*

You've heard this one before. Often the lead story is followed by interviews with coworkers or associates whose comments almost invariably follow one of two main themes:

"He was always a little strange; you know, quiet. Kept to himself a lot, didn't get along with too many people, but came in, did his job, and never caused any real trouble. Nobody ever figured him for a stone killer. Man, we didn't see this one coming."

Or:

"Dammit, I knew it was just a matter of time till something like this happened. That guy was bad news, a ticking bomb, and we all knew it. But there were no precautions or any real kind of discipline at all. We tried to tell management, but they just got annoyed, said there was nothing they could do, and told us not to stir up trouble. When he finally snapped, we were sitting ducks."

People always tell me you don't get rich selling bad news, and this is the chapter nobody likes to read. That's because if the prospect of a violent incident happening at *your* workplace is too scary to contemplate it's probably more comfortable to hide your head in the sand and pretend that "this kind of thing doesn't happen here." Until it does. And then you're faced with skyrocketing medical and mental healthcare costs, a traumatized and alienated workforce, lost business, employee and community lawsuits, and possible criminal charges.

So what's the good news? It's that you can take practical steps right now to minimize the chances of serious violence occurring in your company, instead of just wishing it won't happen. And these practical measures are far less complicated and costly than most managers and executives assume. In survey after survey, one of the things employees say they value most about their companies is the effort the administration makes to keep them safe. And employees who feel that their companies are looking out for them generally are more loyal, are more productive, have less turnover, show less misconduct, and are less likely to file grievances and disability claims. So a safe workplace and a secure workforce are just good business. You've probably heard all this before—so what do you do?

This chapter will describe how corporate executives, supervisory managers, and rank-and-file personnel can work together to set up effective systems for preventing, responding to, and recovering from workplace violence. Most traumatic events encountered in life—such as earthquakes, chemical spills, terrorist attacks, plane crashes, or street crimes—strike suddenly and without warning and often with little control. Correspondingly, medical, mental health, law enforcement, and administrative efforts typically focus on treating victims, survivors, their families, and other stakeholders after the fact.

Once again, recall a cardinal principle from Chapter 1 that *the best form of crisis intervention is crisis prevention.* For virtually no other type of major tragedy are education, training, and preparation so important in foreseeing and planning for emergencies as in the area of workplace aggression and violence. In many cases, you *can* see this one coming. Consequently, special attention is given to what companies can do ahead of time to reduce the risk of this kind of tragedy.

Workplace Violence: Facts and Statistics

The National Institute of Occupational Safety and Health (NIOSH) reports that homicide is the number one killer of women and the third leading cause of death for men in the workplace, after motor vehicle accidents and machine-related fatalities. The majority of workplace homicides are committed by firearms, and the majority of perpetrators are male. You are twice as likely to be murdered at work than to die from a fall, four times more likely than to be accidentally electrocuted, five time more likely than to go down in a plane crash, and many times more likely than to be killed in a terrorist attack. Most violence is perpetrated by people outside the company, but intracompany violence by employees or ex-employees is not rare and most people find the prospect of being harmed by a coworker far more frightening than by an outsider.

Workplace violence costs U.S. businesses approximately $4.2 billion a year. To put this in more personal perspective, it boils down to a conservative estimate of over $250,000 per incident, in terms of lost work time, employee medical benefits, decreased productivity, diversion of management resources from other productive business, increased insurance premiums, increased security costs, bad publicity, lost business, and expensive litigation costs. In terms of the human cost, most workers polled after an incident say that they are psychologically traumatized by the threat of future workplace violence, and a sizable proportion lose work time due to stress disability.

For the average worker, the chances of being murdered on the job are still remote, but, for every actual workplace killing, there occur over one hundred acts of violence that are not lethal, including fistfights, nonfatal shootings, stabbings, sexual assaults, bullying and harassment, bombings, and arson. In addition, perpetrators who turn deadly often engage in threats and harassing behaviors before their actions escalate to killing, emphasizing the need for early boundary-setting and other preventive interventions.

In fact, a survey by a major national insurance company concluded that verbal abuse and harassment can be even more destructive to employee morale and productivity than physical assault. The reason is ironic: Employees who resort to fisticuffs create a palpable disturbance, cause potentially costly injury, and are an embarrassment to the company. Consequently, they are likely to be assertively disciplined. However "mere" verbal threats, curses, snide remarks, and personal property sabotage (one of my clients had rotten food regularly placed in her desk drawer) typically aren't taken as seriously, because they seem to affect few employees or stakeholders outside the direct targets of the nastiness.

Complaints about such behaviors are often treated by management as nuisances that get in the way of doing business and are thus dismissed with comments like, "Grow up," "Deal with it," "Work it out yourselves," or "Don't make a big deal about it and maybe it'll go away." Of course, this only emboldens the perpetrator to escalate the abuse to more overtly physical aggression that produces serious damage. Then, management pays attention. Alternatively, the persecuted victim, rebuffed by management, feels he has no choice but to take matters into his own hands and retaliates explosively, becoming himself the perpetrator of workplace violence, a dynamic very similar to that noted in many school shootings over the past decade.

The Workplace Violence Cycle

While taking into account individual variations, there appears to be a certain predictable pattern in the evolution of many workplace violence incidents, aptly characterized by forensic psychiatrist Robert Simon. The cycle typically begins when the employee encounters a situation (actual or perceived) that he experiences as antagonistic or stressful. This may be a single overwhelming incident or a capping event to a cumulative series of stressors, thereby becoming the proverbial last straw. The worker reacts to this event cognitively and emotionally, based on his predisposing personality, psychopathology, and life experiences. In the typical workplace violence perpetrator, this reaction often involves a noxious stew of persecutory ideation, projection of blame, and violent revenge fantasies.

As these thoughts and emotions continue to percolate, the individual increasingly isolates himself from the input of others and develops a mindset of self-protection and self-justification in which a violent act may come to be perceived as "the only way out." Blame continues to be externalized and vengeance brews as the worker envisions some version of, "I'll show them they can't do this to me and get away with it." For some individuals, the intolerability of the perceived workplace injustice leads to hopeless suicidality with a retaliatory tinge: "If they can screw me, I can screw them back—big-time. Why should other people go on having what they want and enjoying themselves when I can't? I may be going out, but I'm not going out alone." The perpetrator fantasizes that after he's gone, his Ramboesque exploits will be reported to millions of people around the world; his name will be a household word. Far from meekly slinking away, our hero will leave this world in a blaze of martial glory—just like in the movies.

The actual means of carrying out this commando action is dictated by availability and, in our society, the easy obtainability of firearms usually makes this the method of choice. The operational plan may be executed impulsively and immediately, or it may undergo meticulous planning with numerous revisions. The final step is the violent act itself, which may occur any time from hours to months to years following the final perceived injustice. Vengeance has a long memory.

Who Becomes Violent at Work?

Although stresses and strains abound at many workplaces, those who express their anger in overt acts of violence are (fortunately) still the overwhelming minority. Using the psychological knowledge you've gleaned from preceding chapters, you can have a better understanding of the individual personality dynamics that drive different types of people to commit violence at work. You can use this insight to develop customized intervention strategies of the type discussed in Chapter 10 to prevent crises from escalating to dangerous levels.

At the same time, please understand that even among workers with disorders of personality and psychopathology, violence is still the exception rather than the rule, so I hope you won't think I'm asking you to profile your otherwise peaceful difficult and disturbed employees as a bunch of bombs ready to blow. They're probably not but, as I'll illustrate in more detail next, understanding what makes them tick will help you intervene earlier and more effectively should trouble start to brew.

Workplace violence perpetrators with *paranoid personality disorder* have probably shown a long-standing pattern of misinterpreting the words, actions, and motives of others as being threatening, demeaning, or exploitive. They may lie low and secretly nurse their grudges or they may be quite outspoken in their complaints, often filing numerous grievances and lawsuits before resorting to violence.

Paranoid schizophrenic workers are severely disturbed and show a range of psychotic symptoms during the active phase of their illness, including disorganized thinking and hallucinations; indeed, their sheer level of pathology may make them relatively easy to spot.

Workers with *antisocial personality disorder* are likely to have left a long wake of employment, financial, legal, and personal troubles behind them. They are motivated exclusively by self-interest and will use any means necessary, including violence and intimidation, to get what they want. They are also usually quite impulsive and nonreflective and may thus compound their workplace troubles through poor judgment and thoughtless actions.

Workers with *borderline personality disorder* will experience drastic mood swings, mercurial personal attachments, and extremely intense emotional reactions. Having idealized a particular job setting, supervisor, or workmate, the borderline employee may be plunged into rage-filled despair by a subsequent rebuff or disappointment, real or perceived. Their thirst for vindication and restoration of self-worth becomes an all-consuming passion and may include destructive or violent acts, usually centering on a specific person they have demonized.

Avoidant-dependent employees are characteristically shy and socially anxious and hardly the type to be seen as potentially violent, but if they have made work their whole life and then experience rejection or separation from that job role, then a violent act may seem the only way for this person to "make my point."

Borderline and avoidant-dependent employees often suffer varying degrees of *depression*. Impulsive violence against others and against the self often go together, and the sense of hopelessness that is part of the depressed state may facilitate aggressive acting out if the demoralized worker feels he has "nothing to lose" and decides to take others to the grave with him. Indeed, the most common psychological recipe for workplace violence consists of a mixture of anger, paranoia, and mood disorder

Less commonly, *organic personality disorders* due to brain injury, strokes, dementia, or substance abuse may be associated with short-lived, impulsively violent outbursts that seem more akin to a tantrum, and may be preceded by noticeable impairment in memory, concentration, reasoning, or planning that affects job performance.

Workers with *temporal lobe epilepsy* may occasionally show aggressive outbursts associated with seizure activity. These tend to be short and cir-

cumscribed and to occur in a state of relative disorientation and unaware-
ness, followed by partial or total amnesia for the event.

Intermittent explosive disorder is characterized by sudden outbursts of rage
upon minimal provocation and may be associated with abnormal brain
wave activity. The rage attacks are typically impulsive and unplanned and
are perceived by the perpetrator as uncontrollable, although consciousness
is retained, memory for the event is variable, and personal remorse is often
expressed at losing control.

Alcohol and drug abuse can exacerbate violence from almost any other
cause. In so-called *pathological intoxication,* even small amounts of alcohol
can trigger intermittent explosive rage attacks, and the two syndromes often
go together.

Workers who have themselves been victims of violence may experience
posttraumatic stress disorder. They bring their hypersensitivity and hair-trigger
reactivity to the job site, where seemingly minor jibes and hassles can set
them off.

Workplace Violence Prevention

At the risk of repetition, the best form of crisis intervention is crisis prevention. Yet despite the growing recognition of workplace violence as an occupational problem, denial still appears to be the coping method of choice
among U.S. employers. Only a quarter of companies surveyed offer formal
training to any employees in dealing with workplace violence and less than
10 percent offer such training to all employees in the company.

It doesn't have to be this way. In fact, at the start of the twenty-first
century, if someone is going to "go postal" on the job, that person is *least*
likely to be a postal worker. That's because, in the past decade, the U.S.
Post Office has undertaken an effective program to reduce violence at
work. By responding in a similarly forthright manner, the retail trade,
which in the 1980s and 1990s had accounted for more than one third of
workplace violence deaths, has managed to cut its rate of homicides in half
over the past decade.

If your company is serious about preventing violence, it will have clear,
strong, fair, consistent, and clearly written policies against violence and
harassment. There will be effective grievance procedures, firm security

programs, a supportive managerial environment that gives employees reasonable control over their work, relatively open and trusting communication, and periodic training in resolving conflicts through team building and negotiation skills. Organizations must have a clearly stated policy of zero tolerance for violence. This should be conceptualized as a safety issue, the same as with rules about fire prevention or storm emergency drills. Company policies should state clearly that any manner of threatening remark or gesture in the workplace is unacceptable and that anyone who engages in such behavior will face disciplinary action. All threats should be thoroughly investigated, albeit with reasonable sensitivity to all parties. Having official rules that apply to everyone makes enforcement objective and impersonal.

However, in order to prevent your workplace from becoming a caricature of some totalitarian, thought-police regime of political correctness, these policies and procedures should leave room for well-informed managerial discretion and basic common sense. Definitions of reportable behavior, with examples, should be established, distributed, and role-played, as necessary. Just as crucial is putting in place plans that specify how threats and offenses are to be reported and to whom, as well as a standardized protocol for investigating threats. Other policy and procedure points include security measures, complaint and grievance procedures, and services available for dispute mediation, conflict resolution, stress management, safety training, and mental health services. Most companies can develop and write up these protocols themselves. Organizations with large, diverse, or complex workforces may want to avail themselves of knowledgeable outside consultants.

Workplace Violence: Response to Emergencies

Sometimes, despite your best efforts at prevention, a dangerous situation begins to brew and a violent incident becomes a distinct possibility. Other times, the incident just explodes and personnel have to respond on the spot. What do you do? Part of your pre-incident emergency planning will have included a contingency plan for evacuating employees and others and alerting authorities, but you still may find yourself trapped in the position of having to stabilize the situation until help arrives.

The following guidelines have been adapted from AlGene Caraulia and Linda Steiger's program of *nonviolent crisis intervention* for human services personnel and from management psychologist Charles Labig's direct work with corporate crisis prevention and intervention. As always, these recommendations do not take the place of a comprehensive on-site planning, preparation, and training course, but they can serve as an interim practical guide to responding to behavior-based emergencies of many types, including workplace violence.

Recognizing Warning Signs of Impending Violence

Nonspecific red flags that an employee may be on the verge of losing control include disorganized physical appearance and dress; a tense facial expression or other body language; signs of intoxication or inappropriate use of dark glasses or breath mints to mask alcohol or substance abuse; severe agitation; verbal argumentativeness or outright threats, especially to specific persons; and the presence or evidence of weapons. Aside from these general indicators, you, as a manager, probably know (or should know) the people who work for you as well as anybody. So be alert to any significant changes in their appearance, mood, or behavior and take action as early as possible to prevent things from boiling over into a violent confrontation.

Defusing a Potentially Dangerous Situation

A potential workplace violence crisis can be thought of as occurring in several stages, each with its own set of recommendations for defusing danger. Like all protocols, don't think of these as an unvarying sequence of discrete steps, but rather as general categories of response that can change course or blend into one another, depending on the person and the circumstances.

In the *anxiety phase,* the employee is becoming increasingly overwhelmed and agitated, and the response that is most needed at this stage is support. The focus of the intervention should be on how the employee feels and what his concerns are. This involves rapport building and active listening, the mainstay of crisis intervention.

> "You seem upset about something, Fred. Whatever's going on, I hope you'll let me help you out."

In the *defensive phase,* the employee comes to feel increasingly trapped and out of options. The response needed here is a directive one in which the employee is shown a safe and dignified way out of the danger zone. Helpful techniques involve encouraging and modeling self-control, redirecting anger, using calming body language, giving limited choices, and gently but firmly setting limits.

> "I know you're angry about the last suspension, but I don't want you to do anything that's going to hurt you further. C'mon, take a deep breath and let's step into the atrium and talk this out. Or do you want to go down to the cafeteria and get a cup of coffee? I'm buying."

In the *acting-out phase,* the employee has already lost some control. The appropriate response is professional control and containment. Until the cavalry gets there, focus on the employee's immediate behavior, set clear and reasonable limits, and use calming speech and body language. If he has not yet been violent and security or law enforcement officers have arrived, use them to leverage cooperation from the employee.

> "Okay, Fred, I hear you; you made your point. Let's pull this thing back, okay? We can replace the computer, but I need you to drop the chair and do whatever the security people tell you until we get this thing sorted out. I called the authorities here because I don't want anyone to get hurt."

In the *tension-reduction phase,* the crisis has largely passed and the employee should be ready to accept help in reducing his level of anxiety and anger. Assuming no serious harm was done and the employee is not actually in custody, the appropriate response is a supportive type of rapport that is helpful, understanding, and calm. Reinforcing a controlled and face-saving ending to the potentially dangerous episode is often the best insurance that it won't be repeated.

Handling a Violent Episode

When the situation looks like it's getting beyond the point where you can defuse it adequately, then safety comes first. The rule is: *When in doubt, get the hell out.* Pay attention to the environment and to potential dangers, make a mental note of possible escape routes, and think about how to call for outside assistance. If you find yourself absolutely trapped in a potentially dangerous situation, heed the following guidelines, to be supplemented by adequate training and practice.

Initial action. If possible, don't become isolated with the potentially dangerous employee unless you have made sure that security precautions have been taken to prevent or limit a violent outburst. Nevertheless, sometimes an interview or a disciplinary session begins benignly enough only to abruptly start spiraling out of control. If this happens, casually interrupt the interview to call and request something while actually calling for help. Here's where your planning pays off if you have a prearranged signal for just such an emergency. Some authorities recommend telling the person you are calling for help in order to maintain credibility in the interaction and because this may actually reassure some individuals who are feeling out of control. However, other employees may panic and attack you if they think you're calling for backup. Assess the situation and use your judgment.

Body language. Don't behave in ways that could be interpreted as aggressive or threatening, such as moving too close, staring, pointing, or displaying provocative facial expressions or postures. Try to stand at an angle facing the employee—not directly in front of him, which could be interpreted as a challenge, and not behind him, which may signify a possible "sneak attack." Observe the general rule of standing "two quick steps" away from a dangerous individual. Some authorities recommend asking the employee if you can sit down, as this may constitute a less threatening figure. Then encourage him to be seated as well. If you're already standing, and it looks safe, try to slowly and unobtrusively maneuver yourself toward a doorway or other point of quick exit and always be scanning the environment for points of escape, but be careful not to antagonize the employee. Always move slowly and keep your hands where they can be seen.

Communication style. Keep the employee engaged in a conversation about his feelings or about a specific problem, but avoid egging him on. Venting should not escalate to ranting. Keep the conversation going, pace it, and modulate your voice. Don't shout, put a sharp edge on your voice, or use threats. Conversely, don't mumble or speak hesitantly so that the employee has trouble understanding you, which he may find irritating. Give the employee your undivided attention and use empathic listening skills, such as simple restatement of the employee's concerns to show that you're "getting it."

Use common sense and your own judgment, but generally don't attempt to logically reason with an employee who is under the influence of drugs or alcohol or is clearly irrational or psychotic. The purpose of your communication is not to try to talk him out of his gripes or delusions, because you won't. Conversely, don't pretend to agree with the employee's distorted point of view because the inherent deceptiveness and insincerity of this gesture may further infuriate him. Rather, show empathy and concern for his real or imagined plight and suggest alternative ways of resolving the crisis.

When in doubt, shut up. Use silence as a tactic and let the employee talk, as the more energy and adrenaline he expends, the sooner he will fatigue and the easier it will be to control the situation. However, avoid seeming like you're ignoring the employee and answer when spoken to. Also, if his own speech seems to be agitating himself further, use verbal and nonverbal calming techniques to ratchet down the tension level while continuing to let him talk.

Communication content. Don't argue, give orders, or disagree when not absolutely necessary. Don't push your own authority or blather on in an officious, know-it-all manner. Conversely, don't be overly placating or patronizing and don't condescend by using childish responses that are cynical, satirical, or insulting. Be careful with attempts to lighten the situation with humor. Persons under extreme stress tend to be very literal and concrete, and even well-intentioned levity may be misinterpreted as mocking or dismissive.

Don't make promises you can't keep, except possibly to buy time in emergency situations. Avoid complex "why" and "what" inquiries that put the employee on the defensive; rather, use simple, direct, close-ended, yes-or-no questions. Calmly and simply explain the consequences of further violent behavior without provocation or condemnation. Set limits and give choices between two alternatives: "I want to talk with you about this, Fred.

Do you want to sit down here or go outside for a smoke?" Try to de-escalate slowly, moving from step to step toward less agitated behavior.

Scene control. Where there's a commotion, people may flock to the scene, either to help or just to gawk. Don't allow a number of interveners to interact simultaneously with the employee in multiple dialogues, as this can be confusing and irritating. Have one intervener take charge. If this person is clearly ignored or rejected by the employee, try to find someone who can establish better rapport. Any physical restraint or takedown procedures should be carried out by personnel with specialized training in this area. Don't allow an audience to gather around the employee, cheer him on, insult him, or shout at him from a distance; this includes the media. Anyone who has no business being there should leave immediately. If professional crisis negotiators or law enforcement officers show up at the scene, brief them as thoroughly as possible and then let them take charge.

Guns and Weapons

Psychiatrist William Dubin has developed a set of guidelines for mental health clinicians who may confront an armed patient in an institutional setting. In my training programs, I've adapted these recommendations to the requirements of business managers who may be abruptly faced with an armed life-and-death confrontation with an employee.

The first thing to do upon seeing the weapon is acknowledge it with a neutral and obvious remark—for example, "I see the gun." Maintain your distance, keep your hands visible, and move slowly. Never tell the employee to drop the gun or attempt to grab it, as he may have another weapon concealed or may simply overpower you. As rapport develops, and if the employee appears ambivalent about using the weapon, request that he point it away while you talk. Appeal to his sense of competence and control: To avoid an "accident," ask if he will at least decock the gun (revolver) or put the safety catch on (semiautomatic pistol).

If the employee seems willing to surrender the weapon, don't ask him to hand it over, but rather have him unload it; place it down in a safe, neutral corner; and back away. Some authorities recommend that the intervener then slowly pick up the gun and neutralize it, being careful not to point it at the employee, as this may give him an "excuse" to pull another concealed weapon or otherwise attack you. However, any contact with the weapon on your part can be dangerous, because you don't know whether he'll suddenly change his mind and think you're trying to attack him. Therefore, to avoid being baited into "going for" the gun, wait until the employee has put it down safely and then ask him to calmly walk out of the room with you, leaving the weapon behind.

One of the principles of crisis negotiation is that the more time that passes without the person's firing the gun or otherwise injuring anyone, the lower the likelihood of violence occurring. Initially, however, you should comply with whatever reasonable and safe demands the armed employee may make ("Sit over there." "Get my supervisor on the phone.") and take special care to avoid agitating him further. Continue to talk to the employee (unless he tells you to be quiet), reasonably empathize with the perceived grievance or his feelings about it, and acknowledge that he is in control of the situation.

Try to appear calm, but not nonchalant or cocky and not intimidating, confrontational, or argumentative. Encourage the armed employee to talk out his concerns, but remember the difference between venting and ranting; the former serves to blow off steam, whereas the latter can cause the pot to boil over. Employ the relevant defusing strategies discussed above (and reinforced by your training) until the crisis is safely and successfully resolved or qualified professionals have taken control of the scene.

Workplace Violence Intervention with Mentally Disordered Employees

The best formal workplace violence training courses will provide you with the behavioral tools you need to defuse a variety of potentially dangerous situations involving employees. However, what they may not offer is a more fine-tuned and focused approach to individual personality styles and psychological disorders that might be fueling or exacerbating the crisis. In this section, you'll learn how to apply the principles of practical psychology from earlier chapters to specific, targeted defusing strategies for different types of employees who may threaten the safety of your workplace.

Potentially Violent Schizophrenic Employees
Maybe this is an otherwise adequate employee who has gone off his medication or undergone a recent life crisis. The most common factor motiva-

ting aggression in a schizophrenic employee is some form of *persecutory delusion* that may or may not be accompanied by corresponding *command hallucinations* that order the person to do something. These individuals are usually in a state of extreme fear and agitation in response to these delusions and hallucinations, often tinged with anger at the supposed persecutors.

For example, voices may tell the employee that he and the company he works for are vile and wicked, and that the only way to atone for their collective sins is to "save them by cleansing them with blood." Or the individual may interpret a TV newscast about airport security as a warning about his former boss's attempts to plant a monitoring device in his body. If the person is already predisposed to aggressive behavior, the response to these delusions and hallucinations may take a violent turn, from impulsive attacks during his regular work shift to well-planned, commando-like tactical campaigns involving weapons and hostages.

In negotiating during a crisis with a schizophrenic employee, remember that the predominant underlying emotion is likely to be some combination of fear and anger, so the use of calming techniques may seem like the obvious choice. However, schizophrenic individuals tend to be less responsive to normal emotional cues, so don't expect an immediate response. Often the basis for communication in these situations comes from the person's need to explain himself and his motives, so by all means let him talk, interjecting only when his speech tone and content suggest that he is ranting himself out of control with his own words.

In dealing with the potentially violent schizophrenic employee's delusions, a kind of constructive ambivalence may prove to be the most effective stance. That is, neither agree nor disagree with the delusional ideas or motives. On the one hand, attempting to falsely buy in to the person's delusional system may come off as phony and insincere and thus erode rapport. Remember that even psychotic individuals are not necessarily stupid, and they may know if you're playing them. On the other hand, trying to "talk some sense" into the psychotic employee will be equally ineffective and may quickly brand you as just another clueless or treacherous enemy. A better strategy is to acknowledge the content of the delusion and try to ally yourself with the employee's perspective and perception of the situation while keeping the focus on present reality.

Manager: Let me understand this. The people with you in that workers compensation office have been monitoring your home computer and the GPS in your car and telling you to commit crimes so they can blackmail you and discredit your disability claim. Is that right?

Employee: No, that's not it. You just don't get it. Why is it so hard for everybody to understand?

Manager: Okay, sorry, please explain it to me again slowly, because I want to make sure I understand what you're telling me.

Employee: [Explains the conspiracy theory again.] Okay, now do you see what I'm up against?

Manager: Well to be honest with you, I don't have the electronics expertise to know how they can set up these things, but if that's what you think they're doing, it must make you feel pretty mad and scared. I wonder if there's a way to get more information on this before anyone gets hurt.

Potentially Violent Paranoid Employees

This diagnostic category will often overlap with the previous one in the form of paranoid schizophrenia, characterized by paranoid delusions and persecutory hallucinations. However, all levels of paranoia may be seen in the workplace, including in individuals with paranoid personality disorder who are not overtly psychotic but may harbor fixed suspicions and self-referential beliefs that boil to the surface under stress. If confronted with an overwhelming crisis, paranoid individuals may feel compelled to take drastic, violent action in their own defense.

In communicating with a potentially violent paranoid employee, forget about changing his mind or reasoning him out of his belief. One of the characteristics of paranoid beliefs is their imperviousness to disputation. Paranoid subjects are also exquisitely sensitive to attempts to fool or manipulate them and are often quite perceptive in this regard, so stay away from tricks and stratagems. Straightforwardness and calmness are the keys to a successful intervention with this employee.

If possible, open the dialog in a logical, factual, respectful, and unemotional manner: "Mr. McGill, I'm Ned Simpson, the assistant manager of the finance department. You and I have worked together before. I want to hear your side of this so we can keep everyone safe." Keep your voice calm and even, but not at such a monotone that it sounds contrived and artificial.

Ask for the employee's view of the situation and request clarification if necessary.

If the employee gets angry, keep your cool and request further clarification of his complaint. Allow productive ventilation but, as always, beware of the individual self-escalating into a rage. If this starts to happen, use distraction techniques, again, without being too obvious about it. As with schizophrenic employees, if frankly delusional material comes up, try to sidestep it, but without making the employee think you're dismissing or disrespecting him. Keep things clear and direct, and focus the intervention on solving concrete problems.

> **Employee:** They're all trying to get me, first my wife's family and now you damn people. What do I have to do to convince you I mean business!
>
> **Manager:** I want you to know we've notified the authorities to make sure nobody gets hurt. I don't know about those family members you mentioned, but once everybody's safe, I'd bet people here at the company would be more likely to listen to your point.

Potentially Violent Depressed Employees

Depression in a potentially violent employee presents a special kind of problem for managers during a crisis. Depressed employees may be despondent and suicidal and therefore especially dangerous precisely because they have nothing to lose by taking other people to the grave with them. If a coworker or boss has a bad past history with the employee, the only agenda may be to have an audience for his act of desperate revenge. Other depressed employees may not be overtly suicidal but may still be relatively unresponsive to communication due to simple emotional and behavioral inertia, associated with a feeling of "nothing left to live for."

Without being patronizing, the stance of a nurturing parental model or supportive authority figure may appeal to a depressed person because it provides a framework of structure and control. As a manager, if you have had a previously good relationship with this employee, you may be in a unique position to capitalize on this role. Don't verbally rush the person; rather, begin the conversation at a slow pace and gradually pick up the tempo as you go along. Begin with open-ended questions and allow for long pauses before the answers come. If this goes nowhere, ask simple, direct, closed-ended questions. Use reflection of feelings as necessary. If the employee begins to dwell on a painful, unjust past or a bleak, purposeless future, try to keep the time perspective grounded in the present. Avoid deep religious or philosophical issues, if possible, but if the employee seems intent on discussing these, let him speak, and use gentle verbal direction to keep things focused on the here and now.

If the employee brings up suicide, address it forthrightly. If he doesn't explicitly mention it, but nevertheless seems suicidal, gently but directly inquire. Ask what he's thinking of doing. Usually, attempts to talk him out of it are of little avail, but find out what's important to him, and try to give him a glimpse of a better future. Avoid admonishments along the lines of, "Think how your family will feel if you kill yourself." Remember, a suicidally depressed person already feels worthless and hopeless—you don't want to add to that.

A better strategy is to "postpone" the suicide, rather than attempt to dissuade the person.

> **Manager:** Look, William, I know you think this is the only way out now, but give me a little while, okay? I know I can't talk you out of what you're going to do, but let me understand why this is happening, okay? I really want to understand this.

If there seems to be an opening, offer the promise of immediate help— that is, if the employee works with you to end this crisis without harm, you'll see that he gets taken to someplace safe to talk to someone right away. Be sure to be able to back up this promise.

Potentially Violent Avoidant-Dependent Employees

As discussed in Chapter 2, these two personality types are often combined, with the employee being generally shy and socially anxious, but perhaps latching on to one person, usually a trusted coworker or manager, who becomes the psychological lifeline to the employee's sense of identity and purpose in life. If he then experiences rejection or separation from that person or job, it will feel like the end of the world, and some employees may feel driven to do *anything* to restore that connection, including pleading, stalking, or threatening violence to convince the rejecting person to "take me back—or else." Incidentally, many domestic violence perpetrators also fit this profile.

In negotiating with a potentially violent avoidant-dependent employee, try to provide a firm, supportive presence, in essence replicating the role of a competent and caring parental figure. It is very important for the intervener to help the insecure avoidant-dependent employee find a resolution to the crisis that doesn't leave him feeling like he's failed again, which may impel him to do something even more desperate "to show them I mean business." If possible, let the initial ideas for peaceful resolution come from the employee himself, expand and refine them with your own good suggestions and, as much as possible, make it seem like everything positive that happens is the employee's idea, adding your own mentorlike praise and support.

Potentially Violent Antisocial-Psychopathic Employees

As we saw in Chapter 4, antisocial personalities, sometimes referred to as psychopaths, are ruthless and remorseless, but they can also be quite shrewd in a cunning-conning type of way and are often skilled at manipulating and intimidating those around them. When they can't achieve their aims by guile, they may quickly resort to threats or acts of violence to get their way.

Forget forming any kind of empathic bond. Their complete self-centeredness and lack of any real human attachment mean that other people represent nothing more than human bargaining chips to antisocial employees, to enable them to achieve some utilitarian purpose, to "get what's mine" from the company. Revenge is also a powerful motive in these individuals. A potentially violent episode may erupt when the antisocial employee is surprised during an act of sabotage or confronted with his misdeeds and can conjure up no clever way to talk himself out of the jam.

Paradoxically, the antisocial employee's natural cold-bloodedness can actually facilitate the intervention if you can convince him that deescalating the crisis is the easiest way for him to escape the worst consequences of his actions. Appeal to his self-interest: "Ending this peacefully now will result in a lighter penalty"; "Don't give the police an excuse to move in and take you out"; "You can always get a smart lawyer later and beat this," and so on.

But remember that, even more so than for other employees, a key element in intervention with antisocial individuals is the tried-and-true adage:

Don't try to outbullshit a bullshitter. Antisocial personalities live by their wits and their strength, and their greatest thrill comes from tricking and intimidating other people. At the same time, much like the paranoid, they are exquisitely sensitive to being fooled themselves, and they may react with rage if they think you're trying to play them. Promise only what you can deliver.

As for tone, a reasonable, problem-solving approach probably works best—be involved, but unemotional. You want to keep things somewhat bland because psychopaths are power trippers and thrill seekers, and the last thing you want to do is egg him on; at the same time, you don't want things to get too draggy, or the antisocial employee may feel the need to do something more exciting to pump up the adrenaline. Be as straightforward as possible, and realize that virtually nothing this person says can be taken at face value. Communicate cautiously and straightforwardly and try to stall for time until help arrives.

Potentially Violent Borderline Employees

The borderline personality shows a pattern of instability in interpersonal relationships, a fragile self-image, wild emotional swings, vengeful anger, and self-damaging impulsiveness. As discussed in Chapter 3, many borderlines manage to hold it together at work, functioning well—even superlatively—in the eyes of casual observers, only deteriorating into minipsychotic episodes under external or self-induced stress. This is when they may turn violent.

The borderline employee's potentially violent crisis is most likely to be relationship based, as in the case of a fired worker coming back to the job site to even the score of a real or imagined betrayal, or a passed-over employee feeling the sting of rejection. White-hot righteous anger is often the key motivating emotion, as borderlines' scorched-earth policies toward those who have spurned them blot out any glint of reason or empathy. In many cases, they may not have any utilitarian demands at all—they just want the offender to suffer. Again, this pattern is also seen in many domestic violence scenarios.

If caught in a crisis situation with a borderline employee, use the relationship factor to your advantage. Try to build rapport and diffuse toxic emotions. Try to show the employee that you're on his side by providing soothing reassurance, empathy, support, and structure. Because many borderline individuals are so starved for nurturing human connection, they may actually be very susceptible to such rapport-building approaches. The downside is that their feelings can turn on a dime: When they feel you've connected with them, they completely love and trust you, but if they suddenly believe you've crossed them or let them down, they'll want you worse than dead.

So carefully take your cue from the borderline employee. Commiserate and try to understand. Be alert for signs of suicide or violence. Try to preclude impulsive action by gently guiding the employee to safe alternatives or switching the discussion to the reasons for the person's pain and outrage. As with other types of employees in crisis, encourage talking, but be cautious not to let blowing off steam escalate into an explosive loss of control. Be especially careful about involving supervisors, coworkers, family members, or other third parties, who may inflame the situation.

Workplace Violence Recovery

Sometimes the worst happens, and a violent incident stuns and horrifies the workplace. People may be killed, others physically wounded, some held hostage, and many emotionally traumatized. In the aftermath of such a dramatic episode, executives, managers, and the psychologists they consult with typically must engage in an intensive collaboration to facilitate the recovery of affected personnel and the company as a whole.

Workplace Violence Response Patterns and Syndromes

Individuals affected by workplace traumatic events may include injured employees, workers remote from the scene, witnesses and innocent bystanders, family members, first responders such as police or paramedics, stakeholders such as suppliers or customers, or any others connected to the trauma.

Management consultant Joseph Kinney has observed that reactions to a workplace violence trauma will generally fall into three main groups. A few individuals (the first group) will recover quickly without any formal mental health intervention. A number of these seemingly stoic souls may be internalizing their pain and grief only to unload it at a later date, but most people in this small group just possess a natural resilience that enables them to recover quickly. People in the second, and largest, group will require brief psychological counseling to regain their previous level of confidence, security, and safety, but most will recover and move on. Finally, a third, smaller group will develop serious and persisting psychological disorders, such as anxiety, depression, phobias, or posttraumatic stress disorder that may require more extensive psychotherapy or other clinical services. A few of these employees may file claims for stress disability.

For many employees, the workplace is a second family, an alternative community. Traumatic events destroy one's sense of effectiveness, usefulness, mastery, and personal control within that community. Some victims assume a stance of being overly in control, trying to ensure that they will never be vulnerable again. Others try to regain control by blaming themselves for what happened. The implicit assumption is that if the victim did something to put himself or herself in harm's way, then he or she can change that behavior for some imagined "next time" so that this bad outcome won't happen again; blaming the company, supervisor, or coworkers is an analogous process.

To make matters worse, other employees may distance themselves from the victims to avoid "contagion" or to search for some aspect of the victim's behavior that "caused" the violence (a form of relational disenfranchisement all too familiar to victims of sexual assault). This reinforces the victimized employee's further withdrawal and produces a vicious cycle of alienation, recrimination, and despair.

In general, a sense of meaningful purpose in work and in life is disrupted in the wake of workplace violence. Survivors don't feel safe, no longer regard daily life at work or home as predictable or controllable, and lose their motivation to carry on the mission of the company or the trajectory of their own careers. Unless handled competently, this can have disastrous effects on company morale and the bottom line.

Plans, Policies, and Procedures

A particularly fruitful collaboration among executives, managers, and mental health professionals involves proactively setting up policies and procedures for responding to the aftermath of a workplace violence incident. Many of these originated in specialized settings such as mental health clinics or law enforcement agencies and have been developed for the corporate world by psychology and management experts such as Steve Albrecht,

Raymond Flannery, Joseph Kinney, and Michael Mantell. Here, I'll summarize the main points that your individualized company plan should include.

Media and public relations. A specially designated media spokesperson should brief the media and, more important, shepherd them away from grieving employees, family members, and eyewitnesses. A firm, forthright, proactive, and sincere approach to providing information is preferred, from someone in a high position within your organization or, alternatively, a qualified outside public relations spokesperson or firm. Companies should always be prepared to provide a concerned and honest answer to the question, "What is this organization doing for the survivors and the victims' families?"

Employees and families. Someone should be designated to notify the victims' families of the incident and be ready to offer them immediate support, counseling, and other services. Personnel managers should arrange time off for grieving and traumatized employees as appropriate. Following the initial stages of the incident, the mental health clinician should help managers and supervisors find ways for the employees to memorialize slain victims.

Law enforcement, physical security, and cleanup. Someone should be assigned to immediately check, protect, and restore the integrity of the company's data systems, computers, and files. A representative should be designated to work with local law enforcement. The crime scene should be kept intact until law enforcement has gone over the area. A cleanup crew for the site of the attack should be available, pending approval from law enforcement investigators. Exquisite sensitivity to surviving staff's feelings about "cleaning up the mess like nothing happened" is essential, and such cleanup operations should be conducted in as respectful, even solemn, a manner as possible.

Legal measures. In-house legal counsel or your company's outside law firm should be notified about the incident and, if necessary, be asked to respond to the scene. They should advise company executives and managers as to appropriate actions immediately following the incident and in the weeks and months ahead. Always remember that the greater the honest concern shown by the company for its employees, families, and stakeholders, the lower the level of contentious litigation that is likely to occur in the months and years to come.

Mental health mobilization. In the best case, planning will have included detailed preparation and practice drills with the company psychologist or outside mental health consultant. In most cases, it simply means that the mental health clinician has become sufficiently familiar with the organization to know how to gather critical information and to respond promptly and effectively at the time of a crisis. Unfortunately, in many organizations, postincident mental health services are farmed out to generic employee assistance program (EAP) counselors who, competent enough to handle routine mental health issues, have little or no training in posttraumatic stress syndromes or corporate crisis intervention.

Company representatives should know how to contact their mental health professionals immediately and arrange for the clinicians to meet first at top levels of the organization for executive briefings, and then schedule meetings with anyone in the organization who needs to talk about what happened. A critical incident debriefing area should be established for the responding mental health professionals. Optional crisis intervention services should be made available for all potential workplace violence victims outside of immediate survivors or employees. A follow-up schedule should be arranged for the clinicians to return for further services as needed or for referral of employees to their private offices for follow-up counseling.

Restoring Order: Posttrauma Crisis Management

In the immediate aftermath of a workplace violence incident, available personnel must begin the process of accounting for slain, injured, and surviving employees while awaiting the arrival of posttrauma professional service providers. Company officials must communicate the message that all personnel and their family members will be provided the utmost care and concern. You must recognize that many of your employees are destabilized, demoralized, and disoriented, and that they are looking to company authorities to restore order and their sense of confidence and mental equilibrium. This is a crucial time. Failure to demonstrate constructive leadership following a crisis can leave a corrosive stain on the morale of your company that will be hard to expunge. The following steps are designed to help affected companies express concern and restore order following a work-place violence trauma.

1. *Demonstrate concern and caring* for those who have been harmed by the trauma. The clear message that employees and other organization stake-holders need to hear is that management is going to do everything humanly and administratively possible to care for those affected by this tragedy.

2. Within the limits of privacy and security, *open up communication chan-nels and control rumors*. Describe what actions the company is taking to assist in recovery and what measures are being developed to reduce the risk of this kind of trauma happening again.

3. *Assess the organization's personnel and business requirements* to restore business performance. Inform employees what it will take to get things back to normal.

4. Following the immediate and short-term crisis interventions, *arrange for the posttrauma mental health team to return* to the workplace on a periodic basis to counsel and debrief employees as needed.

5. *Conduct a thorough postincident investigation.* Remember one of the principles from Chapter 1: 20/20 hindsight = 20/20 insight = 20/20 fore-sight. Questions asked during the postincident investigation may concern the nature of the perpetrator; his relationship to the organization and with coworkers and supervisors; his history of disciplinary action or termination; his role as a customer or other outsider; the actions that led to his dissatisfac-tion as an employee or a customer; any restraining orders or other legal actions and their enforcement; workplace stressors that may have been in-volved; financial pressures; drugs, alcohol, mental illness, or personality dis-orders; any warning signs that should have been heeded; and the company's overall security and threat assessment procedures.

In general, if there is any positive outcome that can emerge from a workplace violence incident, it is what can be learned to reduce the chances of the same kind of tragedy happening in the future. To the extent that this is accomplished, a greater sense of control and safety will allow your traumatized company to heal itself and get back to business.

Role of Executives and Leaders

What is needed is a strong message from top management that emphasizes the company's willingness to take appropriate responsibility, address the causes of the incident in a forthright manner, provide services for all who need them, and pursue every necessary step and reasonable action to ensure, as much as humanly and organizationally possible, that something like this never again catches the company unprepared. Indeed, as we'll see in Chapter 12, all successful managers, at every level, manifest the qualities of true leadership in both ordinary and critical circumstances.

Tough at the Top

Organizational Stress Management and Leadership

You're a conscientious manager—you've proven that by reading this book. And by now you realize (if you didn't know it already) that no matter at what level in the organization you manage, you couldn't be good at what you do if you didn't possess the essential qualities of leadership.

Indeed, a recurrent theme of this book has been that most organizations are only as good as their leaders. No matter how democratized the decision-making process in an organization becomes, someone still has to make the difficult command decisions, to sit at the desk on which the proverbial buck often drops with a thud. If that person is you, then you probably know both the exhilarations and the pressures of that role. So now we turn the practical psychology spotlight on you. This chapter describes the elements of good leadership in two types of supervisory and managerial situations: command decision making during stressful critical incidents and the daily challenges of running a healthy organization.

Command Decision Making Under Critical Stress

Effective management involves showing leadership in both the extraordinary and the mundane challenges at work. For purposes of continuity with

Chapter 11, we'll deal with the emergency aspect first and discuss what a competent command leader actually thinks, says, and does during a major crisis of almost any type.

In my management seminars for emergency services administrators, after we go through all the protocols and strategies for dealing with a critical incident, I'm almost always asked some version of the following question: Why are some leaders just better at it than others? That is, during critical incidents, what allows one leader to remain calm and focused in the heat of battle, while another is more likely to fold under pressure? Are certain managers just "born leaders" or is superior command leadership a quality that can be learned?

Actually, as with all human traits and skills, it's a little of both: a combination of innate talent, bolstered and refined by hard work and proper training. Think of the professional athlete, artist, or musician. Certainly, without a natural gift for his or her sport or skill, all the training in the world won't take the individual past the B range. But raw talent alone is insufficient—the athlete or artisan has to work at developing that skill to its ultimate level to attain and stay in the A+ zone. In fact, research shows that those individuals at the top of their fields never coast; if anything, they put in many times more effort than those with less innate talent. That is, they take what's great and make it even greater. This applies both to individuals and to organizations.

It's the same with the kind of decision-making and people-influencing skills that constitute true leadership. By dint of intellect, temperament, and personality, some individuals may be natural-born leaders. Nevertheless, without honing those skills in the real world of managing people under stress, this will remain a largely undeveloped potential.

With that in mind, the following is a representative inventory of behaviors, skills, and personal traits that form the basis for effective incident command leadership, as developed for emergency response and military teams by crisis specialist Rhona Flin, and that I've adapted to the requirements of most kinds of organizational crises.

Communication

This involves both input and output. The effective leader quickly and accurately assimilates what others tell him or her from a morass of often rushed, confused, and conflicting information and is able to translate complex plans and strategies into specific, focused directives to appropriate personnel.

▓▓ *CASE STUDY.* Claire had been the branch manager for only a few weeks when the bomb threat occurred early one morning just before opening for customers. Having carefully studied the bank's policies and procedures for emergencies, she knew what to do. She ascertained which employee had received the threat and what information he had obtained from the caller. She visually surveyed the premises via her security camera array. She quickly punched in the security code on her phone, which alerted both internal security and local law enforcement. Then, she punched in the general alert code that alerted the employees to assemble in the main area and went out to brief her troops.

Team Management

The effective leader coordinates the efforts of individual team members into a united force. He or she is able to delegate responsibilities as needed but can quickly jump in and take personal control where necessary.

▓▓ *CASE STUDY.* Claire told Charles and Monica to go to each office to notify any employees who may not have received the alert. They were also to check the restrooms. At all times, they were to keep in verbal contact with Claire through their phone headsets. Everyone was told to be on watch for anything suspicious, but not to touch anything or take any other action other than to get as quickly as possible to the main area.

Decision Making Under Stress

It's not enough to keep from panicking under life-and-death conditions; the effective command leader must be able to think clearly and make critical split decisions under pressure. This requires the ability to distinguish signal from noise, to take in and quickly distill the relevant environmental data to come up with a useful response. The key is not to be relaxed, but to maintain an optimal arousal state of focused concentration without distracting anxiety.

::::: *CASE STUDY.* When Claire got to the main area, the employ-ees were milling around buzzing with questions. Should they leave? Could they call their families? Was help on the way? Cell phone in one hand, Claire waited for a callback from corporate headquarters while she instructed the employees to ask their questions one at a time. When the callback came through, she took the information and then turned back to the employees, shushing them long enough to give them a quick update on what was going on, all the while being alert for arriving police and paramedics and keeping in contact with Charles and Monica.

Planning, Implementing, and Evaluating

Grace under pressure does little good if the leader lacks the cognitive skills to quickly and efficiently size up a situation, rule in and rule out the appro-priate actions, implement those actions, and then accurately assess their effects on the overall crisis management situation. For skilled critical inci-dent leaders, this cyclical process seems to evolve as a seamless, coordinated flow—which is why competent crisis leaders always seem to make their job of managing emergencies look easy. It *isn't* easy, but skill, practice, and experience provide the level of expertise that almost always makes the lead-er's decisions the right ones.

::::: *CASE STUDY.* Emergency services were here! Claire told the employees to stay put while she went out to meet with them to determine whether it was safe to leave. The bomb squad quickly examined the entranceway to the building to ascertain whether it was secure and then told Claire to have the employees begin to exit the building single file. While doing so, Claire made a quick head count and remembered to check in with Charles and Monica, calling them back to the main area so that the police could continue searching the building for stragglers. In re-sponse to Claire's ring tone, Monica answered immediately—but where was Charles? Claire told Monica to return at once to the main area, which Monica did with two other employees whom she had gathered up in her search. But still no Charles.

Claire briefed the police and let them know of Charles's last whereabouts.

Emotional Stability

Undergirding the traits of superior leadership lies a certain basic emotional ballast and stability of character. Often referred to as "charisma" or "chops," this leadership quality is more than just the brashness, swagger, and popularity that these terms sometimes imply. Rather, it consists of a calm, purposeful, self-assured interpersonal style that inspires the troops with confidence and commands respect without having to fish for it. This kind of leadership loyalty can't be bought, coerced, or cajoled—the team members will go out on a limb for this leader because they absolutely trust his or her judgment and commitment to the job and to their own well-being.

> CASE STUDY. "Hey, where's Charles?" one of the employees suddenly called out. The other employees started to get nervous and a few who were Charles's friends wanted to go back into the building to search for him. "That's the professionals' job," Claire told them. When they insisted, Claire pulled rank, looked them right in the eye, and said, "You haven't known me very long, but believe me when I say that we're not leaving anyone behind. But for your own safety, you have to leave the building now." Something about the way she said it and how she had handled the whole episode so far made the employees believe her and back off. Claire turned to finish briefing the police search team about the missing Charles when who should come running down the hall but you-know-who. It turned out that Charles had lost his earpiece in one of the restrooms he was checking and, rather than go back and look for it, he had decided to return to the main area as quickly as possible. For all the commotion, no bomb was found and the employees returned to work later that afternoon.

Organizational Stress Management and Supervisory Style

Most of the time, it is not a major critical incident that supervisors and administrators have to deal with. Most busy managers have to make all sorts of minor and midlevel command decisions and judgment calls continually throughout every day. Insights from practical psychology can help managers manage their own stresses and become the kinds of leaders their people will respect.

Managerial Stresses

Private corporations and public agencies have undergone important changes in recent decades, some in line with changes in the larger business world, others more specific to their own industries, and all, according to law enforcement executive trainer James Sewell, potential sources of stress for today's managers.

Middle managers, especially, have many masters, from senior-ranking supervisors to top executives, city and county leaders, citizen and community groups, the media, employee union groups, even their own families. In any hierarchical organization, middle managers are responsible *for* the people below them and *to* the people above. This task is frequently complicated by poor communication through different levels of command and by an emphasis on exceptional failures rather than more common successes (the *you're-only-as-good-as-your-last-screw-up* principle).

Middle- or upper-level managers may feel isolated from the daily realities that employees face, leading to perceived lack of "street cred" and resulting friction: "Easy for the boss to tell us what to do; he's not out here every day." As public and private organizations across the country face tightening budgets, opportunities for advancement tend to shrink, as do opportunities for lateral moves to other departments or other jobs, and managers may feel stuck in a career rut, leading to frustration, demoralization, and burnout.

Demands for greater technical proficiency in the new wirelessly wired world, as well as adaptation to innovative types of business practices, require that managers maintain adequate education and training, for both themselves and their personnel, at the same time that resources for such retooling may be dwindling. There is rarely time to get everything accomplished, schedules are maxed out, and the manager always feels just one unscheduled emergency away from chaos. Seemingly arbitrary directives from above may force managers to change policies and routines, further destabilizing daily schedules and protocols and leading to potential confusion and resentment at all levels of the organization.

For example, new programs may be pushed through from above without appropriate planning, training, or support, creating unfunded mandates in terms of both time and money. Even when middle managers try to institute their own productive policies and protocols, these may be swept away by political fiat if the higher-ups decide that there are (in their view) more important things for the department or company to do. Increased time away from family and frayed nerves upon returning home further erode the manager's support system. And all the time, the harried manager gets the feeling that the street-level troops are scrutinizing him or her for signs of weakness or disingenuousness.

A vicious cycle may thus ensue whereby deteriorating morale within the department leads to poor employee performance, resulting in either lackadaisical supervision as a form of managerial capitulation or draconian discipline to "keep the lid on," which further erodes troop morale. Resentful employees then continue to shirk duties and/or escalate misconduct (see Chapter 10), which leads to more customer complaints; censure by upper executives; and finally, perhaps, to a complete overhaul of the department or organization, often by a new administration that is sent in to "clean things up." Unfortunately, without addressing the core problems, the pattern soon begins again.

Manager Supervision Styles

I hope this book has made clear that typologies are useful if they help us to understand and more effectively deal with real people and problems. But they can be counterproductive if they serve only to stifle creative thinking by pigeonholing people into rigid categories. In this spirit, I present a typology of managers that I've adapted from police psychologist Robin Engel's work with law enforcement and public safety agencies and that can be applied to the needs of public organizations and private companies of many types. My goal is that you'll find this helpful in your own self-assessment and in your efforts to improve your managerial skills.

Traditional managers. "It's called *work* for a reason." These managers have high levels of task orientation and expect their employees to do their jobs with little complaint. They are more directive in their decision making and expect their subordinates to produce measurable outcomes, particularly in the areas of sales or production, along with the necessary paperwork and documentation. Consistent with their emphasis on authority, discipline, control, and chain of command, these managers are more likely to give advice and instruction to subordinates but less likely to reward them. Not surprisingly, traditional managers spend significantly less time engaging in informal encounters with employees and have little interest in participating in extracurricular activities or socializing.

Active managers. Managers in this category prize their willingness and ability to go out in the field and do their own share of grunt-level work. They are authoritative and directive, but unlike the authoritarian traditional managers, they tend to inspire loyalty and group cohesion among their subordinates by "walking the walk." However, their emphasis on a my-way-or-the-highway approach to supervision risks choking their troops with micromanagement. Generally, they seem to be the kind of supervisors who are promoted to management positions because they genuinely earned it, but are just not comfortable being "desk jockeys" and have not quite mastered the skills of delegation and positive reinforcement as supervisory training tools.

Innovative managers. Generally more amenable to innovative changes in the workplace, these managers are more likely to encourage employee feedback and to support independent problem-solving efforts. They expect their subordinates to embrace new initiatives and work philosophies enthusiastically, which might not always be realistic. They are less concerned with rigidly enforcing rules and regulations or other task-oriented activities and favor a relations-oriented approach to supervision that relies more on coaching and mentoring than direction and discipline. Overall, they would prefer to delegate than micromanage. These managers also spend far more of their time directly interacting with customers and other stakeholders in the organization.

Supportive managers. These managers generally get high marks for supporting and protecting their troops from what they see as unfair actions on the part of both their own organizational higher-ups and obnoxious elements in their customer base. They are the most likely to be cheerleaders and boosters for the employees under their command. Like the innovative manager, they support individual initiatives and creative approaches to work; however, they may have a tendency to permit their troops to slack off on certain necessary functions, such as documentation, attendance, and discipline. In fact, these kinds of managers may be ripe for exploitation by less well-meaning subordinates and may unknowingly abet misconduct, abuse, or corruption by being too nice and shielding their employees from the consequences of their actions.

· · · · · · ·

Because workplaces are heterogeneous, no one single supervisory style should be considered the best or perfect standard for all managers. In some settings, making nice is the best policy; in others, you've got to crack the whip. In many workplaces, you may have to do a little of each and everything in between. Indeed, it would be ideal if we could blend the positive qualities of each style and winnow out the negatives. The policy implication is that executives and administrators should recognize the need for better training of first-line supervisors to achieve the organization's goals.

Managing Organizational Stress: Guidelines for Managers

How do you deal with organizational stress at your company? When I ask this question of managers, I usually get more eye rolls, accompanied by a collective mirthless chuckle. That's because the endemic stresses that build up cumulatively over time are often a symptom of systemic problems within the company. So what does top management do? Instead of taking the difficult but necessary steps of instituting crucial organizational changes, they frequently contract with outside mental health clinicians or motivational seminar purveyors to conduct flowery-sounding stress management or team-building courses, as if a few generic classes on diaphragmatic breathing, diversity awareness, ethics, or anger management will make a dent in the individualized problems that confront your company's personnel every day.

Having been both student and teacher of such courses, I can attest to the palpable cynicism that often seethes through the room as the classes become either droning monologues by the instructor, with students sullenly refusing to participate, or deteriorate into angry bitching sessions that only serve to further inflame and entrench the departmental bitterness against an uncaring administration that is seen as trying to "straighten us out by throwing a course at us."

However, there are a number of measures, as articulated by law enforcement executive trainer James Sewell, that you as a manager can adapt and use to constructively address stress within your own department. Although these measures don't necessarily require a psychologist to implement successfully, they are based on a few practical psychological principles of leadership.

Show Yourself

To be effective, a leader must be visible and accessible. You must be seen by the troops as being actively involved in running the department, receptive to constructive feedback, and sincerely committed to both the welfare of your personnel and the competent performance of their duties. Especially in the presence of organizational changes or upheavals, the ideal leader acts as a bedrock of stability and consistency. The troops should know that you can be counted on to do the right thing, to not confuse urgency with crisis, and to handle problems effectively. The best way to teach is by example: "Walk the walk" of commitment and integrity; don't just preach about it. This often involves putting in the extra time and effort it takes to be an effective manager, not just living by the clock.

Give Respect to Get Respect

Remember that the workplace is, fundamentally, a tribal family. As we've just seen, individual management styles may vary, from formal and hierarchical to casual and egalitarian. And employee personalities and psychopathologies may cover the wide spectrum of topics discussed in the preceding chapters. Yet it is striking how the core elements of respect and integrity have a powerful impact on the productivity and well-being of virtually all employees and suffuse through successful organizations of every type of chain-of-command structure, from laid-back California technogeek firms to no-nonsense military units. As I hope I've made clear throughout this book, the purpose of achieving greater understanding of those you work with is to be able to motivate them as people, not manipulate them as specimens.

Troops always know when their leaders are treating them fairly and will usually strive to reciprocate. Unfortunately, many leaders confuse *respect* with *fear,* as in "I'm the boss, so you'd better respect me, or else." Remember that people will kowtow to you out of fear, but only as long as they have to, or until someone more fearful comes along to knock you off your rock. But people who *respect* you will remain loyal even when they don't have to, because true respect is built on consistency, trust, and integrity.

Expect the Best and Reward It

Being respectful doesn't mean tolerating slackers. If your workers signed on for a tough job, you have every right to expect them to do it. Don't be afraid to demand excellence, but don't neglect to back this up by freely acknowledging and rewarding your troops' honest effort and hard work. Delegate responsibly and avoid micromanaging, but know when to step in and get your hands dirty when you have to. As we've discussed in previous chapters, make a good-faith effort to rehabilitate underperforming or misbehaving employees, but know when to cut your losses and don't let a truly bad apple continue to rot your organizational barrel. Show your troops that the rules apply fairly to everyone.

Ask for Feedback and Use It

Managing fairly and respectfully means you can't be afraid of constructive feedback from above and below and that you're always ready and willing to learn and expand your knowledge base. A skilled manager never makes subordinates afraid to confront him or her with conflicting or unpalatable data if the goal is to improve the overall performance of the department or the organization. Indeed, this is one of the main ways problems are identified before they become crises (see Chapters 10 and 11).

True leaders are not afraid to be wrong if the correction will lead to being right the next time; that's the essence of the 20/20/20-hindsight/ insight/foresight principle. You can never promise your employees that you will always agree with them, implement their suggestions, and accede to their requests. But you can guarantee that you will always *listen*, and being *heard* is a sign of being acknowledged and respected that will resonate with an employee of virtually any personality type.

Maintain a Culture of Knowledge

Knowledge comes from many sources, from formal textbooks and academic courses to on-the-job training to practical field experience to self-study and personal improvement. You already believe this or you wouldn't be reading this book.

Education and the incremental acquisition of knowledge also work in the other direction, too, and true leaders will make continuing education and training a priority of their troops' involvement in the organization. Many public and private organizations encourage continuing education and some even link formal academic credits to pay bonuses, but the ideal leader should set the example of making new learning a virtue in itself. Aside from the training necessary to do their jobs, people should not be forced to cram extra information into their brain if they don't want to, because the last thing I want you to do is turn learning into a punishment. A much more effective strategy is to create what I call a *culture of knowledge* where becoming smarter about any aspect of your work is not something regarded as a nerdy indulgence, but is seen as an admirable exercise in self-development as a true craftsperson or professional. Again—you're already doing it.

Pick Your Battles and Fight Them Wisely

Any kind of organizational reform isn't easy, and it doesn't happen overnight. Even if you're the type of committed manager discussed in this chapter, you'll often find your head banging up against a recalcitrant corporate or governmental bureaucracy that's used to doing things the old way and expects you to straighten out your own house—however, often without giving you the latitude, resources, or authority to make the truly needed changes. But if you're a manager of integrity, your rank-and-file personnel will genuinely appreciate your efforts to improve conditions on their behalf. And they'll comply with required changes on their part if these are seen as being fair and equitably distributed throughout the organization. In other words, it's not all or nothing: A manager with a vision can almost always accomplish something valuable, even if external circumstances force the reality to fall far short of the ultimate goal.

Role of the Psychologist in Organizational Stress Management

My professional colleagues would consider me remiss if I didn't mention some of the specific roles played by psychologists who consult to organizations. In addition, as a manager, you may be curious as to what exactly our profession can offer in the way of helping your company to manage the challenge of organizational change or just the stresses of daily work life.

Direct Clinical Services

Psychologists and other mental health professionals can see employees and their families in individual or group therapy sessions to deal with personal or professional stresses that may affect their performance at work. Employees will avail themselves of this resource to the extent that its legitimacy and usefulness are supported and modeled by the organizational leadership.

This is not just a nice idea but a practical one that makes fiscal sense. In a study reported by Tori DeAngelis in the *APA Monitor,* 250 public safety workers who received stress counseling were compared to a matched control group of 100 workers who did not. Four or five counseling sessions were initially provided, and referral was made to a mental health professional if more treatment was needed. The counseled group showed less depression, less anxiety, and less somatic concerns, and there was a two-thirds decline in sickness-related absences. As for cost-effectiveness, it was found that the brief counseling of that group of employees resulted in a savings of approximately $200,000 in sickness absence.

Interestingly, work-related problems were only the second most important issue dealt with in counseling. The single greatest source of stress for these workers was related to marital and personal problems and addressing these issues adequately in treatment made the biggest difference in terms of nuts-and-bolts cost containment for healthcare outlays. This highlights the importance of companies providing the necessary mental health resources for employees to deal with the stresses of their personal lives because these problems will inevitably affect how they perform at work.

Education and Training

Psychologists can provide training in organizational stress management in the form of departmental workshops and seminars, formal academic courses at local universities or community colleges, short minicourses, in-service training, brown-bag lunch meetings, or any other venue that will enhance learning and mastery of stress management, communication, conflict resolution, and work efficiency skills. Again, support from upper management is crucial in implementing and sustaining these programs.

Management Coaching

Psychologists with expertise in industrial/organizational and management psychology can provide coaching and consultation services to assist in organizational change, personnel management, executive coaching, and departmental crisis management. It's hoped that as companies increasingly recognize that all work, even the most technical, ultimately involves real human beings, their use of these practical psychological services will continue to expand.

Conclusions

Within business organizations of all types, stress is typically multidirectional: from the top down, from the bottom up, and from side to side. Like all close-knit social groups, a workplace is a tribal family unit, in which the cycles of work, love, hate, loyalty, jealousy, honor, betrayal, life, and death are played out on the template of each employee's unique personality style and psychological dynamics. As such, organizations have an intimate stake in the health, fitness, and well-being of their members. To the extent that employees and their managers and executives respect and trust one another, those organizations will run smoothly and profitably and will serve their clients, customers, and communities effectively and honorably. Your understanding of the practical psychology of work will help make you the manager customers respect, administrators listen to, and employees want to work for.

Bibliography and Further Reading

Albrecht, Steven. *Crisis Management for Corporate Self-Defense*. New York: AMACOM Books, 1996.

American Psychiatric Association. *Diagnostic and Statistical Manual of Mental Disorders*. 4th ed. (text revision) Washington, DC: American Psychiatric Association, 2000.

Anderson, Lynne M., and Christine Pearson. "Tit for Tat: The Spiraling Effect of Incivility in the Workplace." *Academy of Management Review*, 1999, 452–471.

Argenti, Paul. "Crisis Communication: Lessons from 9/11." *Harvard Business Review*, December 2002, 103–109.

Blount, Ernest C. *Occupational Crime: Deterrence, Investigation, and Reporting in Compliance with Federal Guidelines*. Boca Raton, FL: CRC Press, 2003.

Blustein, David L. *The Psychology of Working: A New Perspective for Career Development, Counseling, and Public Policy*. Mahwah, NJ: Erlbaum, 2006.

Blythe, Bruce T. *Blindsided: A Manager's Guide to Catastrophic Incidents in the Workplace*. New York: Portfolio, 2002.

Buckingham, Marcus. "What Great Managers Do." *Harvard Business Review,* March 2005, 70–79.

Caraulia, Algene P., and Linda Steiger. *Nonviolent Crisis Intervention: Learning to Defuse Explosive Behavior.* Brookfield, MA: CPI Publishing, 1997.

Casciaro, Tiziana, and Miguel Lobo. "Competent Jerks, Lovable Fools, and the Formation of Social Networks." *Harvard Business Review,* June 2005, 92–99.

Ciulla, Joanne B. *The Working Life: The Promise and Betrayal of Modern Work.* New York: Times Books, 2000.

Collins, James C. *Good to Great: Why Some Companies Make the Leap . . . And Others Don't.* New York: Harper Business, 2001.

DeAngelis, Tina. "Workplace Stress Battles Fought All Over the World." *APA Monitor,* January 1993, 22.

Dezenhall, E., and John Weber. *Damage Control: Why Everything You Know About Crisis Management Is Wrong.* New York, Portfolio, 2007.

Dubin, William R. "Assaults with Weapons." In Burr S. Eichelman and Anne C. Hartwig, eds. *Patient Violence and the Clinician.* Washington, DC: American Psychiatric Press, 1995.

Dubrin, Andrew J. *Your Own Worst Enemy: How to Overcome Career Self-Sabotage.* New York: AMACOM Books, 1992.

Einarsen, Stale. "The Nature and Causes of Bullying at Work." *International Journal of Manpower* 20 (1999): 16–27.

Engel, Robin S. "Supervisory Styles of Patrol Sergeants and Lieutenants." *Journal of Criminal Justice* 29 (2001): 341–355.

Engel, Robin S. "Patrol Officer Supervision in the Community Policing Era." *Journal of Criminal Justice* 30 (2002): 51–64.

Ferris, Gerald R., Pamela Perrewe, and Sherry Davidson. "Political Skill at Work." *Organizational Dynamics* 28 (2000): 25–37.

Fischler, Gary, and Nan Booth. *Vocational Impact of Psychiatric Disorders: A Guide for Rehabilitation Professionals.* Gaithersburg, MD: Aspen, 1999.

Flannery, Raymond B. *Violence in the Workplace.* New York: Crossroad, 1995.

Flin, Rhona. *Sitting in the Hot Seat: Leaders and Teams for Critical Incident Management.* New York: Wiley, 1996.

Friedman, Raymond A., Simon Tidd, and Steven Currall. "What Goes Around Comes Around: The Impact of Personal Conflict Style on Work Conflict and Stress." *International Journal of Conflict Management* 11 (2000): 32–55.

Garner, Gerald W. *Common Sense Police Supervision: A How-To Manual for the First-Line Responder.* 2nd ed. Springfield, IL: Charles C Thomas, 1995.

Gilliland, Burl E., and Richard James. *Crisis Intervention Strategies.* 2nd ed. Pacific Grove, CA: Brooks/Cole, 1993.

Gini, Al. *My Job, My Self: Work and the Creation of the Modern Individual.* New York: Routledge, 2000.

Goleman, Daniel, Richard Boyatzis, and Annie McKee. *Primal Leadership: Realizing the Power of Emotional Intelligence.* New York: Harvard Business School Press, 2002.

Grote, Dick. *Discipline Without Punishment: The Proven Strategy That Turns Problem Employees into Superior Performers.* 2nd. ed. New York: AMACOM Books, 2006.

Hedlund, Jennifer, George B. Forsythe, Joseph A. Horvath, Wendy Williams, Scott Snook, and Robert J. Sternberg. "Identifying and Assessing Tacit Knowledge: Understanding the Practical Intelligence of Military Leaders." *Leadership Quarterly* 14 (2003): 117–140.

Hoffman, Edward. *Psychological Testing at Work: How to Use, Interpret, and Get the Most Out of the Newest Tests in Personality, Learning Styles, Aptitudes, Interests, and More.* New York: McGraw-Hill, 2002.

Johnson, Pamela R., and Julie Indvik. "Rebels, Criticizers, Backstabbers, and Busybodies: Anger and Aggression at Work." *Public Personnel Management* 29 (2000): 165–173.

Kidwell, Roland, and Christopher Martin, eds. *Managing Organizational Deviance.* Thousand Oaks, CA: Sage, 2005.

Kinney, Joseph A. *Violence at Work: How to Make Your Company Safer for Employees and Customers.* Englewood Cliffs, NJ: Prentice-Hall, 1995.

Klein, George. "The Effect of Acute Stressors on Decision Making." In James Driskell and Eduardo Salas, eds. *Stress and Human Performance.* Hillsdale, NJ: Erlbaum, 1996.

Labich, Kenneth. "How to Fire People and Still Sleep at Night." *Fortune,* June 1996, 65–72.

Labig, Charles E. *Preventing Violence in the Workplace.* New York: AMACOM Books, 1995.

Lax, David, and James Sebenius. *The Manager as Negotiator.* New York: Free Press, 1986.

Leonard, Dorothy, and Walter Swap. *Deep Smarts: How to Cultivate and Transfer Enduring Business Wisdom.* Boston: Harvard Business School Press, 2005.

Lerbinger, Otto. *The Crisis Manager: Facing Risk and Responsibility.* Mahwah, NJ: Erlbaum, 1997.

Le Storti, Anthony J. *When You're Asked to Do the Impossible: Principles of Business Teamwork and Leadership from the U.S. Army's Elite Rangers.* Guilford, CT: Lyons Press, 2003.

Lowman, Rodney L. *Counseling and Psychotherapy of Work Dysfunctions.* Washington, DC: American Psychological Association, 1993.

Maccoby, Michael. "The Power of Transference: Why People Follow the Leader." *Harvard Business Review,* September 2004, 77–85.

Maddi, Salvatore R., and Deborah M. Khoshaba. *Resilience at Work: How to Succeed No Matter What Life Throws at You.* New York: AMACOM, 2005.

Mantell, Michael, and Steve Albrecht. *Ticking Bombs: Defusing Violence in the Workplace*. New York: Irwin, 1994.

Millon, Theodore. *Personality Disorders in Modern Life*. New York: Wiley, 2000.

Mitroff, Ian I. *Managing Crises Before They Happen: What Every Manager Needs to Know About Crisis Management*. New York: AMACOM Books, 2001.

Namie, Gary, and Ruth Namie. *The Bully at Work: What You Can Do to Stop the Hurt and Reclaim Your Dignity on the Job*. Naperville, IL: Sourcebooks, 2000.

Nicholson, Nigel. *Executive Instinct: Managing the Human Animal in the Information Age*. New York: Crown Business, 2000.

O'Reilly, Charles A., and Jeffrey Pfeffer. *Hidden Value: How Great Companies Achieve Extraordinary Results with Ordinary People*. Boston: Harvard Business School Press, 2000.

Peak, Kenneth J., Larry Gaines, and Robert Glensor. *Police Supervision and Management in the Era of Community Policing*. 2nd ed. Upper Saddle River, NJ: Prentice-Hall, 2004.

Perrewe, Pamela L., Gerald R. Ferris, Dwight D. Frink, and William P. Anthony. "Political Skill: An Antidote for Workplace Stressors." *Academy of Management Executive* 14 (2000): 115–123.

Pfeffer, Jeffrey, and Robert Sutton. *Hard Facts, Dangerous Half-Truths, and Total Nonsense: Profiting from Evidence-Based Management*. Boston: Harvard Business School Press, 2006.

Potter-Efron, Ronald T. *Work Rage: Preventing Anger and Resolving Conflict on the Job*. New York: Barnes & Noble, 1998.

Quick, James C., Jonathan Quick, and Debra Nelson. *Preventive Stress Management in Organizations*. Washington, DC: American Psychological Association, 1997.

Roberts, Brent W., and Robert Hogan, eds. *Personality Psychology in the Workplace*. Washington, DC: American Psychological Association, 2001.

Robinette, Hillary M. *Burnout in Blue: Managing the Police Marginal Performer.* New York: Praeger, 1987.

Rostow, Cary D., and Robert Davis. *A Handbook for Psychological Fitness-for-Duty Evaluations in Law Enforcement.* New York: Haworth, 2004.

Schouten, Ronald. "Sexual Harassment and the Role of Psychiatry." *Harvard Review of Psychiatry* 3 (1996): 83–100.

Serpas, Ronald W., Joseph W. Olson, and Brian D. Jones. "An Employee Disciplinary System That Makes Sense." *The Police Chief,* September 2003, 22–28.

Sewell, James D. "The Law Enforcement Executive: A Formula for Success." *FBI Law Enforcement Bulletin,* April 1992, 22–26.

Sewell, James D. "Managing the Stress of Organizational Change." *FBI Law Enforcement Bulletin,* March 2002, 14–20.

Shapiro, David. *Neurotic Styles.* New York: Basic Books, 1965.

Simon, Robert I. *Bad Men Do What Good Men Dream: A Forensic Psychiatrist Illuminates the Darker Side of Human Behavior.* Washington, DC: American Psychiatric Press, 1996.

Sperry, Len. *Handbook of the Diagnosis and Treatment of the DSM-IV Personality Disorders.* New York: Brunner-Mazel, 1995.

Sperry, Len. *Corporate Therapy and Consulting.* New York: Brunner/ Mazel, 1996.

Sperry, Len. *Psychological Treatment of Chronic Illness: The Biopsychosocial Therapy Approach.* Washington, DC: American Psychological Association, 2006.

Sternberg, R. J. "Managerial Intelligence: Why IQ Isn't Enough." *Journal of Management* 23 (1997): 475–493.

Stone, Anthony V. *Fitness for Duty: Principles, Methods, and Legal Issues.* Boca Raton, FL: CRC Press, 2000.

Stone, Florence M. *Coaching, Counseling, and Mentoring: How to Choose and Use the Right Technique to Boost Employee Performance.* 2nd ed. New York: AMACOM Books, 2007.

Strauser, David R., and Dreena G. Waldrop. "Reconceptualizing the Work Personality." *Rehabilitation Counseling Bulletin* 42 (1999): 290–301.

Susskind, Lawrence, and Patrick Field. *Dealing with an Angry Public: The Mutual Gains Approach to Resolving Disputes.* New York: Free Press, 1996.

Thibault, Edward A., Lawrence M. Lynch, and R. Bruce McBride. *Proactive Police Management.* Upper Saddle River, NJ: Prentice-Hall, 2004.

Wagner, Rodd, and James K. Harter. *12: The Elements of Great Managing.* New York: Gallup Press, 2006.

Weisinger, Hendrie. *The Power of Positive Criticism.* New York: AMACOM Books, 2000.

Weitzel, Thomas Q. "Managing the Problem Employee: A Road Map for Success." *FBI Law Enforcement Bulletin,* November 2004, 25–32.

Yandrick, Rudy M. *Behavioral Risk Management: How to Avoid Preventable Losses from Mental Health Problems in the Workplace.* San Francisco: Josscy-Bass, 1996.

Yudofsky, Stuart C. *Fatal Flaws: Navigating Destructive Relationships with People with Disorders of Personality and Character.* Washington, DC: American Psychiatric Publishing, 2005.

Other Works by the Author

Miller, Laurence. "Neuropsychological Concepts of Somatoform Disorders." *International Journal of Psychiatry in Medicine* 14 (1984): 31–46.

Miller, Laurence. "Neuropsychological Assessment of Substance Abusers: Review and Recommendations." *Journal of Substance Abuse Treatment* 2 (1985): 5–17.

Miller, Laurence. "Tourette Syndrome and Drug Addiction." *British Journal of Psychiatry* 147 (1985): 584–585.

Miller, Laurence. "Conversion, Paranoia, and Brain Dysfunction." *British Journal of Psychiatry* 148 (1986): 481.

Miller, Laurence. "The Emotional Brain." *Psychology Today,* February 1988, 34–42.

Miller, Laurence. "To Beat Stress, Don't Relax: Get Tough!" *Psychology Today,* December 1989, 62–63.

Miller, Laurence. *Inner Natures: Brain, Self, and Personality.* New York: St. Martin's Press, 1990.

Miller, Laurence. "Neuropsychodynamics of Alcoholism and Addiction: Personality, Psychopathology, and Cognitive Style." *Journal of Substance Abuse Treatment* 7 (1990): 31–49.

Miller, Laurence. "Psychotherapy of the Brain-Injured Patient: Principles and Practices." *Journal of Cognitive Rehabilitation* 9 (1991): 24–30.

Miller, Laurence. "Psychotherapeutic Approaches to Chronic Pain." *Psychotherapy* 30 (1993): 115–124.

Miller, Laurence. *Psychotherapy of the Brain-Injured Patient: Reclaiming the Shattered Self.* New York: Norton, 1993.

Miller, Laurence. "Toxic Torts: Clinical, Neuropsychological, and Forensic Aspects of Chemical and Electrical Injuries." *Journal of Cognitive Rehabilitation* 11 (1993): 6–20.

Miller, Laurence. "Civilian Posttraumatic Stress Disorder: Clinical Syndromes and Psychotherapeutic Strategies." *Psychotherapy* 31 (1994): 655–664.

Miller, Laurence. "The Epilepsy Patient: Personality, Psychodynamics, and Psychotherapy." *Psychotherapy* 31 (1994): 735–743.

Miller, Laurence. "Psychotherapy of Epilepsy: Seizure Control and Psychosocial Adjustment." *Journal of Cognitive Rehabilitation* 12 (1994): 14–30.

Miller, Laurence. "Toxic Trauma and Chemical Sensitivity: Clinical Syndromes and Psychotherapeutic Strategies." *Psychotherapy* 32 (1995): 648–656.

Miller, Laurence. "Workplace Violence in the Rehabilitation Setting: How to Prepare, Respond, and Survive." *Florida State Association of Rehabilitation Nurses Newsletter* 7 (1997): 4–8.

Miller, Laurence. "Malingering in Brain Injury and Toxic Tort Cases." In Eric Pierson, ed. *1998 Wiley Expert Witness Update: New Developments in Personal Injury Litigation*. New York: Wiley, 1998.

Miller, Laurence. "Not Just Malingering: Recognizing Psychological Syndromes in Personal Injury Litigation." *Neurolaw Letter* 8 (1998): 25–30.

Miller, Laurence. *Shocks to the System: Psychotherapy of Traumatic Disability Syndromes*. New York: Norton, 1998.

Miller, Laurence. " 'Mental Stress Claims' and Personal Injury: Clinical, Neuropsychological, and Forensic Issues." *Neurolaw Letter* 8 (1999): 39–45.

Miller, Laurence. "Workplace Violence: Prevention, Response, and Recovery." *Psychotherapy* 36 (1999): 160–169.

Miller, Laurence. "Workplace Violence and Psychological Trauma: Clinical Disability, Legal Liability, and Corporate Policy. Part I." *Neurolaw Letter* 11 (2001): 1–5.

Miller, Laurence. "Workplace Violence and Psychological Trauma: Clinical Disability, Legal Liability, and Corporate Policy. Part II." *Neurolaw Letter* 11 (2001): 7–13.

Miller, Laurence. "How Safe Is Your Job? The Threat of Workplace Violence." *USA Today Magazine*, March 2002, 52–54.

Miller, Laurence. "Posttraumatic Stress Disorder in School Violence: Risk Management Lessons from the Workplace." *Neurolaw Letter* 11 (2002): 33, 36–40.

Miller, Laurence. "What Is the True Spectrum of Functional Disorders in Rehabilitation?" *Physical Medicine and Rehabilitation: State of the Art Reviews* 16 (2002): 1–20.

Miller, Laurence. "Personalities at Work: Understanding and Managing Human Nature on the Job." *Public Personnel Management* 32 (2003): 419–433.

Miller, Laurence. "Police Personalities: Understanding and Managing the Problem Officer." *The Police Chief,* May 2003, 53–60.

Miller, Laurence. "Command Leadership Under Fire." *Law and Order,* June 2005, 26.

Miller, Laurence. *Practical Police Psychology: Stress Management and Crisis Intervention for Law Enforcement.* Springfield, IL: Charles C Thomas, 2006.

Miller, Laurence. "Psychological Principles and Practices for Superior Law Enforcement Leadership." *The Police Chief,* October 2006, 160–168.

Index

About the Author

Laurence Miller, Ph.D., is a clinical and forensic psychologist, an educator and trainer, an author and speaker, and a management consultant in Boca Raton, Florida. Dr. Miller is the police psychologist for the West Palm Beach Police Department and mental health adviser for the Florida Highway Patrol. He conducts civil and criminal forensic psychological evaluations and testifies as an expert witness in court. He maintains an independent practice in consulting, counseling, and psychotherapy in which he evaluates and treats workers, managers, and executives, as well as a range of other patients and their families. Dr. Miller is an instructor at Palm Beach Community College and is on the adjunct faculty at Florida Atlantic University. He conducts local, regional, and national continuing education programs and training seminars for mental health and legal professionals, executives, managers, and employees. Dr. Miller is the author of more than two hundred print and online publications pertaining to the brain, behavior, health, criminal justice, civil law, business management, and organizational psychology. He is a frequent guest on radio and television programs and a respected commentator and sought-after expert for local and national news media. Dr. Miller can be contacted at 561-392-8881 or online at docmilphd@aol.com.